This publication explores and theorises urban qualities of con[illegible]evelopments in thriving global c[illegible]g so, it combines theoretical and practical perspectives. Its aim is to positively affect the future of urban developments, providing a manifesto for a relational, collective and diverse future for our cities. The project is not to be understood as a complete urban design scheme; rather, it highlights the conditions under which an ideal urban development project could flourish. It debates contemporary planning culture and provides a vehicle to discuss the relations between the development of a particular site and the city in its entirety, between urban processes and resulting forms, between active and passive planning, and their political and ethical dimensions.

CW01640439

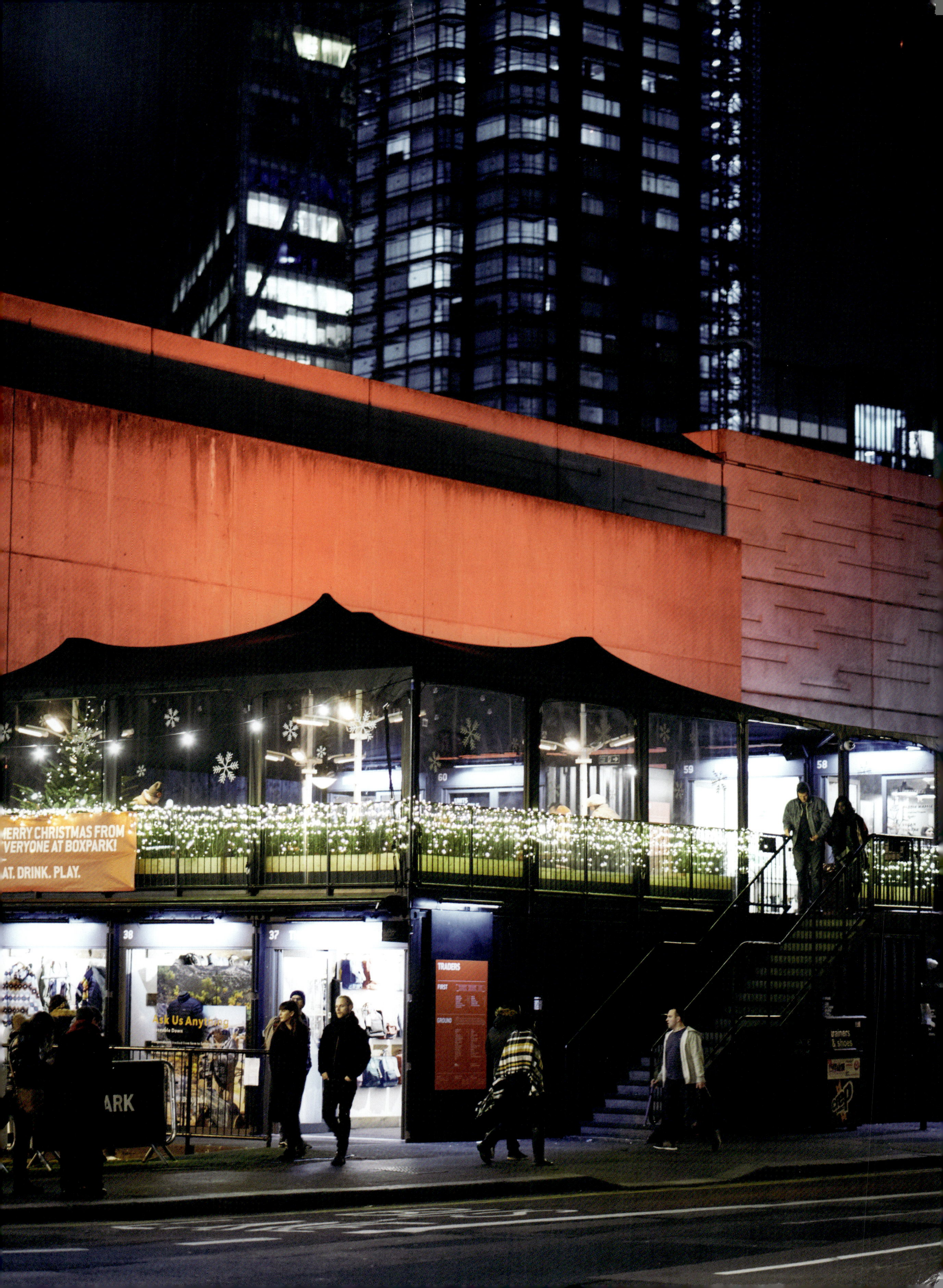
MERRY CHRISTMAS FROM
EVERYONE AT BOXPARK!
EAT. DRINK. PLAY.
TRADERS
Ask Us Anything
ARK

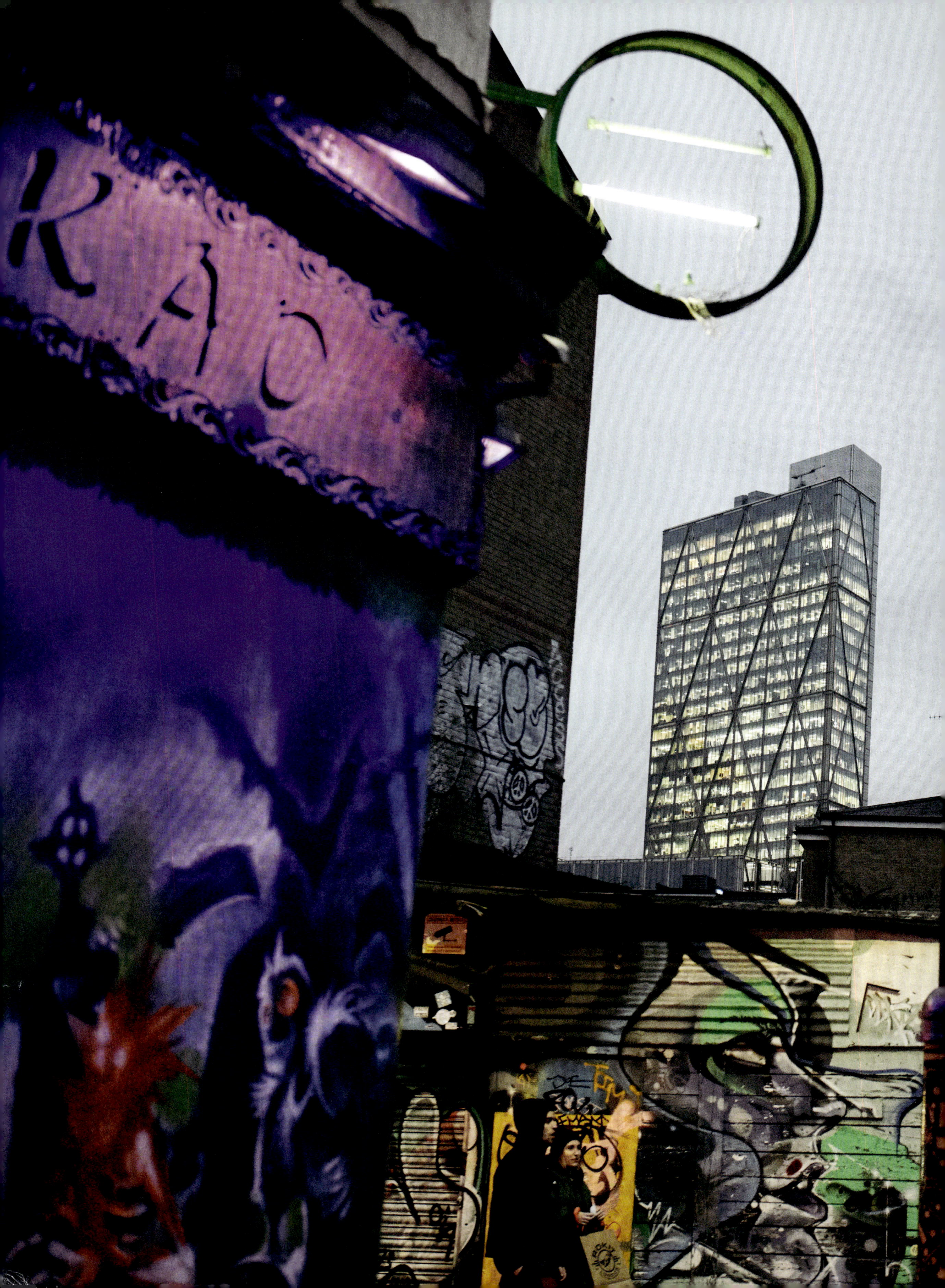

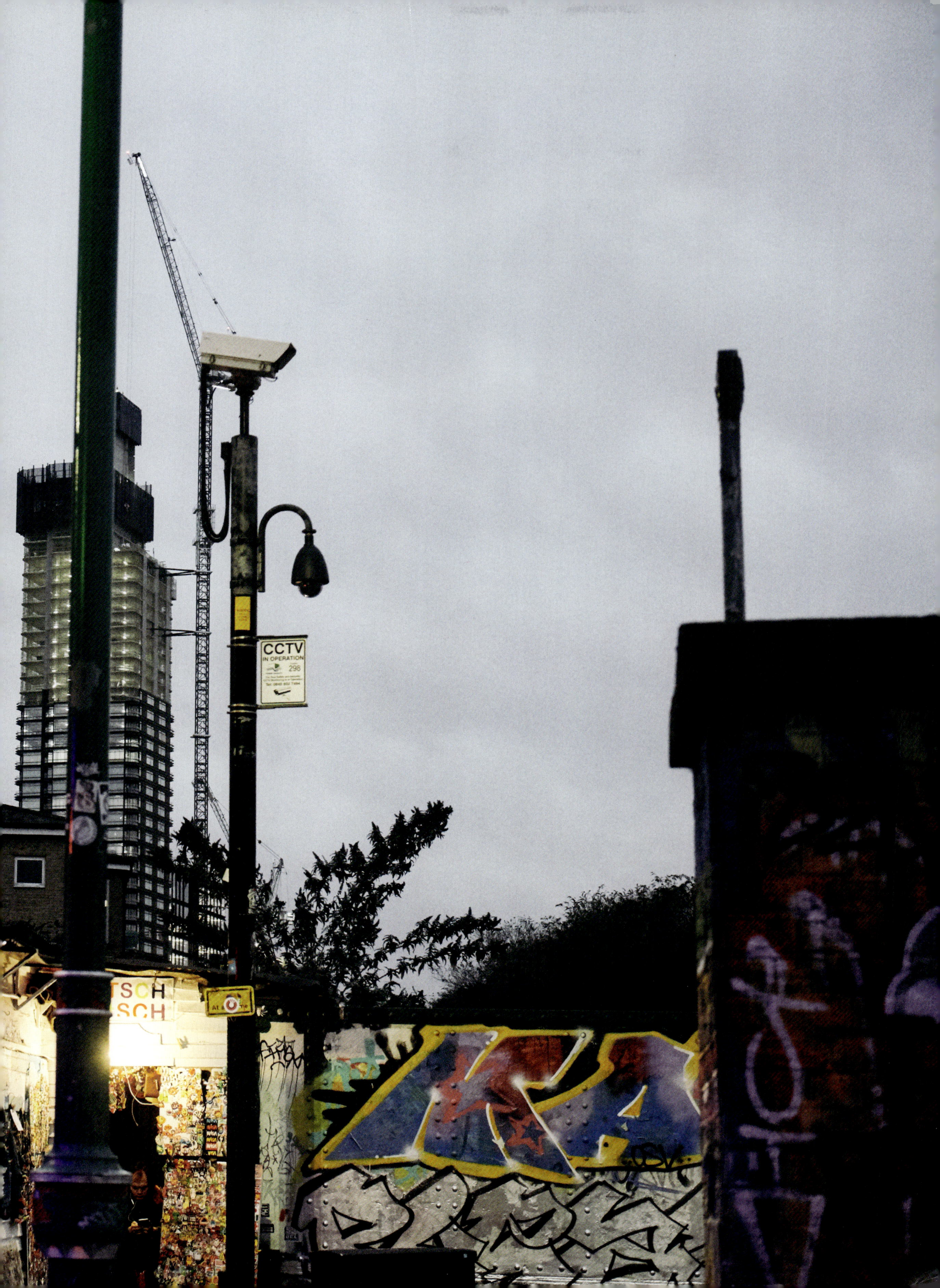
CCTV
IN OPERATION
298
TSCH
SCH

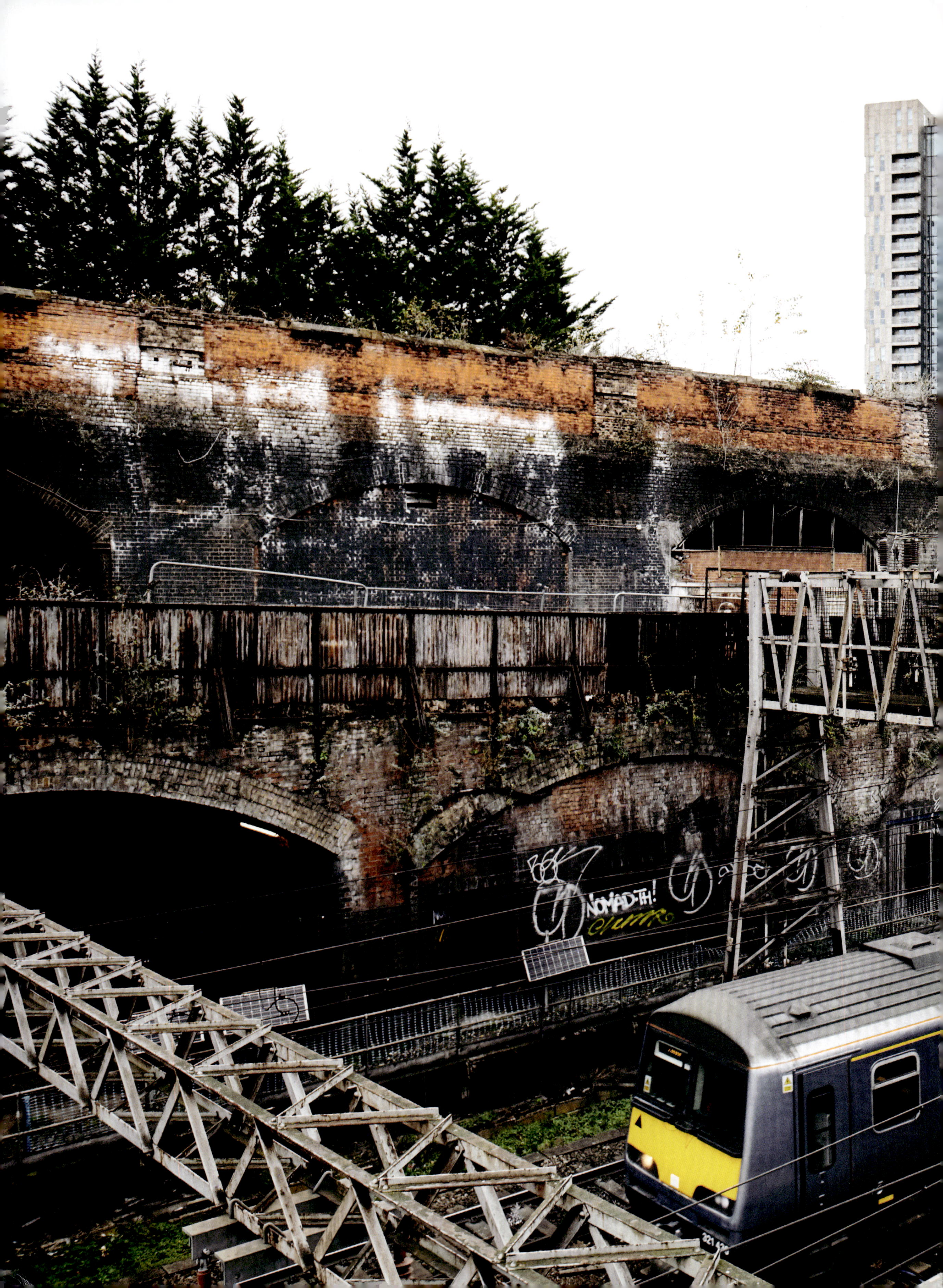
NOMAD-TH!

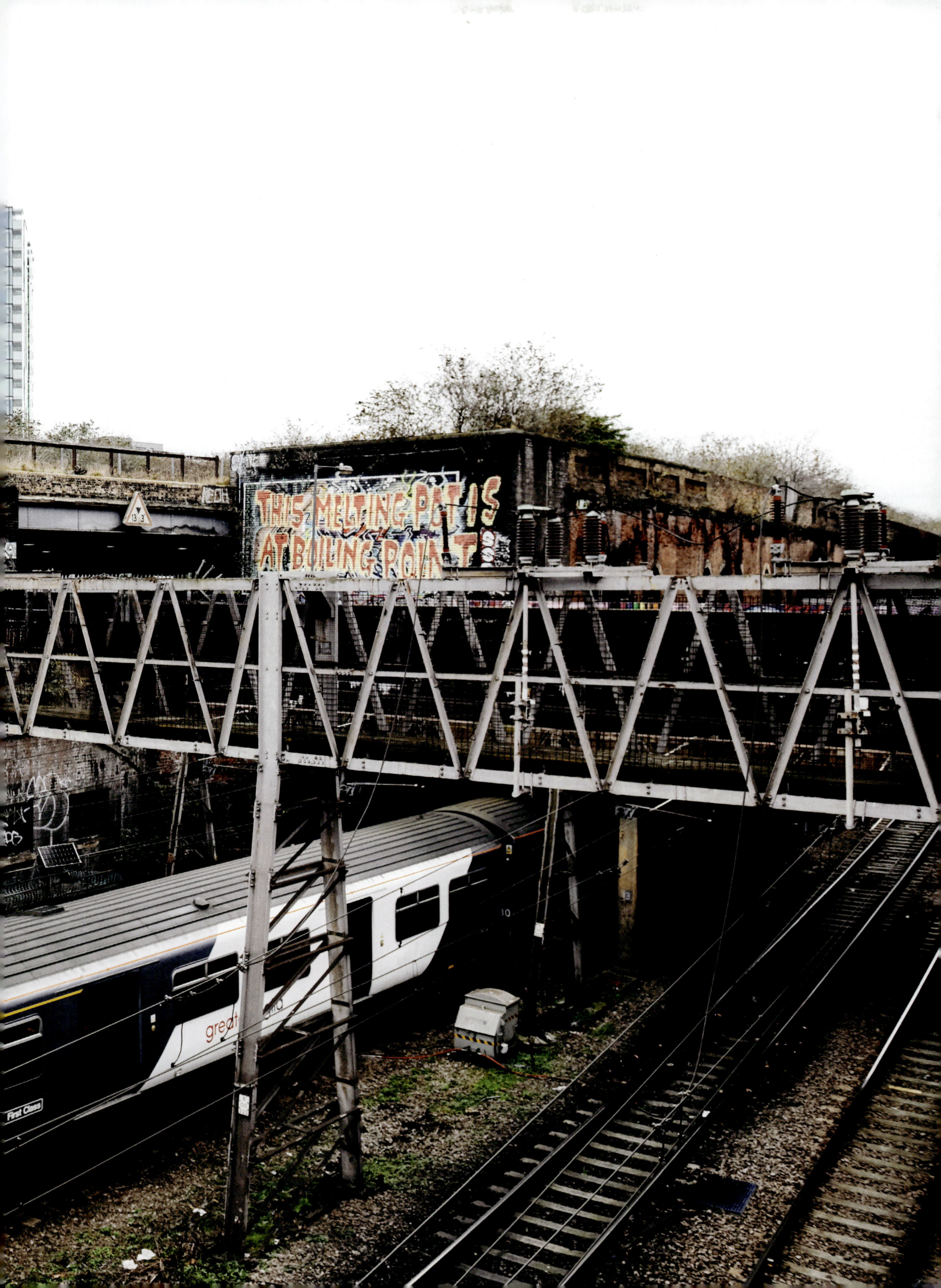
THIS MELTING POT IS
AT BOILING POINT
First Class

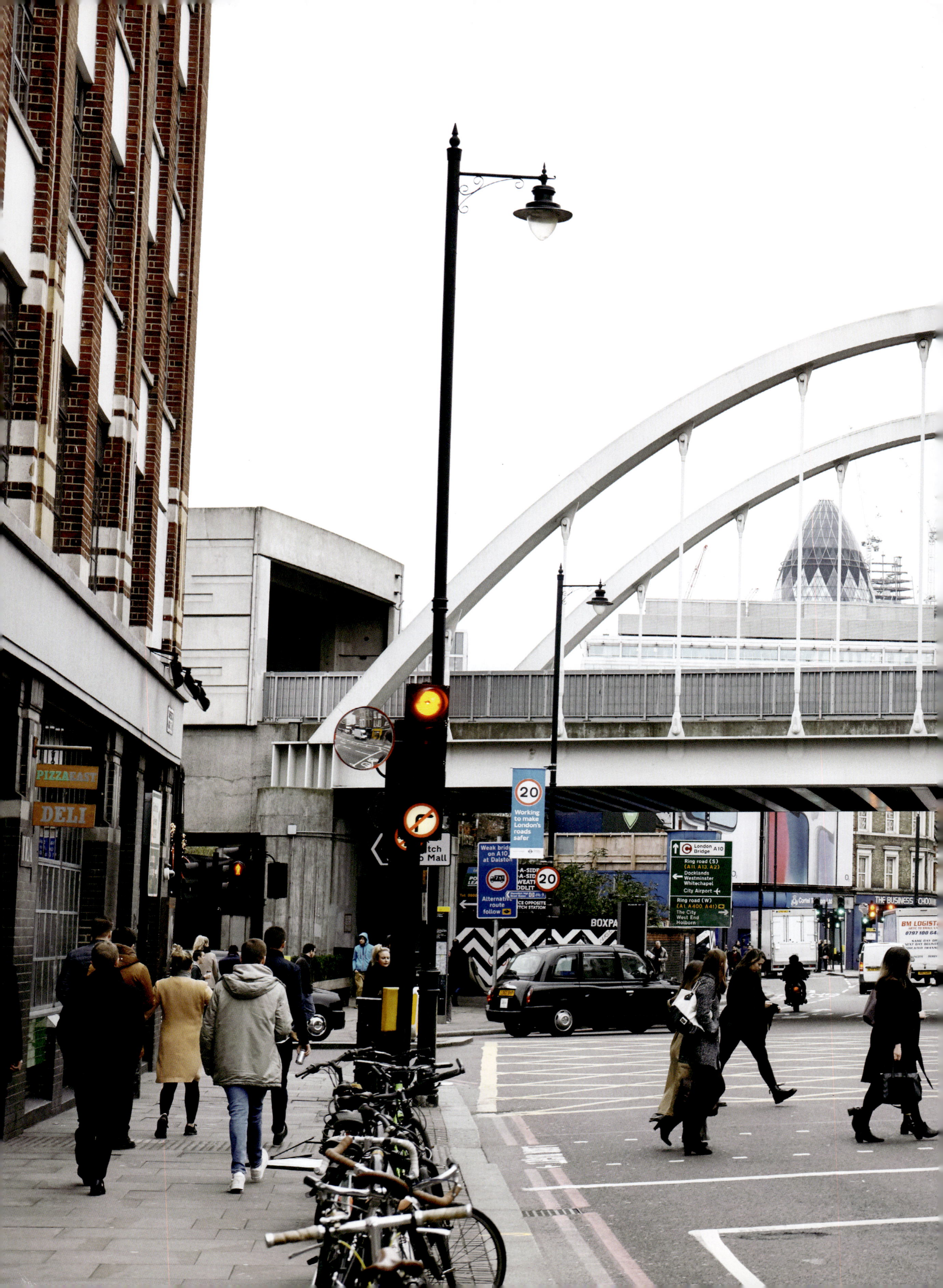
PIZZAEAST
DELI
20
Working to make London's roads safer
Alternative route follow
20
London Bridge A10
Ring road (S) (A11, A13, A2)
Docklands Westminster Whitechapel
City Airport
Ring road (W) (A1, A400, A41)
The City West End Holborn

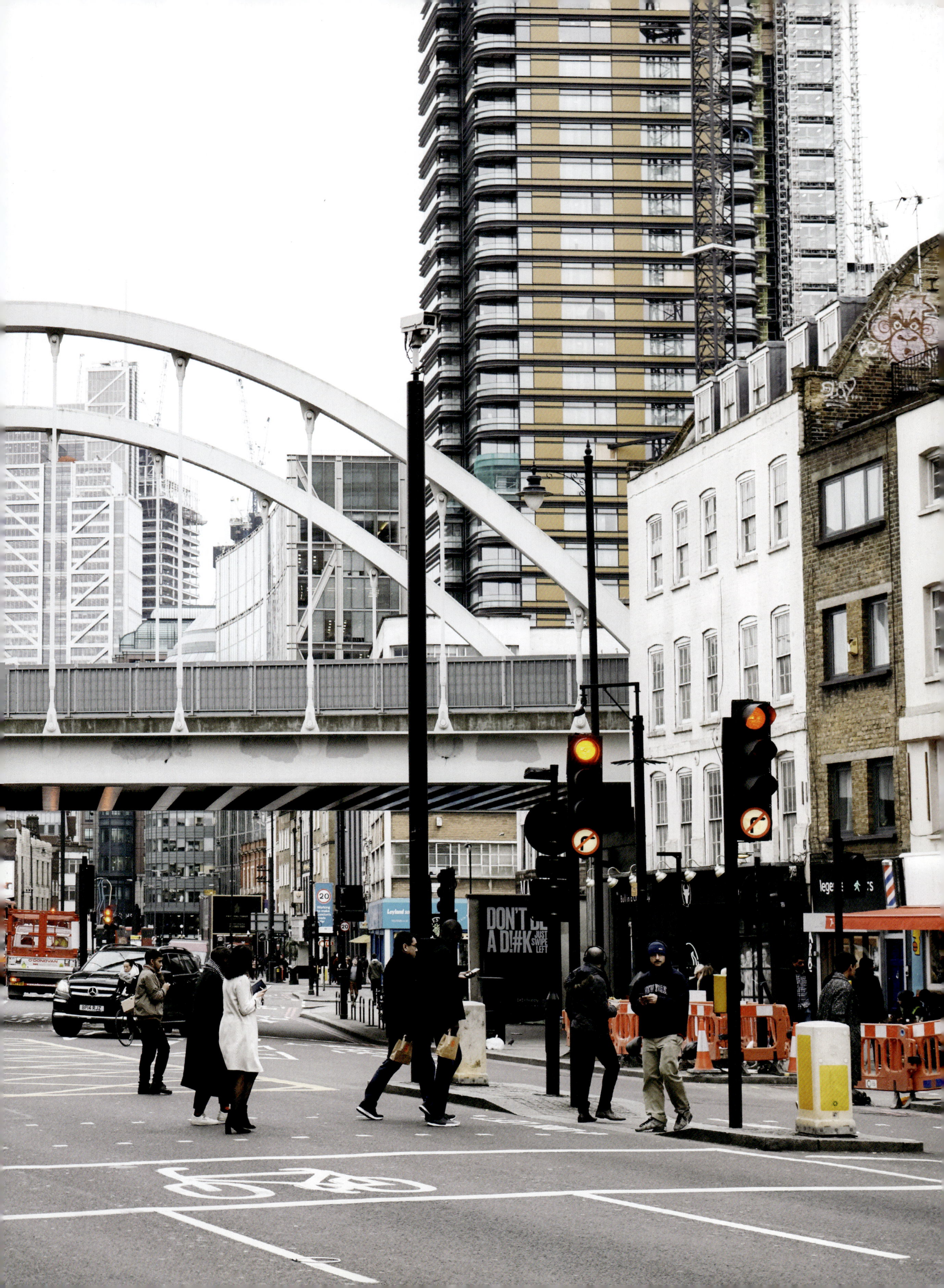
DON'T
A D!#K
JUST SWIPE LEFT
20

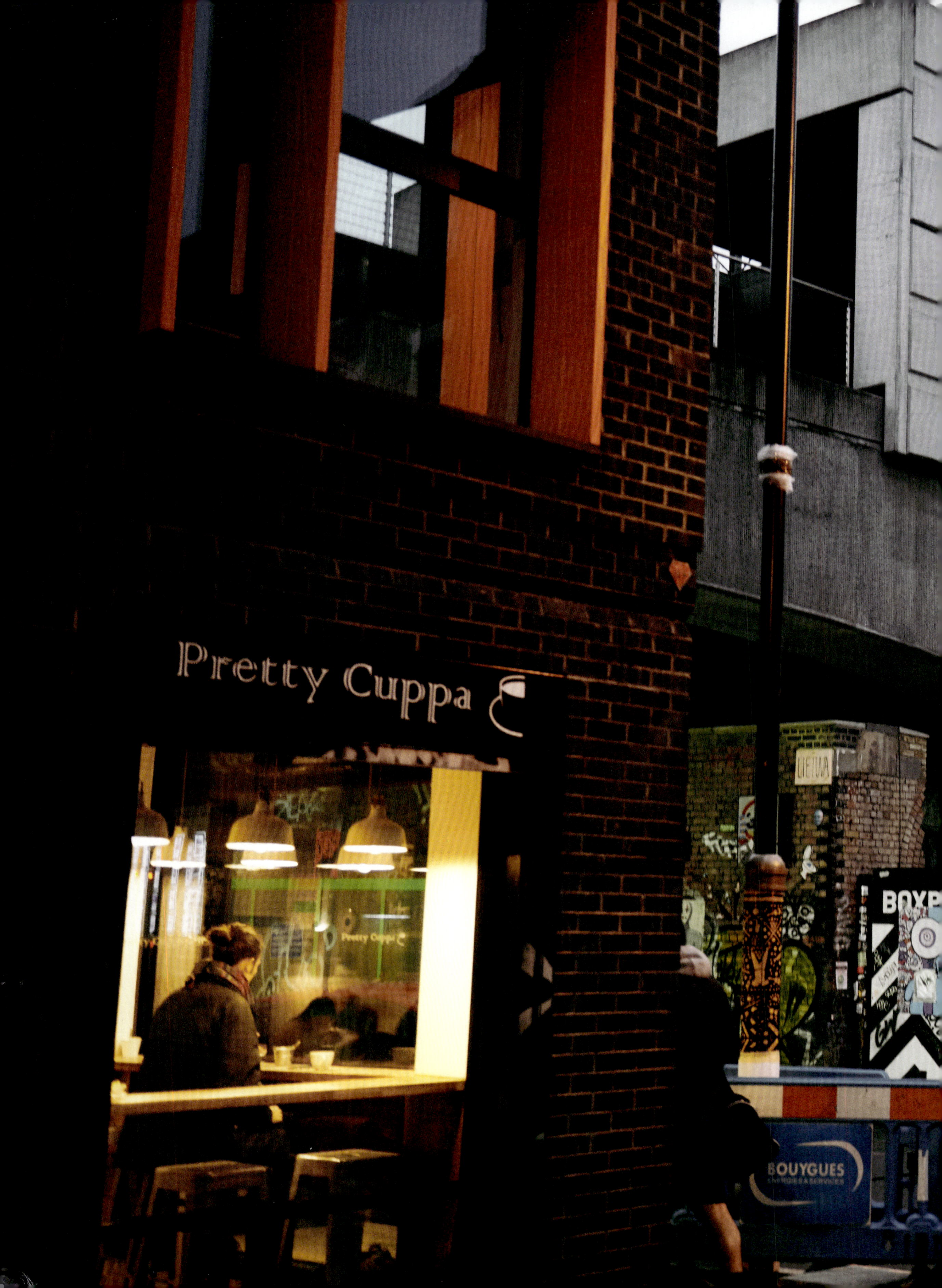
Pretty Cuppa
LIETUVA
BOUYGUES

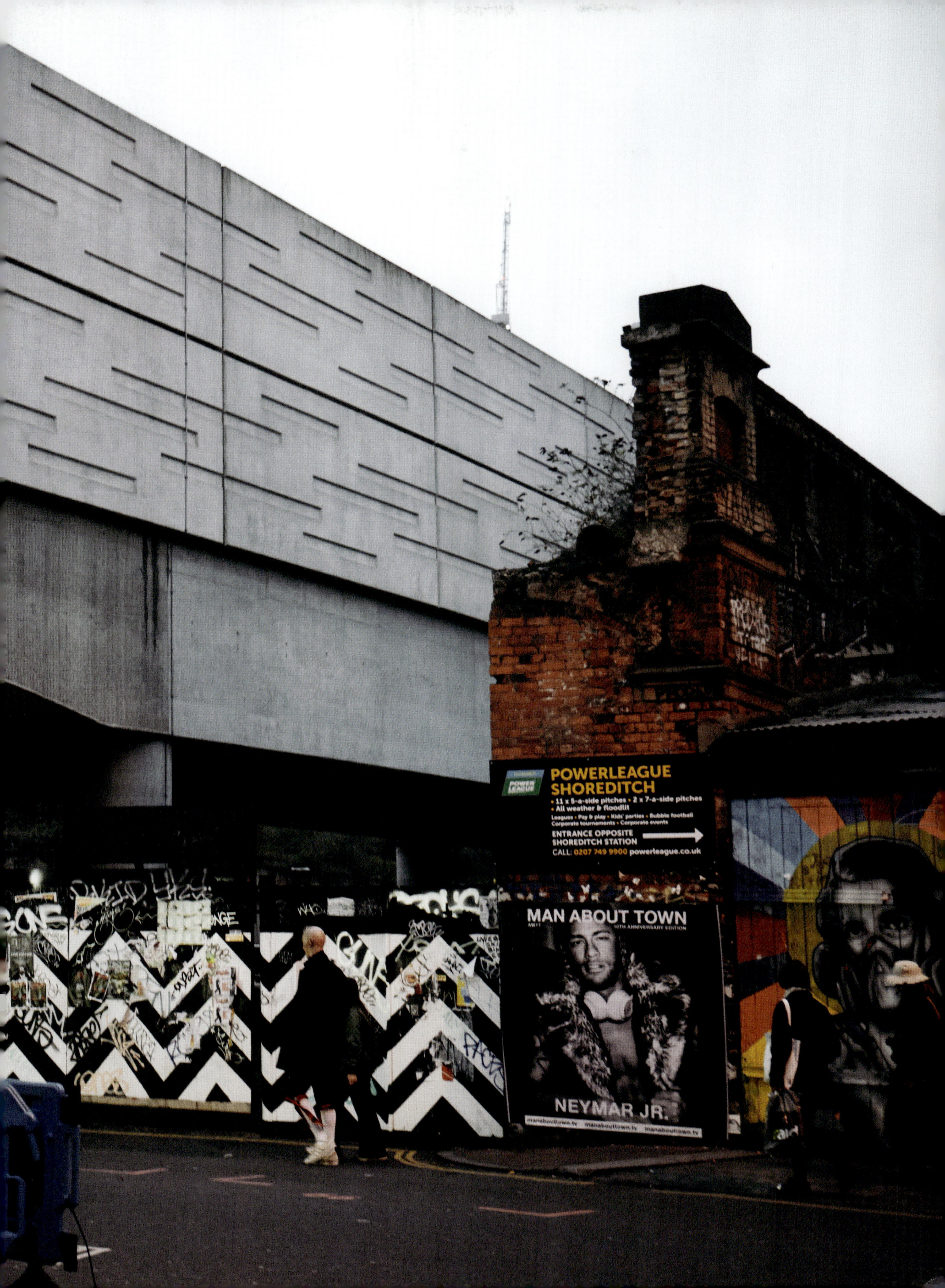
POWER LEAGUE
POWERLEAGUE SHOREDITCH
• 11 x 5-a-side pitches • 2 x 7-a-side pitches
• All weather & floodlit
Leagues • Pay & play • Kids' parties • Bubble football
Corporate tournaments • Corporate events
ENTRANCE OPPOSITE SHOREDITCH STATION
CALL: 0207 749 9900 powerleague.co.uk
MAN ABOUT TOWN
AW17
10TH ANNIVERSARY EDITION
NEYMAR JR.
manabouttown.tv manabouttown.tv manabouttown.tv

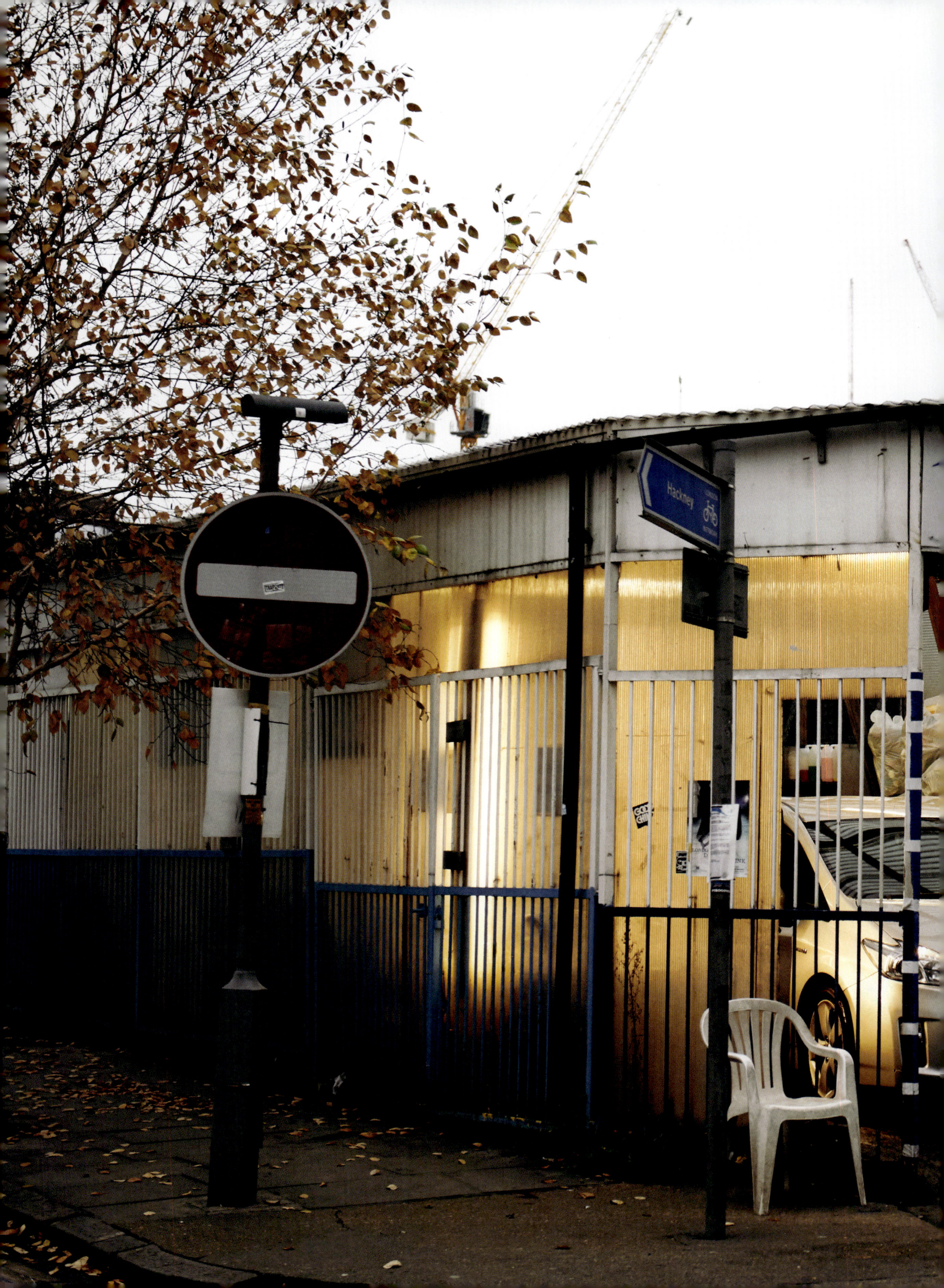
Hackney

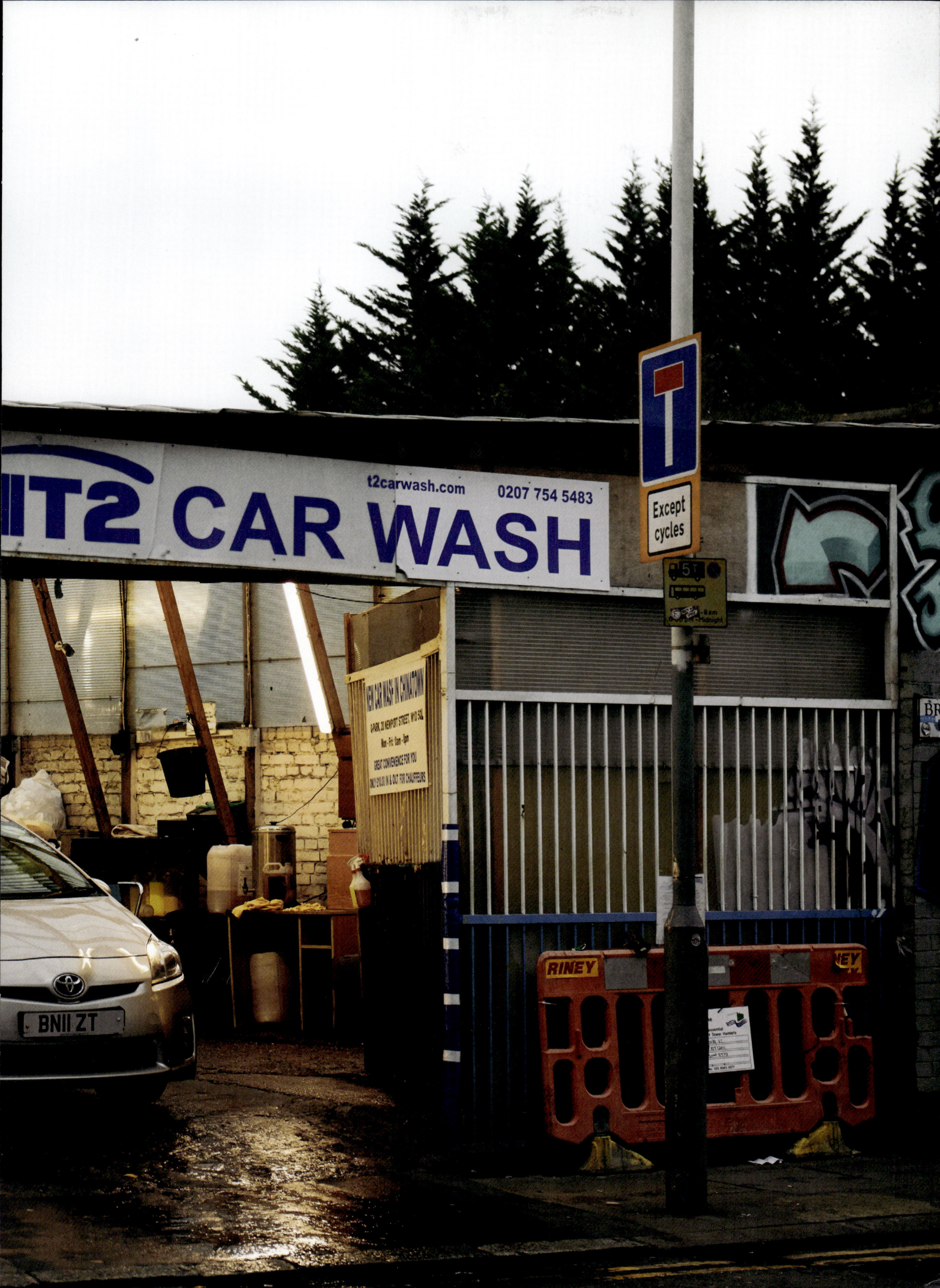

CAR WASH
t2carwash.com
0207 754 5483
Except cycles
NEW CAR WASH IN CHINATOWN
GREAT CONVENIENCE FOR YOU
RINEY

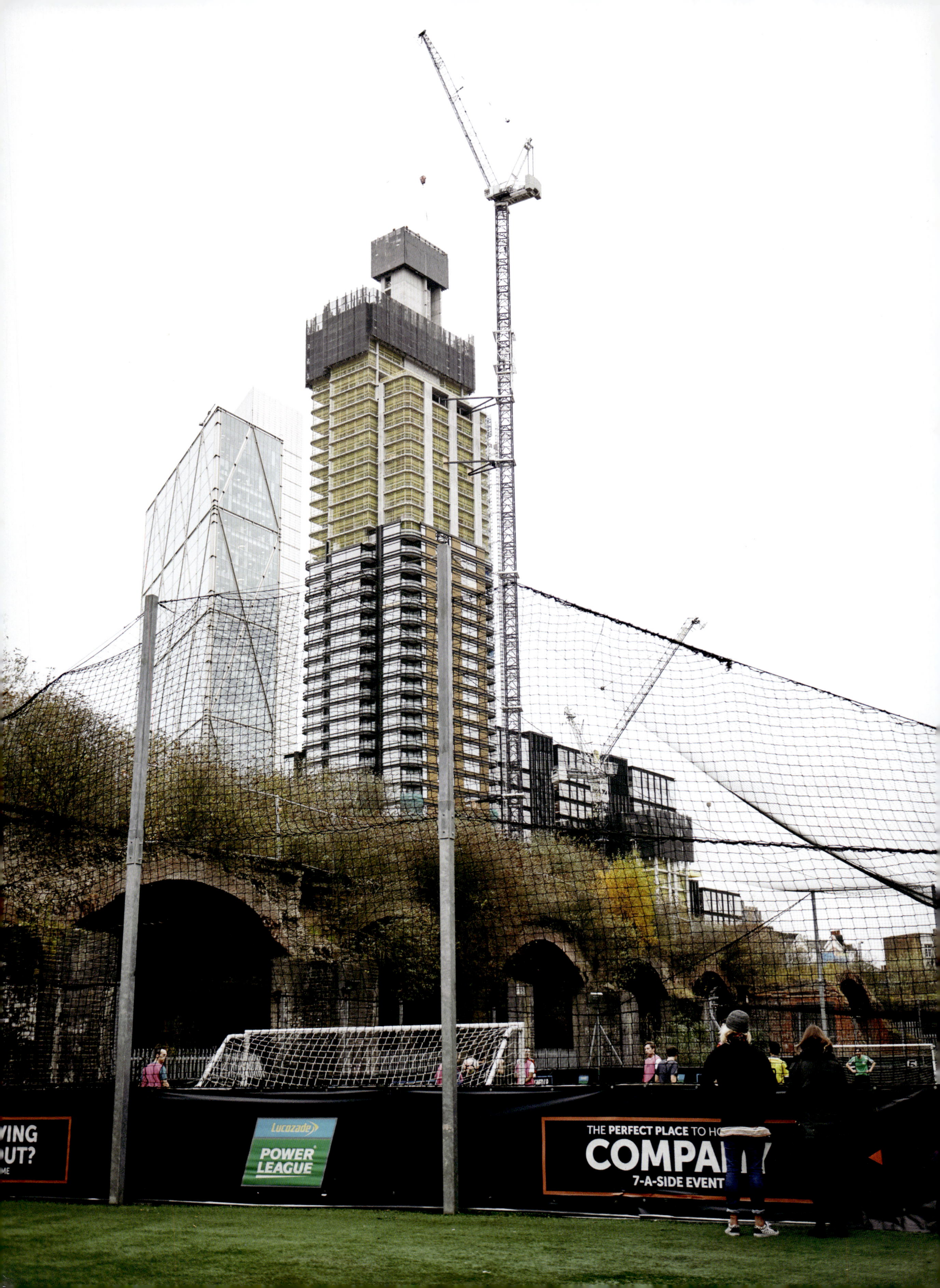
VING
OUT?
Lucozade
POWER LEAGUE
THE PERFECT PLACE TO HO
COMPA
7-A-SIDE EVENT

On Planning — A Thought Experiment

Edited by Simon Kretz and David Chipperfield

Contributions by Benno Agreiter, Christian Weyell and the Institute for Urban Design, Prof. Kees Christiaanse, ETH Zurich.
With photographs by Benjamin McMahon.

Editors
Simon Kretz, David Chipperfield

Authors
Benno Agreiter, David Chipperfield, Simon Kretz,
Christian Weyell

Photography
Benjamin McMahon

ETH Zurich Department of Architecture
Research and Design Team
Institute for Urban Design, Prof. Kees Christiaanse,
ETH Zurich: Benno Agreiter, Kees Christiaanse,
Joris Jehle, Eirini Kasioumi, Simon Kretz,
Christian Weyell
Institute for Landscape Architecture, Prof. Günther Vogt:
Ilkay Tanrisever, Günther Vogt

David Chipperfield Architects Team
Olivia Lawrence Bright, David Chipperfield

Students
Project Team 'Eastward Bound': Benjamin Artero,
Jil Kugler, Noah Richner, Mark Zahran
Project Team 'Urban Catalyst': Mathieu Bulliard,
Graziella Gini, Adrian Kröpfli, Nicolas Wild
Project Team 'Towards Ownership Diversity':
Christopher Aebi, Nicole Bucher,
Franziska Matt, Delia Wymann
Project Team 'Vertical Zoning': Laura Bernard,
Leandra Krummenacher, Androniki Prokopidou,
Sarah Stähle
Project Team 'Neighbourhood Centre':
Nik Bieri, Ileana Dan, Tobias Germann,
Samuel Meier
Project Team 'Metropolitan Park':
Demian Derron, Niti Malik, Alina Wyder
Project Team 'Walk in the Park': David Brückmann,
Yannick Dvorak, Tim Kappeler, Samuel Thomas
Project Team 'Bishopsgate Courtyards':
David Gössler, Alexandra Grieder,
Jan Helmchen, Alisa Labrenz
Project Team 'London Line': Martin Achermann,
Charly Jolliet, Gabriel Souto, Felix Tran,
Daniel Zielinski

Models/Diagrams
Simone Michel, Thorben Westerhuys

Supported by
The Rolex Mentor and Protégé Arts Initiative, Geneva

This book is the result of a year-long dialogue between David Chipperfield and Simon Kretz – two architects of different generations and backgrounds. The collaboration was enabled by the Rolex Mentor and Protégé Arts Initiative, through which David Chipperfield was invited to be mentor for architecture for 2016–17. The programme was established in 2002 with the aim of contributing to global culture by seeking out gifted young creative professionals from around the world and bringing them together with leaders from their respective fields for a period of mentoring and creative collaboration. This philanthropic programme covers seven disciplines: architecture, dance, film, literature, music, theatre and the visual arts.

This project explores and theorises qualities of contemporary urban developments in thriving global cities, such as London, Berlin, Paris, New York, Amsterdam and Zurich. Its aim is to positively affect the future of urban developments. The publication combines theoretical and practical perspectives, which are naturally closely related to each other. The first chapter contains a short theoretical essay, critically discussing purely market-oriented urbanism and providing a manifesto for a relational, collective and diverse future for our cities. The second presents a case study which exemplifies and further investigates the theoretical reflections. Developed in partnership with the Institute for Urban Design at ETH Zurich led by Professor Kees Christiaanse, Benno Agreiter, Eirini Kasioumi, Simon Kretz and Christian Weyell, thirty-six students conducted a design-based investigation of the Bishopsgate goods yard, a highly debated urban development site in East London. The study consists of nine different design proposals, each highlighting specific potentials and investigating the limits and constraints of the site. These nine thought experiments are then synthesised in order to provide a multi-scalar urban strategy. The presented strategy is not to be understood as a complete urban design scheme; rather it highlights the conditions under which an ideal urban development project could flourish. Therefore, it debates the contemporary planning culture and provides a vehicle to discuss the relations between the development of a particular site and the city in its entirety, between urban processes and resulting forms, between active and passive planning, and their political and ethical dimensions. These reflections are the cornerstones of the dialogue and are assembled into a thesis in the third chapter.

1 Introduction

As architects, we often demonstrate an ambivalent attitude towards the discipline of urban planning. On the one hand we might think it unnecessarily restrictive and not sufficiently sophisticated to respond to real conditions, while on the other we celebrate the results of clear planning visions. The relationship between planning and architecture continually fluctuates. Previous generations of architects have regarded architecture and planning as fundamentally linked disciplines, and depended on this union to create their visions. This was evidently the case in post-war Europe, where reconstruction and new attitudes to the city and its traffic motivated innovative ideas about the city and society.

The gradual loss of confidence in Modernism, however, not only affected architecture but our attitude to planning too. Societies unhappy with large and failing housing estates, drastic traffic planning and unsatisfactory urban conditions, saw large-scale planning visions as dangerous. In Britain, this was combined with growing scepticism of the public sector, regarding it as inefficient and out of touch. Protected bureaucracy was questioned and replaced by a new orthodoxy – a belief that the private sector was better organised and less wasteful. Of course, privatisation also meant that the public purse could benefit from the ideology of efficiency and enterprise.

In Britain today, as we contemplate our withdrawal from the European Union, we realise that we are making a dramatic decision about the nature of society. It is not just an issue of sovereignty but of our attitude to regulation and the British tendency to view it as the enemy of enterprise. Nothing can demonstrate this Anglo-Saxon approach better than a quick glance at London's developing skyline, which can only be explained as the result of enterprise and private competition. We cannot believe that this operation has been carried out for the common good, and we must question to what degree citizens have benefited from this transformation. If the post-war period suffered from overly ambitious visions of planners and architects, the recent period of development demonstrates the loss of common criteria and the collapse of what we might now quaintly describe as 'urban design'.

As the pendulum swings once again, there is a growing realisation that proactive planning has an important role in defining a balance between the motivations and tendencies of the free market and the concerns of wider society. The London skyline has been changed predominantly within the defining boundaries of the commercial district, which is somewhat immune to normal civic concerns. While the City of London might assume a civic appearance, it conceals a place largely devoid of other domestic urban characteristics. The radical transformation within its boundaries has not, therefore, really affected its nature, only its commercial performance and competitiveness.

With Pandora's box now open, this approach has jumped beyond the walls of the City and developers have moved the investment machinery into other parts of London. This has met surprisingly little effective resistance, only the inconvenience of a planning process that must be negotiated and managed. This is partly a generalisation, and the stump of our planning system that remains is fighting as hard as it can to resist the worst excesses of investment-led speculation. However, it has become evidently clear that our planning process earns little respect, status or resources.While some of the changes in wider London are a consequence of the improvement of infrastructure and transport, it is mostly motivated by the speculative exploitation of rising land values. This development not only takes the form of one-by-one improvements or densification, but of large-scale redevelopment projects which often involve imported typologies and changes in the scale, morphology and social structure of the city. In its most explicit form, this urban development comes in neat vertical stacks through the construction of towers – the cleanest method of investment with minimal engagement with the place, touching the ground and the neighbourhood as lightly as possible. These are not the romantic and ideological towers of the Modern movement imbued with the inspiring, if flawed, idea of the modern city and new society. Such investment projects have little patience for the conventional issues of urban regeneration and city planning. Meanwhile planners and politicians try to civilise this process as much as their powers allow and can be justified in light of the celebrated commercial advantages of investment, job creation and income generation. It is undeniably a giant industry that brings great wealth to the city and ensures the success of the larger economy, and in many ways London has benefited from this commercial energy, continuing its prosperity through the process. However, the fragmented city that is left in its wake forces us to ask some fundamental questions.

The work that we present in these pages is the result of a collaboration between Simon Kretz and myself. Through our conversations, and by comparing the free-market-driven Anglo-Saxon approach with the approaches applied in the more social democratic atmosphere of Switzerland, we have tried to understand what the fundamentals of a realistic and healthy planning approach could or should be. Given that the standard objections are inevitably practical and commercial in nature, it was important to test these principles in a 'real' context, or at least to borrow the market-led conditions that justify the Anglo-Saxon approach. We used London as an example of a growing global tendency to encourage private development of our cities, and the parallel assumed acceptance that planning is only a reactive procedure.

Our hypothesis was that the failures of the London planning system are not exclusively due to the conventionally blamed culprits of greedy developers, talentless architects, lazy planners and obstructive communities, but rather to the process itself. The dismantling of the planning system, the distrust of professional advice, and the withdrawal of resources from planning authorities have placed the initiative in the hands of the investors. However, this brings neither good results nor is it as commercially efficient as we might suppose. Taking a wider view, it is evident that the planning process is inefficient, and the commercial inefficiency is ultimately paid for by increasing the volume of development at the expense of local communities.

The exercise that we undertook has attempted to unpick some of these issues, which often seem to be protected by their own complexity. The evolution of the proposals for Bishopsgate goods yard demonstrates all of the components of a typical urban planning struggle: a large and complex urban site, previously peripheral, valued on one hand by planners and local communities for its potential to contribute to the urban and social structure, while on the other, highlighted for its development potential, albeit somewhat compromised by its conditions and restrictions. The redevelopment has been debated for more than ten years and features a cast of investors primarily driven by the market for land and development, a local community representing diverse concerns with little voice other than protest, a complicated urban condition including protected industrial heritage fabric, two local planning departments stuck between these concerns, and finally the involvement of the Mayor of London.

While we set out with a hypothesis we wanted to prove, we felt that it was important to try to apply as much objective analysis as possible to the experiment. For this we thank the students and staff of the Institute of Urban Design ETH Zurich who developed proposals for the area as a method of demonstrating how more complex issues could be dealt with if they were included as part of the planning context. Through these projects we hoped that the students would prove the potential of a development not only to address the commercial and logistic concerns of the investors but also to engage wider urban and social concerns, and, most importantly, to show that these were not mutually exclusive issues.

We believe that this theoretical work sufficiently demonstrates the essential points of our proposition. Like all good experiments, we have tried to extract some principles, illuminating the points that we set out to investigate. These points are familiar and they all rotate around recurring issues that are commonly understood and yet seem to be consistently ignored. Planning cannot and should not escape the need to be what it purports to be. Planning is not just a facilitation process and certainly should not yield only to the strongest power. It cannot deal with the problems that are raised by urgency, investment and logistics alone, but must give presence to those issues that have no other representation. If we believe in the future of our cities we must protect and foster the qualities for which we value them.

David Chipperfield

2 Problem Statement

A Matter of Public Interest

Architecture is, to a certain degree, an autonomous discipline with its own integrity. No other could replace it.[1] Nevertheless, architecture is highly embedded in its cultural and physical context. When considered as a relational concept, not only do people build architecture, but human activities are also in turn structured by it.[2] Therefore, both architecture and human beings can be considered as part of a dynamic and reciprocal relationship. Walls, doors, windows, ceilings, floors, sills, steps, tables, chairs, curtains – all of these elements structure, enable and influence activities. Buildings are active parts of our living environment, of our cities. Each project is, therefore, a contribution to the collective and shared urban realm, and every architectural endeavour has an urban impact. Regardless of its size and complexity, an urban project incorporates intertwining relationships – between people, other animate beings and inanimate objects – and enables new relationships that are as yet undetermined.[3] As such, a successful urban project does not only include the design of the material space per se, but also the concentration of things, people and other living beings. Essentially, it is a mental act: thoughts, ideas and projections that place things, people and other living beings in new and meaningful relationships. But it is not only architecture that shapes our cities; planning and the way planning processes are orchestrated have a profound influence on the physical and social form of cities, on how we live and perceive our daily environment. Architecture cannot solve these issues alone. It could be said that planning can be understood as the generator of the city's urban code, its blueprint and the script for its development, while architecture focuses rather on the city's phenotype, its physical and social manifestation. As a third discipline in this triumvirate, urban design is the mediating link between the other two. Because all three establish a relation between individual development potentials and a collectively shared vision, they are a matter of public interest.

This being said, the editors and authors of this book share an uneasy feeling about many contemporary urban projects and the current developments of the cities in which we live. Cities are booming and the focus of real estate developments has shifted from exurban areas back to the city cores. Finally, long-proposed densification strategies for the city cores meet the taste of capital investment, and in addition the cultural turn has brought architecture to the foreground of public debate. Shouldn't architects be content, especially as buildings with high aesthetic quality are trademarks of many contemporary developments? There is a bitter taste to this ongoing process, however, a darker side: many developments do not seem to provide truly inspiring environments and seldom contribute positively to the urban realm. As urban projects, they tend to fail. Often, development projects are standalone enclaves with spectacular architecture that consume urbanity without providing it. In these contexts, architects have become increasingly marginalised and complicit in the system, and a kind of caricature – the 'starchitect' – has become the emblem of the profession.[4] The reputation of established architects is often (mis)used both to achieve and justify very high floor area ratios. Other projects are less spectacular but often amount to little more than isolated exercises in land valorisation. Thus, their limited urban impact is not only rooted in iconographic singularism but can also reflect their lack of urbanity.

1 For a discussion of themes relating to the autonomy of architecture, see: Ungers, O. M. (1983): *Die Thematisierung der Architektur*. Stuttgart: Deutsche Verlags-Anstalt.

2 For a discussion of sociological concepts in architecture, see: Latour, B. (2007): *Eine neue Soziologie für eine neue Gesellschaft. Einführung in die Akteur-Netzwerk-Theorie*. Frankfurt a. M.: Suhrkamp. / Giddens, A. (1988): *Die Konstitution der Gesellschaft: Grundzüge einer Theorie der Strukturierung*. Frankfurt a. M. / New York: Campus.

3 For a consideration of objecthood in urbanism, see: Kretz, S.; Salewski, C. (2014): 'Urbanität der Dinge'. In: Christiaanse, K. et al.: *Die Stadt als Ressource: Konzepte und Methoden für städtebauliches Entwerfen*. Berlin: Jovis. pp. 167–180.

4 David Chipperfield, in conversation with Simon Kretz and Edwin Heathcote. London, 26.05.2017.

Urbanisation without Urbanity[5]

Urbanisation describes the process producing our built environment such as buildings, infrastructural networks and man-made landscapes, and their societal implications.[6]

Urbanisation leads to an extensive transformation of society and is closely connected historically to the process of industrialisation. Urbanity, however, describes the specific conditions in space and time of how societies arrange, organise and live within the overarching process of urbanisation. Urbanity is the way of life and the form of cohabitation when many different people live in a relatively dense environment and therefore share physical and mental spaces, infrastructures and goods.[7] Unlike the rather inevitable processes of global urbanisation often described as a 'law of nature'[8] or as the new 'empire',[9] urbanity focuses on political ideas, options, choices and the multitude of differences.[10] Urbanisation processes do not automatically lead to liveable forms of togetherness, and often the contrary. While urbanisation seems inevitable, urbanity is a very fragile condition that needs to be cultivated.

This conceptual duality is mirrored in the contemporary production of development sites in global cities. The leading narrative of the free market – often combined with the legitimate liberal fear of the straightjacket of state control – focuses squarely on the influx of capital, production of new jobs and, consequently, economic growth.

The main focus lies on propelling the process of urbanisation, and on efficiency, small government and low taxes. Often, this narrow scope overlooks values of urbanity such as social diversity, interaction and, most importantly, the potential for the inhabitants to appropriate the built environment.[11] The existence of societal forces demanding more (or other) values than just economic growth cannot be denied. These forces gain visibility when development projects exclude specific groups and people start to resist and oppose development projects – as happened with our case study, the project to transform the former Bishopsgate goods yard in central London in 2016. The detailed reasons for opposition may vary from case to case but these projects have one common denominator: they are based on a single focality of urbanisation without fostering urbanity. Small government leads to a lack of real integration of different stakeholders. In addition to this, the lack of a clear and collective strategy leads to high planning insecurity. When combined, development opportunities can turn into expensive and risky undertakings that are perceived as insensitive to their surroundings.

Even though 'urbanity' is often prominently promoted in such development projects, in reality these narratives cannot hide their lack of urban qualities. For those in opposition, urbanity cannot be added like a cherry on a cake. On the contrary, urbanity should be the main ingredient. Such opposition highlights not only the highly conflicted political dimension of contemporary urban production, but also leads to substantial delays, disintegration and frustration on both sides. In these cases, the development's focus on urbanisation starts to harm its core ideals, such as efficiency. At this point, the notions of market friendliness, a swift pace of development, streamlined processes and small government can become mere rhetoric. The often-unmediated clash of values turns projects into political battlefields – a condition that hinders both

5 For a discussion of the two terms, see: Schmid, C. (2016): 'Urbanisierung und Urbanität'. In: Kretz, S.; Kueng, L. (2016): *Urbane Qualitäten*. Zurich: Hochparterre. pp. 14–40.
6 See: Harvey, D. (1982): *The Limits to Capital*. Oxford: Blackwell.
7 See: Wirth, L. (1938): 'Urbanism as a Way of Life'. In: *The American Journal of Sociology*. 44/1, pp. 1–24.
8 See: Ursprung, P. (2010): *Die Kunst der Gegenwart. 1960 bis heute*. Munich: C.H. Beck.
9 See: Hardt, M.; Negri, A. (2002): *Empire*. Cambridge, Mass.: Harvard University Press.
10 See: Lefebvre, H. ([1970], 1972): *Die Revolution der Städte*. Munich: List.
11 Kretz, S.; Kueng, L. (2016): *Urbane Qualitäten*. Zurich: Hochparterre.

urbanisation processes and urbanity. These moments of crisis clearly show that successful transitions from urbanisation to urbanity, and the relation between freedom of privatisation and a certain degree of integration of collective interests, are highly relevant pieces in the complicated puzzle of the production of urban space.

To further investigate the blind spots of urbanisation without urbanity, it is important to mention that contemporary urbanisation processes are far too often solely based on infrastructural logic, investment-driven processes and market analysis. Because of this, those involved tend to forget that infrastructural logic fosters hierarchical relations based on the reduction of complexity, that purely investment-driven processes are often blind to the habitat of human beings while preferring to focus on a very narrow user profile, and that market analysis is fundamentally conservative. This knot of paradigms and dogmas tends to miss opportunities to turn urbanisation projects into vehicles fostering positive forms of urbanity. There are four salient points that we believe can foster such positive forms of urbanity, which can be described as:

A. Articulated spaces
B. Metropolitan spaces
C. Adaptable spaces
D. Inclusive spaces

A. Articulated spaces of tangible relationships

are based on the idea of linking up things – a basic architectonical and urban design quality Bruno Taut once coined 'Proportion'.[12] Articulation, complexity and *differentiation* are its ingredients.[13] Articulation means that things are perceptible and can therefore be placed in new relationships by people. Complexity means that things are tied into multiple relationships and thus have several interpretations. Finally, differentiation means that things may be different from one another but are nonetheless interrelated. The goals are figures of socio-spatial *interaction* in the form of relationship wealth and relationship potential.[14] Relationship wealth is a state between two extremes: on the one hand, boredom means that there are very few relationships or only those of the same type; on the other hand, chaos means that there are too many unrelatable stimuli, making it impossible to act or to make sense of them. The production and sensation of relations creates mental, social and physical embedding and a meaningful environment, and this is, naturally, one of the most important functions of civilisation. In addition, relationship wealth should also be possible in future forms. The city fabric therefore requires another characteristic, identified as 'elasticity' by Bruno Taut in his work on architecture.[15] According to Taut, elasticity ensures usefulness in the future; he writes that 'the relationships between purposes are inextricably intertwined. Apart from that, we do not know what the future will bring. We should therefore make it our duty never to obstruct future development. This means a departure from [...] rigidity.'[16] From this point of view, elasticity equates to relationship potential.

12 Taut, B. ([1935/36], 2009): 'Architekturlehre/Architekturüberlegungen'. In: *Arch+*, Nr. 194, pp. 36–157./ Kuma, K. (2012): *Anti-object: The Dissolution and Disintegration of Architecture*. London: Architectural Association Publications.

13 See: Frampton, K.; Solà-Morales, M. de (2008): *Manuel de Solà-Morales: A Matter of Things*. Rotterdam: NAi.

14 For a definition and a discussion of the two terms, see: Kretz, S.; Salewski, C. (2014): 'Urbanität der Dinge'. In: Christiaanse, K. et al.: *Die Stadt als Ressource: Konzepte und Methoden für städtebauliches Entwerfen*. Berlin: Jovis. pp. 167–180.

15 Taut, B. ([1935/36], 2009): 'Architekturlehre/Architekturüberlegungen'. In: *Arch+*, Nr. 194, pp. 36–157.

16 *Ibid*. p. 120.

B. Metropolitan spaces for a multitude of users

are based on the idea that infrastructurally well-connected development sites should not only be residential or commercial developments, but have an urban impact on many scales. This encapsulates concepts of *centrality* (different uses and programmes for people not living or working on site) as well as porosity and *accessibility*.[17] If central locations lack such an urban impact, the whole metropolitan area suffers from this absence of collective centralities. The integration of multiple scales in one location is described by the concept of transscalarity. It encompasses the knowledge that contemporary urbanisation processes do not only affect specific development sites, but reach out to the metropolitan areas and are highly connected to national and international regulations, capital flows, technological innovations and employment markets.[18] This line of thought leads to the comparison of urbanistic projects with other transscalar disciplines, such as environmental impact studies. Not unlike the analytical concept of the 'ecological footprint' for measuring negative human impact on the Earth's ecosystem[19], an 'urban footprint' could be established as an analogy for positive human impact on a city's socio- and ecosystem. An advantage of such concepts is that they depend on transscalar thinking because they encompass effects on different scales.[20]

C. Adaptable spaces for the everyday

are based on the idea that there is a viable alternative to the concept of public spaces being purely retail-oriented. This alternative is founded on the belief that the public domain can be established without being fixated on retail. Interstitial spaces such as greens, squares, front gardens, corner coffee shops, workshops and pavements become important devices in this context – spatial elements with a long-standing tradition in cities, especially in London. Not only marketability, but also *appropriation* and long-term *adaptability* are core qualities of such quotidian spaces.[21] If existing relationships are rigid, extremely stable and difficult to change, people miss out on opportunities to transform, rearrange or reconfigure their relationships according to their needs. The city cannot, therefore, adapt to new usage requirements, meanings or relationships. The French writer, film-maker and urban theorist Guy Debord once described the historical inner city of Paris as a suppressive 'straightjacket' that forced people to keep to specific courses of action, so they were unable to live their lives themselves but felt compelled to take part in a 'spectacle'.[22] All relationships followed strict capitalist values and could not be changed by the individual. This limited their freedom and left no room for them to make their own decisions.

D. Inclusive spaces formed by diverse stakeholders

are based on the idea that urban qualities such as social diversity or stakeholder complexity should not be seen as narrative add-ons to post-legitimise development projects, but rather as core constitutive forces of urbanity. Urbanity only emerges if multiple uses and interests are collectively able to shape the socio-spatial realm, because urban spaces with a certain density are used by diverse users with different backgrounds and perspectives.[23] The density of uses and users in cities has four socio-spatial effects: the first increases resource efficiency due to the multiple use of spaces by different users, for different purposes. The second effect brings completely different people and groups together due to its multiple uses. This connection may occur through an actual encounter within the physical space, such as in a square. These meetings lead to reciprocal perception and a mutual connection to different environments.[24] According to Hannah Arendt, this type of encounter is the essence of public life.[25] Even if people do not encounter another person directly, they may come to have an indirect relationship due to multiple uses and a shared awareness that they use the same spaces and things. These multiple uses and meanings lead to a third effect, whereby this density of diverse programmes and users may cause rivalry and therefore conflict, for example, if different uses disturb or contradict one another. This causes things to become more disputed. This effect has given rise to the urban culture of social interaction in two different but closely related ways. In order to avoid or reduce unproductive conflicts, relationships within the urban realm are largely structured according to regulations, modes of behaviour and social norms. According to the German sociologist Georg Simmel, the social phenomenon historically described as 'urban' refers to the refined, regulated way of life in urban societies, as opposed to societies shaped by agriculture.[26] This structuring via formalisation and standardisation upholds high relationship density while preventing relationships from collapsing from too many conflicts. Moreover, this culture means that urban societies have a lower risk when it comes to experimenting with new forms of relationship, due to their experience in preventing and reducing conflicts. This explains why cultural, technical and social innovation happens primarily in cities and why urban societies can absorb increasing numbers of new, foreign people and relationships while also fulfilling their own potential for innovation. This innovation potential and the ability to synthesise conflicts is the fourth effect and one of the key elements of successful urban processes in heterogeneous social constellations. When designing an urban project, it is therefore key to integrate a multitude of stakeholders in a very early phase of planning, not only as a political duty to include different perspectives, but also to activate local and specific knowledge, to address conflicts and potential forms of consensus as generating parts of the project, and to use the multi-perspective potential of stakeholder heterogeneity as a tool for robust developments without fixation on a single – and therefore highly vulnerable – perspective. The shaping of the urban realm as a collective and transparent endeavour further helps to avoid frustration, inefficiencies, unnecessary follow-up costs and political mistrust.

All four spatial types highlight core urban qualities such as centrality, diversity, interaction, accessibility, appropriation and adaptability.[27] The absence of these spaces and qualities is an indicator of urbanisation without urbanity. Even though their lack is ultimately a deficiency of the urban form, it is not only the designer who is to blame. The reason for this lies in the nature of urban projects. They are foremost results of long-lasting and highly complicated planning processes, deeply embedded in local planning regimes and in cultural milieus. The chain of decision-making is often very long when it comes to urban projects – it encompasses not only politicians, planners, developers, experts, architects and engineers, but also a public debate including opposing and supporting forces, and land-capitalisation models. Architecture happens to be the most visible element of this chain, but not necessarily its most decisive. Even though architects and urban designers have a high responsibility in the making of urban space – and this responsibility should by no means be extenuated – it is fair to say that good architecture and public spaces which address urban qualities can hardly save badly conceived planning processes. This simple but crucial insight leads us to acknowledge the importance of urban planning and the inherent processes leading to urban projects, and the fundamental forces, convictions and ideologies forming these processes.

17 See: Sennett, R. (2006): *The Open City*. downloads.lsecities.net/o_downloads/Berlin_Richard_Sennett_2006-The_Open_City.pdf, accessed 25.11.2017. / Lynch, K. (1981): *A Theory of Good City Form*. Cambridge, Mass.: MIT.

18 See: Brenner, N. (2014): *Implosions/Explosions: Towards a Study of Planetary Urbanization*. Berlin: Jovis.

19 See: Wackernagel, M.; Rees, W. (1996): *Our Ecological Footprint: Reducing Human Impact on the Earth*. Gabriola Island, BC [etc.]: New Society Publishers.

20 Salewski, C.; Kretz, S. (2017): 'An Assemblage of Assemblers: The 2006 Antwerp Strategic Structural Plan s-RSA', in: *disP the Planning Review*, 208 – Vol. 53.1 (1/2017). Special Edition: 'Assemblages for Innovative Planning: Shaping Processes of Transformation'. pp. 87–98.

21 Heidegger, M. ([1927], 2001): *Sein und Zeit*. Tübingen: Max Niemeyer Verlag.

22 See: Debord, G. ([1976], 1991): *La Société du Spectacle*. Paris: Gallimard.

23 See: Hajer, M.; Reijndorp, A. (2001): *In Search of the New Public Domain. Analysis and Strategy*. Rotterdam: nai010.

24 See: Lefebvre, H. (1974): *La production de l'espace*. Paris: Anthropos.

25 See: Arendt, H. (2010): *Vita activa: oder Vom tätigen Leben*. Munich: Piper.

26 See: Simmel, G. ([1903], 2006): *Die Grossstädte und das Geistesleben*. Frankfurt a. M.: Suhrkamp.

27 See: Kretz, S.; Küng, L. (2016): *Urbane Qualitäten*. Zurich: Hochparterre. / Lynch, K. (1981): *A Theory of Good City Form*. Cambridge, Mass.: MIT.

Planning Cultures

As stated above, today, all global cities face the task of connecting the immense forces of capital investment and real estate development with the idea of the city as a collective place to live, work and enjoy our lives in a constructive and fair way. The coordination of development opportunities and the metabolism of cities may differ from city to city, but the problem has global dimensions. Since all these cities have their own history and therefore their own specific cultural path-dependency, each deals with this common core problem differently. While Paris on the one extreme traditionally cultivates a very strict planning regime in its inner city boundary, London at the other end of the scale stands for a very libertarian attitude toward planning and cultivates one of the least protective planning systems. The municipality of Amsterdam in contrast has a long-standing tradition of very precise planning of whole city areas, famously known as 'Bestemmingsplan', while Berlin is well known for its site-specific policies based on socio-economic strategies. Eventually, all cities have to find their own form of planning or non-planning, and their specific balance between control and laissez-faire.[28] Some choose proactive steering, others cultivate a strategy of passivity.

As we can see, planning is deeply morally charged and culturally embedded, it is political and artistic, economic and logistic. But despite the many differences between cities and their specific path-dependency, the way cities and regions are planned can very well change or be changed.[29] Planning cultures are dynamic. They perpetually transform through adaptation, innovation, evolution and sometimes even revolution; and most of all by mutual learning through exchange. Zurich, for example, operated for decades on a planning system based on zoning-law, defining zones with homogenous building codes and densities. Under the pressure of densification and investment, however, the Anglo-Saxon model was studied and the existing zoning policy was topped up with a rather liberal, deal-based policy for large and strategically relevant sites, where higher densities are allowed. Consequently, Zurich now runs an interesting dual planning system, trying to balance exceptions and homogenous zones. London can be seen as the origin of deal-based planning and an inspiration for many other cities. In the wake of scaling down bureaucracy and contemporary critique of modernist planning fantasies, many cities follow the Anglo-Saxon model of abandoning the idea of comprehensively planning whole cities and move towards a planning system that focuses less on general rules and more on strategic interventions and on specific densification zones.

Therefore, so-called 'opportunity areas' become the most important devices of present-day planning.[30] While the advantages of this planning approach – such as focusing on the most important sites and tailor-made local densification – are highly praised, the downside of extremising inequalities of land values is accompanied by another risk: if 'opportunity areas' are not fully embedded in a shared social and spatial vision of a city's future and therefore not properly used as an opportunity for the whole city, they become inward-looking and disconnected pieces of land that can negatively impact their surroundings. The reasons for this can be threefold: lack of vision, unsuccessful urbanistic integration or too much of a passive and defensive role of the public hand – or all at once.

Combined with the concept of deal-based planning and with a planning process that does not create powerful public forums and proper integration of independent professional experts, 'opportunity areas' become opaque for many. Hence, they can provoke damaging confrontations. Obviously, such planning set-ups have the tendency to be confusing rather than inspiring. People start to feel that the city is something that happens to them, a process in which they have no voice.[31]

Therefore, it is not venturous to state that the lack of a far-sighted integration of development projects is a risky aspect of contemporary planning culture and has the potential to turn the promising notion of an 'opportunity for urbanity' into a disappointing 'opportunistic spawn of urbanisation'.

In this context, the learning process between cities could be reciprocal. Since the planning system of Zurich has a lot to offer concerning the way planning processes are politically embedded and how different agencies take part within these planning processes, its model of including engagement and activism could be studied. Public engament is often both misunderstood and underestimated. A careful study of Zurich's planning system shows that inclusion is not only a resource for our urban future,[32] but also crucial for the credibility of cities and their politics.

In summary, three lessons can be learned. Firstly, even though cities should not blindly adopt models generated in other contexts, learning from each other is a fundamental source of improvement and innovation and should be enhanced. Secondly, the quality and performance of an urban project greatly relies on its genesis, primarily on the planning process and the planning system, both being societal products. Urban form is, to a certain degree, preconditioned by urban processes. Thirdly, there is a strong triangular relation between the contemporary conceptualisation of society, the way planning processes are set up and the phenomenon of 'urbanisation without urbanity'. Its nexus reflects the hegemonic planning culture of today and can be studied in a multitude of cases. The next chapter will investigate one representative example, the project for the former Bishopsgate goods yard in London. It should not be misunderstood as a platform to pronounce disappointment with the urbanistic or architectural layout of the design, but to understand the project as an examplar of many in order to point at a deeper, more cultural problem: the contemporary way of failing to orchestrate individual development potentials with a collectively shared urban vision and the underlying trend to de-cultivate and de-politicise planning.

28 Christiaanse, K. (2004): 'Control & Laissez Faire'. In Christiaanse, K.: *The City as Loft. Projects at the interface of architecture and urbanism*. Rotterdam: NAi. p. 8.

29 See: Sassen, S. (2001): *The global city: New York, London, Tokyo*. Princeton. N.J.: Princeton University Press./ETH Studio Basel (2015): *The Inevitable Specificity of Cities: Napoli, Nile Valley, Hong Kong, Belgrade, Nairobi, Canary Islands, Beirut, Casablanca*. Zurich: Lars Müller.

30 See: Mayor of London (2015): 'City Fringe Opportunity Area Planning Framework'. London: Greater London Authority.

31 David Chipperfield, in conversation with Simon Kretz and Edwin Heathcote. London, 26.05.2017.

32 Hoelzel, F. (2014): 'Zusammenspiel der raumplanerischen und städtebaulichen Planungsinstrumente im Grossraum Zürich'. In: *Stadtregionen planen/Stadsregio's plannen*. Themenheft vom Hochparterre Mai 2014. Zurich: Hochparterre. pp. 24–27.

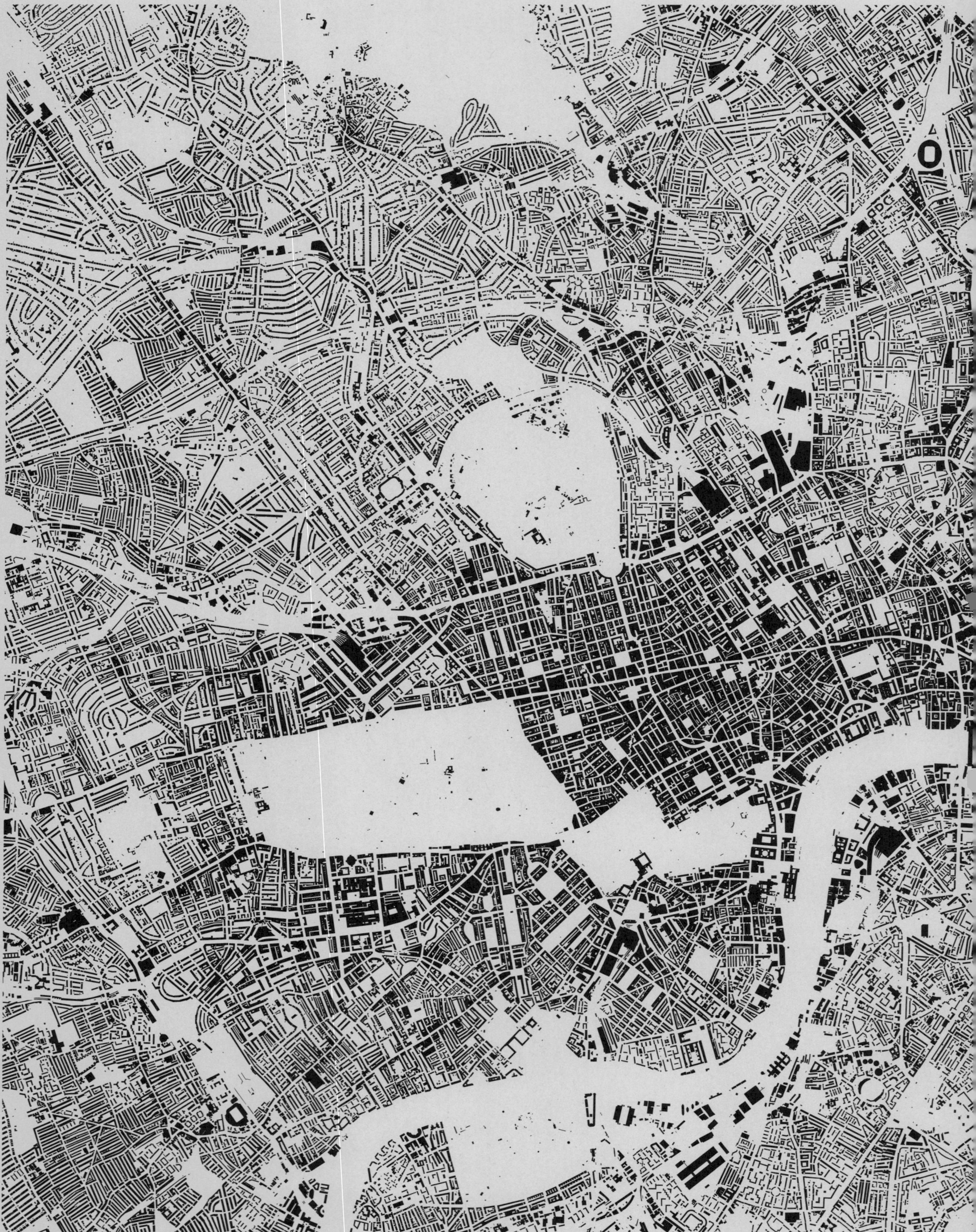

1 Map of London

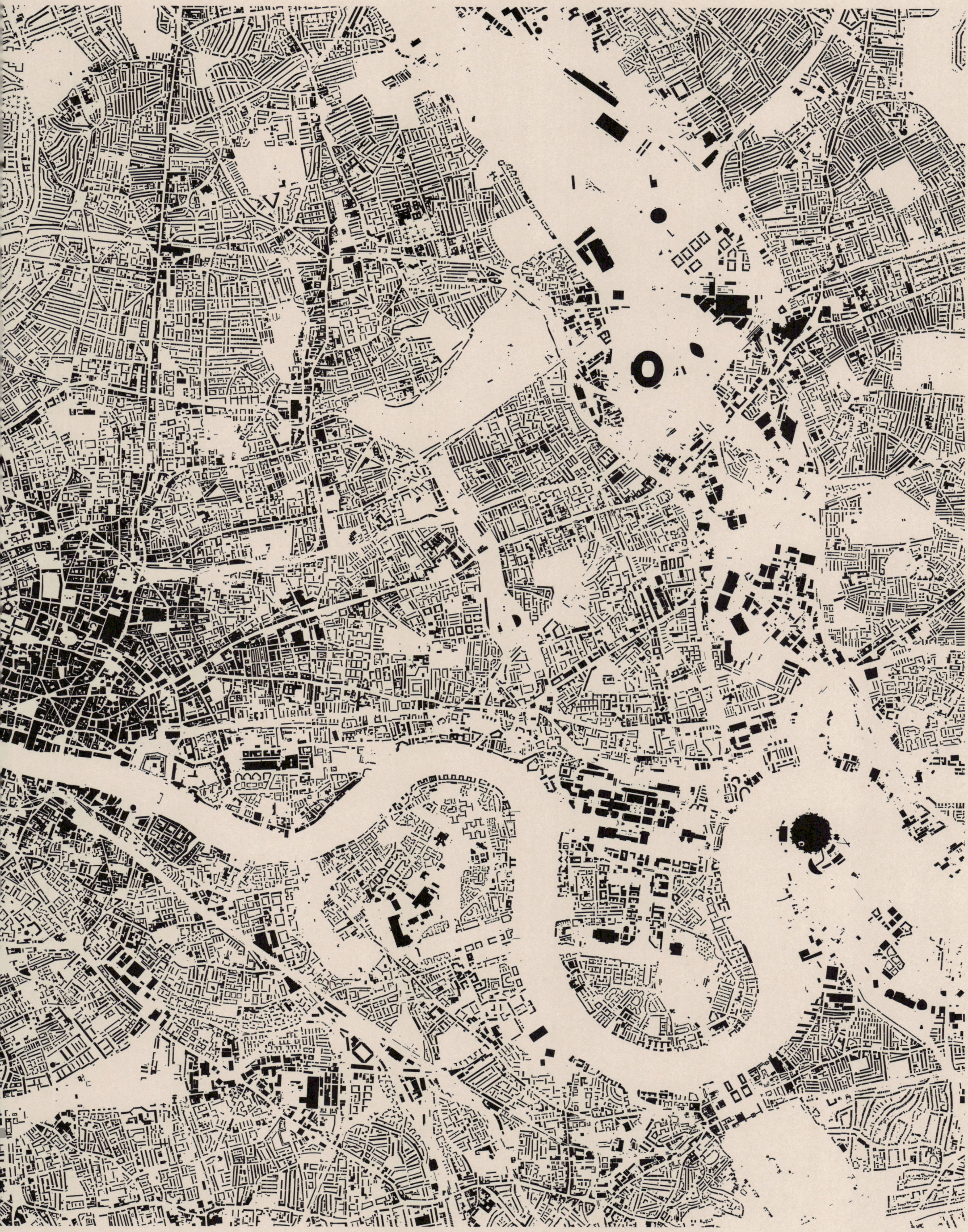

3.1 Case Study Bishopsgate Goods Yard Context and Method

The Confrontational Way

The listed ruin of the former Bishopsgate goods yard lies at the threshold of the City's financial district and the dynamic neighbourhoods of London's East: Shoreditch, Bethnal Green and Whitechapel – including the (in)famous Brick Lane (fig. 1). The history of the site is characterised by discontinuities and profound transformations. Before the Bishopsgate passenger station was built in 1840, the site was an indistinguishable part of a homogenous residential neighbourhood. In 1880, the passenger station was transformed into a goods station and yard. This sparked industrial development in the surrounding neighbourhoods, such as the Truman brewery and various storage buildings (figs. 2 and 3). After the station partly burned down in 1964, these industries suffered as well, creating an urban vacuum in the neighbourhood and particularly on the site. Fenced off, it became a no man's land strewn with industrial ruins and brick railway arches. Eventually, the remaining covered parts and the roof were used for parking cars. Today, the graffiti-covered brick ruin is surrounded by steel and glass facades and serves as a backdrop for street markets, temporary football pitches, trendy 'pop-up' shops, 'local' vintage stores, and organic burger restaurants (figs. 4–6). The farther the City extends into the East, the more the new investments hide behind traditional brick facades. The area around Bishopsgate remains a border zone between the new precariate, creative industries and large financial firms, and gains its attraction from the friction created by its extremely heterogeneous environment (figs. 7–11). Its centre, however, is still a gaping hole in the urban fabric.

An urban project at this location has the potential to become a spatial and programmatical link between these different environments, a public transport node, and a new centrality in London. The site, situated in two boroughs and cut up by various types of infrastructure, poses great challenges to urban design both because of its sheer size and its complex topological relations.

British developers Hammerson and The Ballymore Group bought the site from National Rail in 2002. It was not until 2014 that they presented an 800-million-pound development project, which quickly became one of London's most disputed projects (fig. 12). Following protests from different groups, the authorities rejected the proposal in early 2016. It was considered too insensitive for the surrounding neighbourhoods, provided too little affordable rental space, and lacked urbanistic potential.

The episode also highlights the relatively passive role of the boroughs' planning councils even when it comes to important projects such as the Bishopsgate goods yard. From the start, the developers took the lead, commissioned surveys and made proposals, to which the boroughs could respond. The planning councils had considerably less manpower and were practically bound to take a referee position, rather than actively steering the process. The weak position of planning authorities in the UK is deeply rooted in political culture. Since the Greater London Council (GLC) was abolished by Margaret Thatcher in 1986 and owing to the subsequent culture of deregulation, the borough councils have lost much of their influence through the lack of both competencies and resources. Not even the Greater London Authority (GLA) has the power to make tangible development proposals, declare the Bishopsgate site important for the public or integrate it in a larger urban strategy. The GLA's core actions are to define Opportunity Areas and to call in projects from the boroughs to re-evaluate them. Finally, the considerable difference in power over projects between developers and authorities also has financial roots. The costs for almost all planning processes are borne by the developers. Consequently, authorities are pushed into a passive role. Thus, because the planners and experts are mostly selected by the developers and the key characteristics of projects are necessarily determined by them as well, he who pays the piper calls the tune. Authorities therefore can either comply with the developer's needs and adopt their narratives, or block projects completely. There is hardly room for a collaborative approach to the design process, and to incorporate issues of public interest into the basic design concepts. This rather confrontational approach is hardened by the very complex and often unclear guidelines and laws in planning and building rights, as is exemplified by the percentage of affordable housing, which seems to be a negotiable guideline rather than an absolute stipulation. The authorities are left with a few explicit and non-negotiable paragraphs, such as regarding the protected views corridors, protection of open spaces or access to daylight. The result is a bundle of restrictions and duties for the developers, most often confined to the building site. This inward-looking perspective on projects is further fostered by developers, because they try to reduce possible complexities at the site's edges in order to design more readily realisable designs. Unsurprisingly, the proposal offered by Hammerson and Ballymore has strengths only within the site's perimeter, where their (financial) interests are strongest, while the connections to and integration into the surroundings are weak if existing at all. The project proposed is therefore an excellent example of urbanisation without urbanity.

Understandably, the lack of urbanistic qualities was one of the reasons for the boroughs to object to the proposal. Although the site is located within the boroughs of Hackney and Tower Hamlets, the final decision on the project proposal lies with the Mayor of London, since he can 'call it in' to his office to overrule the boroughs. This is exactly what former mayor Boris Johnson did in 2015 upon pressure from the developers. Despite their legal impotence, however, the boroughs publicly rejected the proposal and the borough of Hackney presented a viable alternative of considerably smaller density and lower building heights. While having merely a rhetorical function, the presentation of this alternative could be read as an attempt to urge the developers to downscale their next proposal. Before the Mayor officially reacted to the application, however, Hammerson and Ballymore withdrew it for reconsideration. In this game of confrontational ping-pong, it is the developers' turn again, while the boroughs and the GLA have to wait for their next application.

Test Planning as Alternative

At this point, the Urban Design Studio at the Institute for Urban Design at the ETH Zurich comes into play. Its aim is to propose a planning method alternative to the duel 'developer vs. city' with the Bishopsgate goods yard as its case: the test planning method.[33] Instead of a rather opaque deal-based process, the proposed method is based on fostering an open debate. Its main goal is to start a broad discussion about the future of the goods yard well before any crucial decisions are made about the core principles of the project. Therefore, nine different scenarios are designed, tested and critically discussed in order to debate the following questions:

How can urban design projects be conceptualised as new centralities in heterogeneous neighbourhoods? How can urban design projects be connected to the urban texture, while having positive urban impacts at the scale of both the neighbourhood and the metropolis?

Principally, all projects aim at gaining knowledge through designing. Therefore, each design can be understood as a *thought experiment* examining and highlighting certain qualities of the existing environment and testing ideas and concepts.

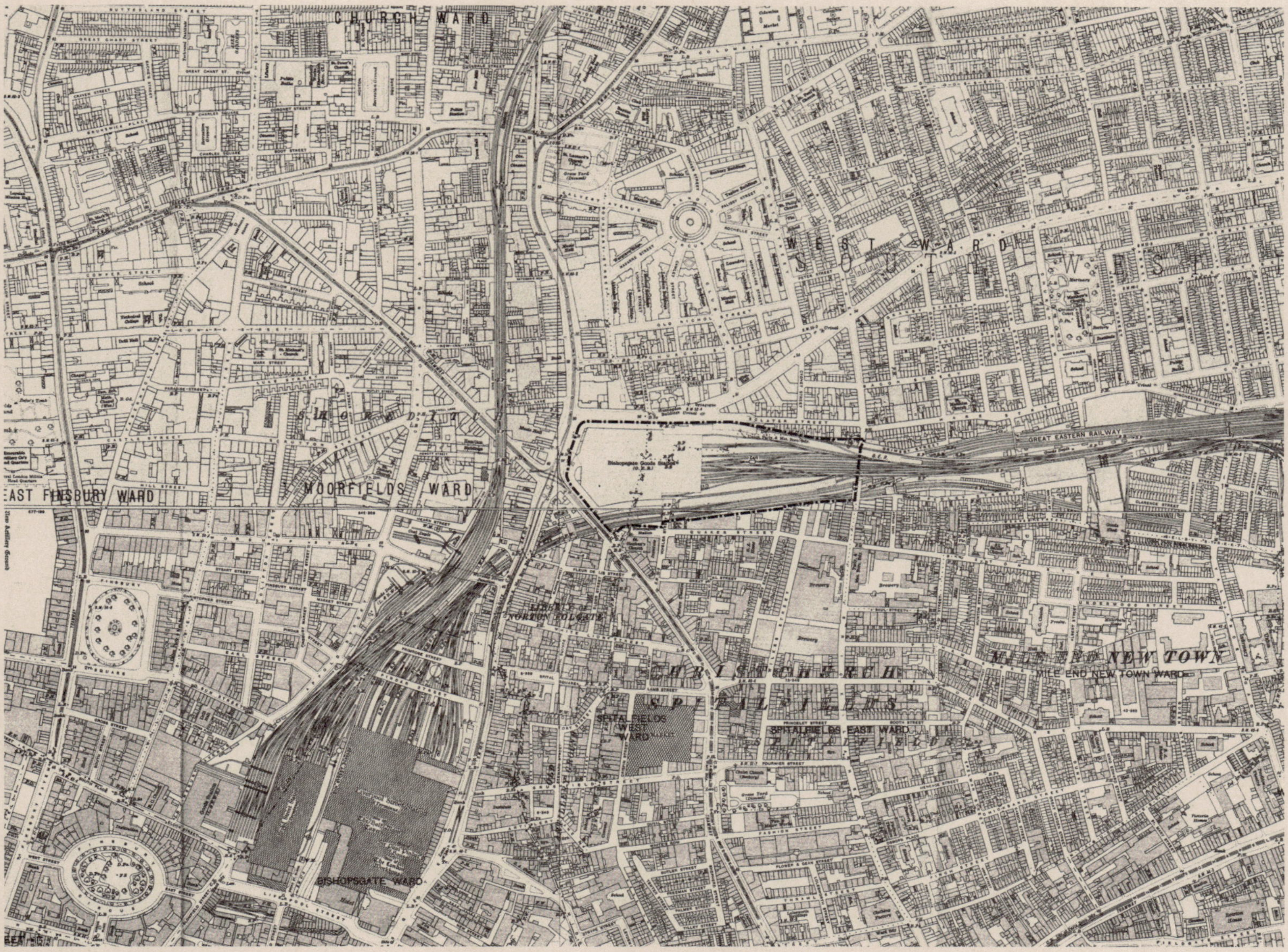

2 Bishopsgate goods yard and the surrounding area, 1916

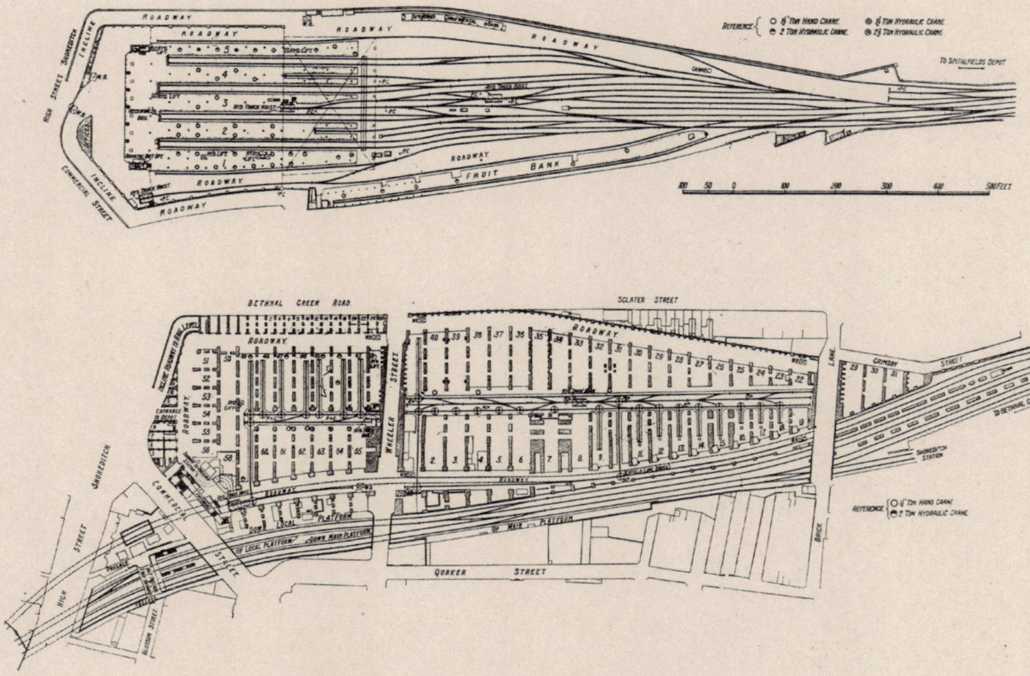

3 Bishopsgate goods yard, established 1881; ground level and roof level floor plan

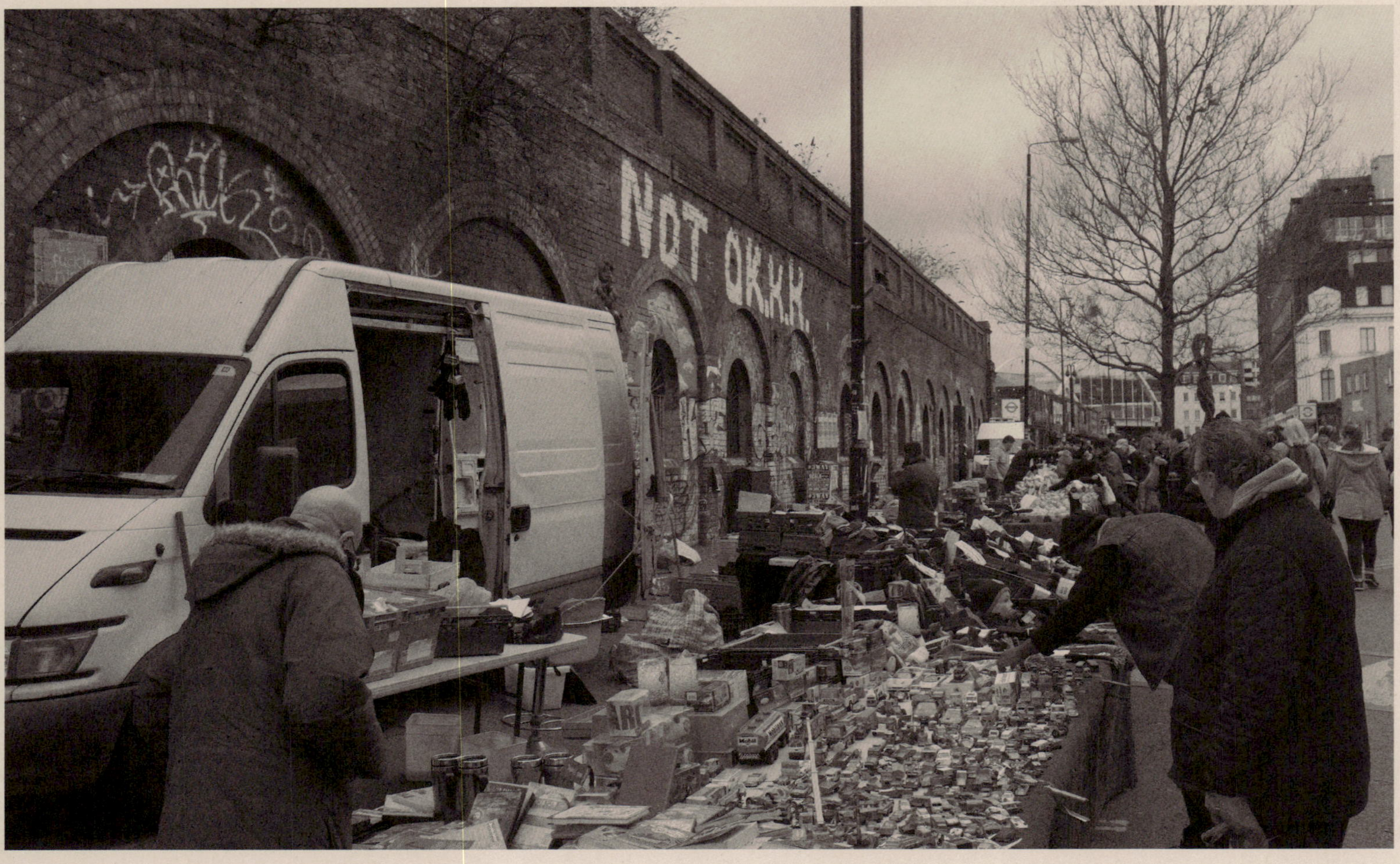

4

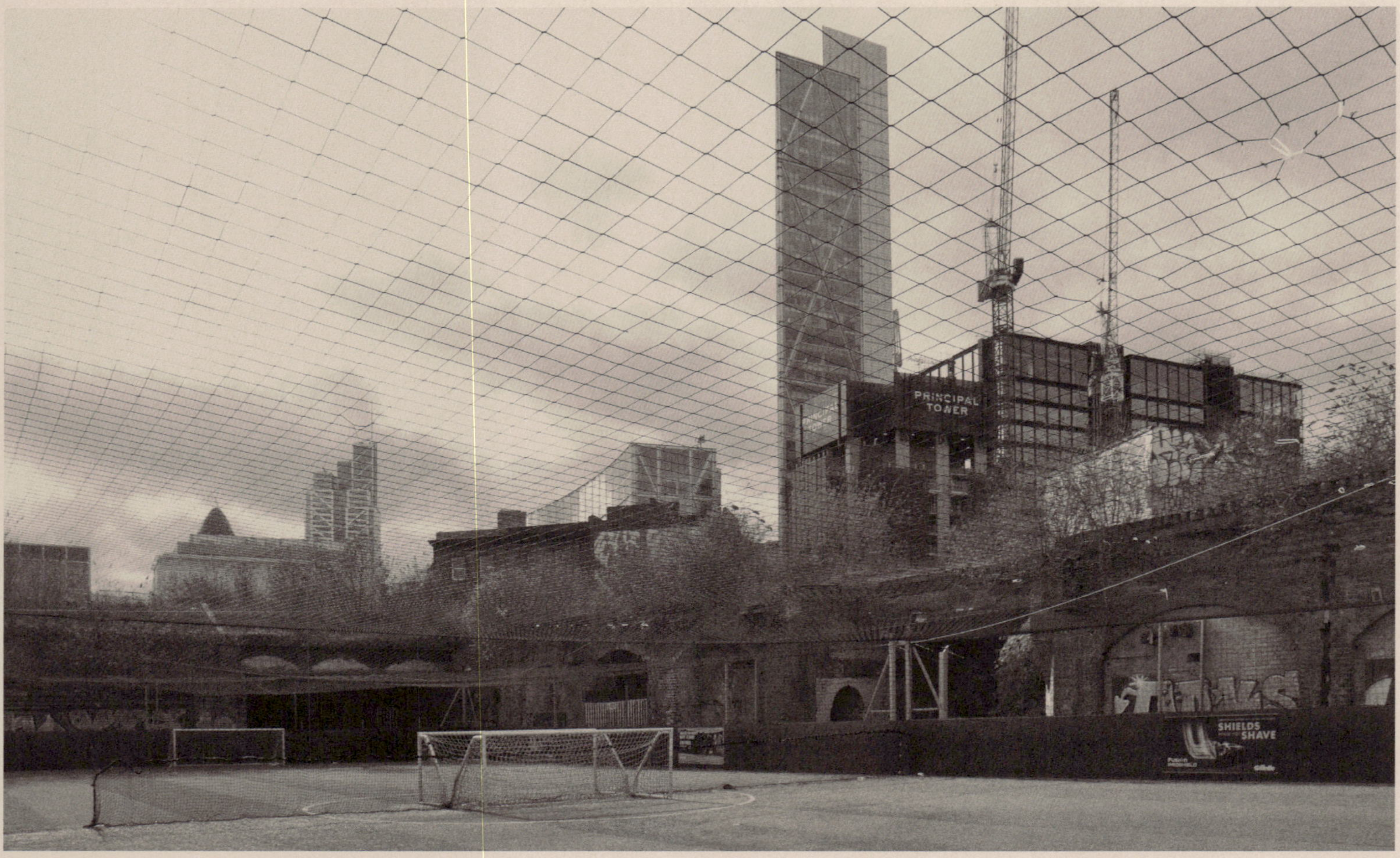

5

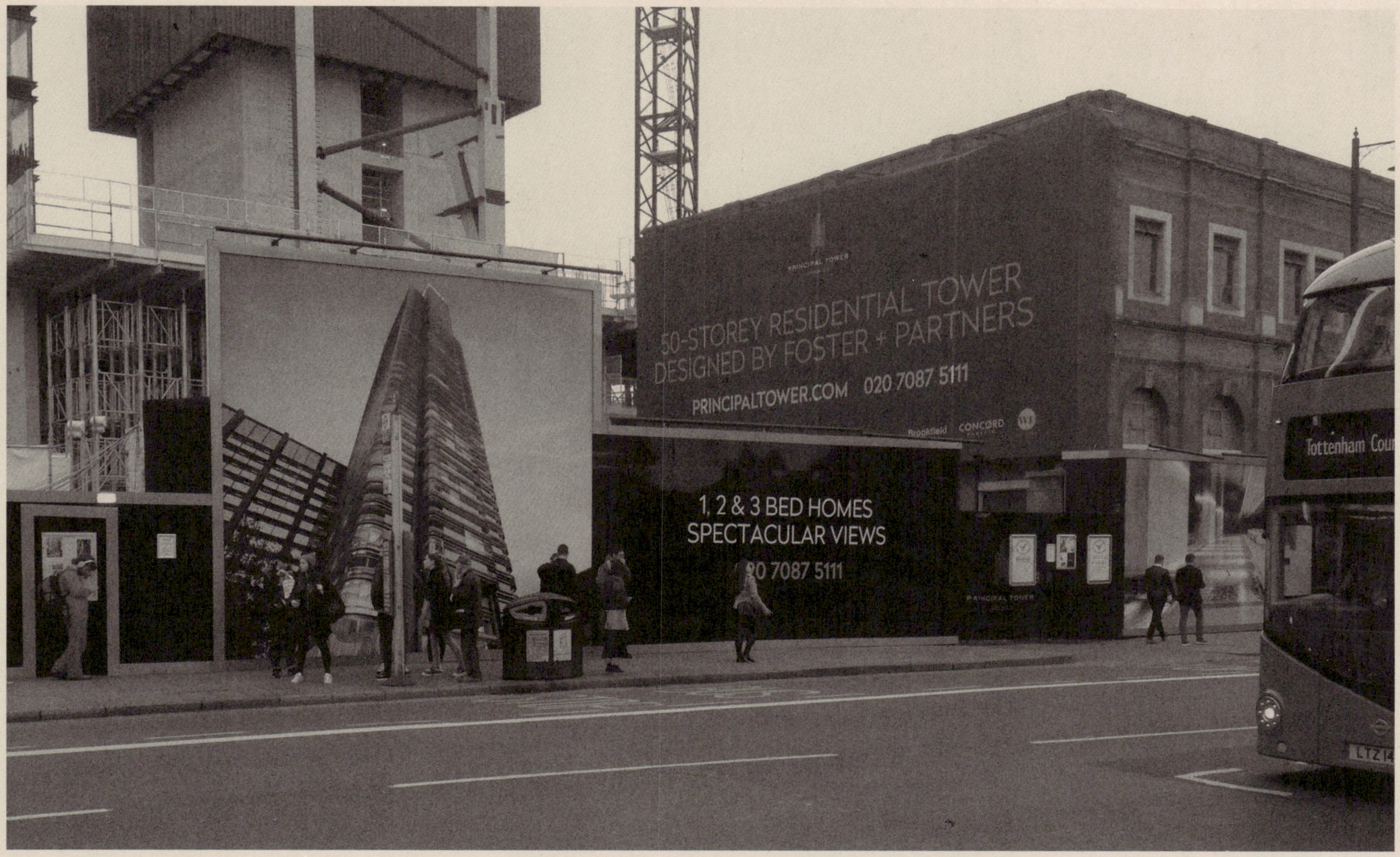
50-STOREY RESIDENTIAL TOWER
DESIGNED BY FOSTER + PARTNERS
PRINCIPALTOWER.COM 020 7087 5111
1, 2 & 3 BED HOMES
SPECTACULAR VIEWS
020 7087 5111

6

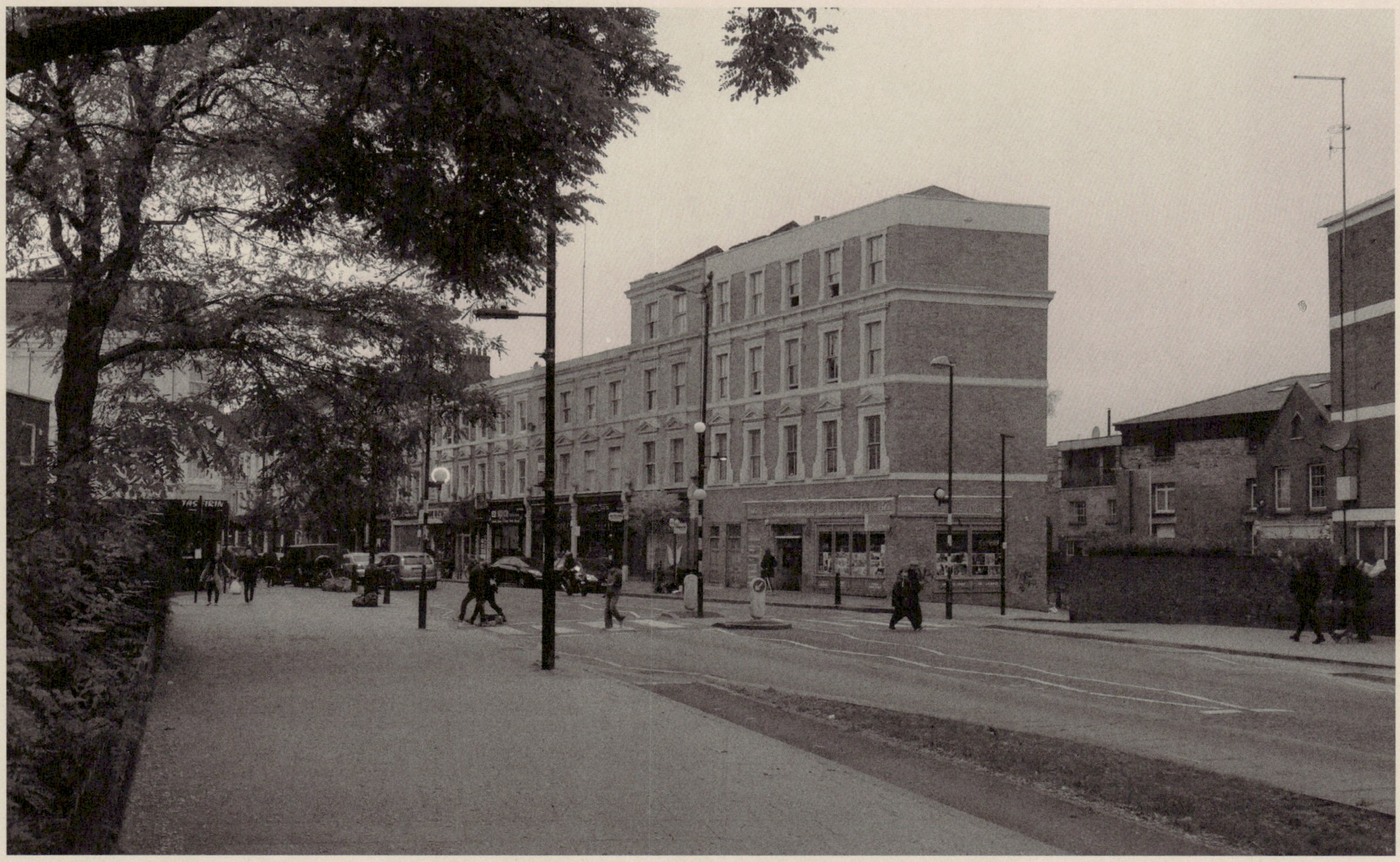

7

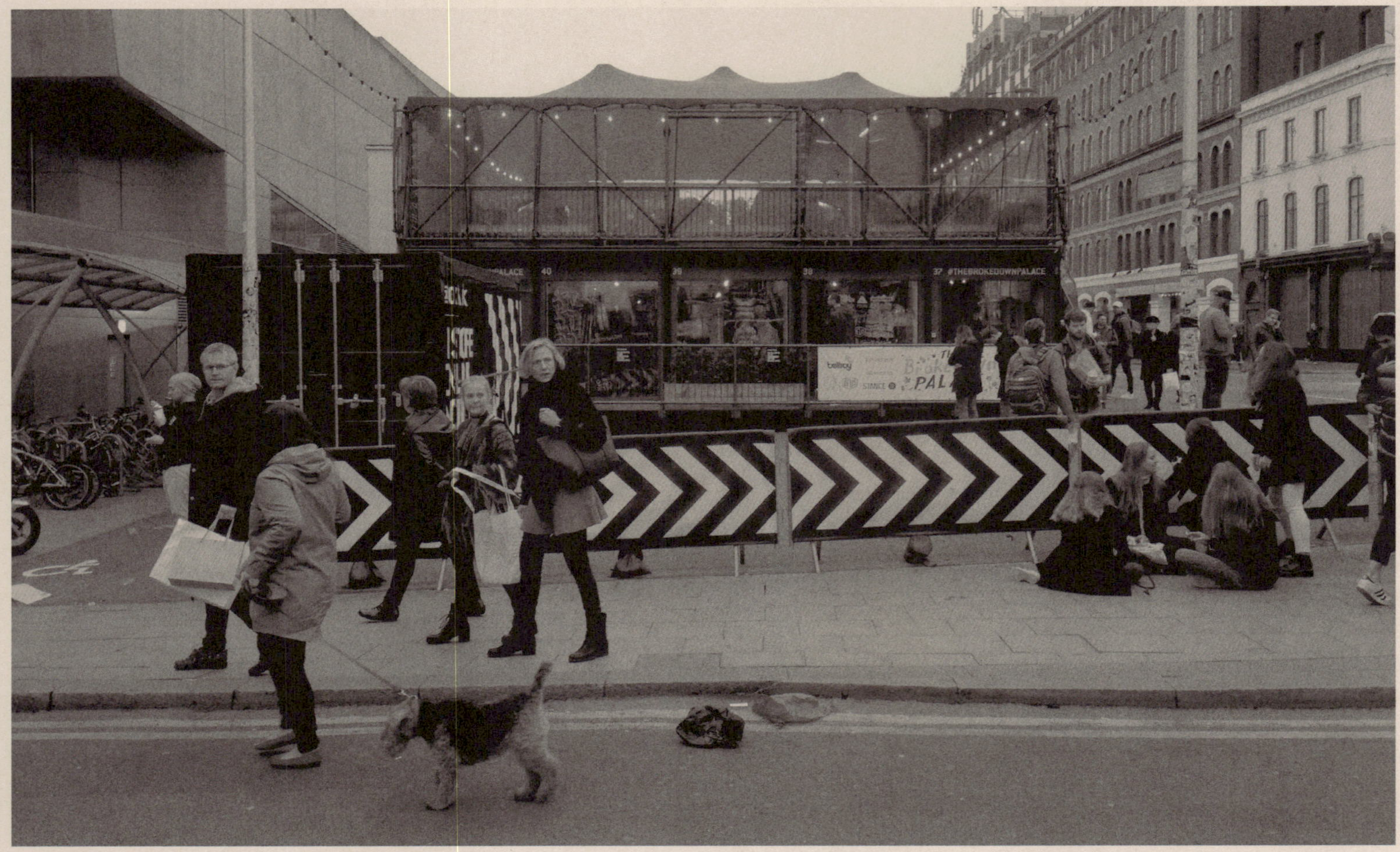

8

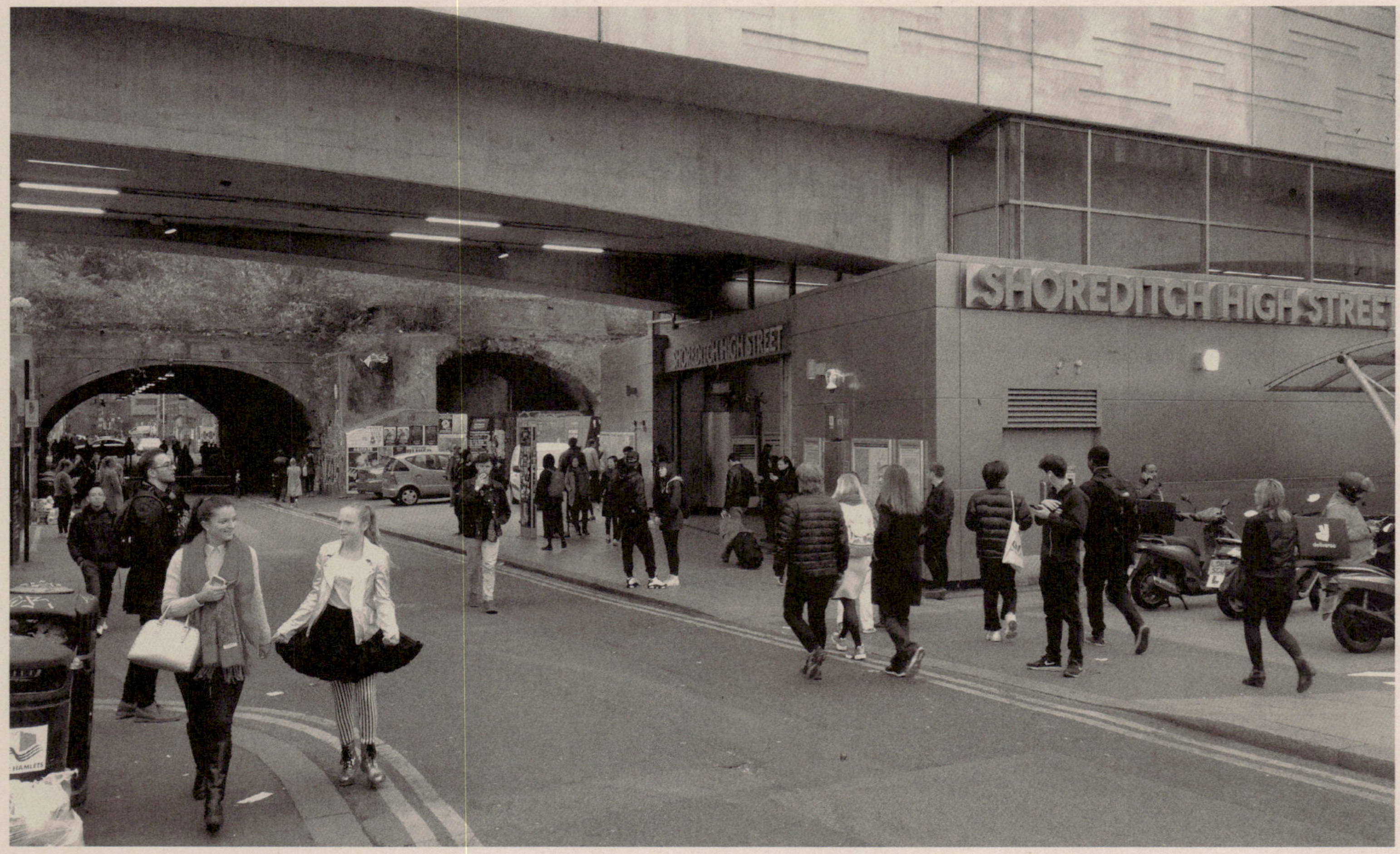

9

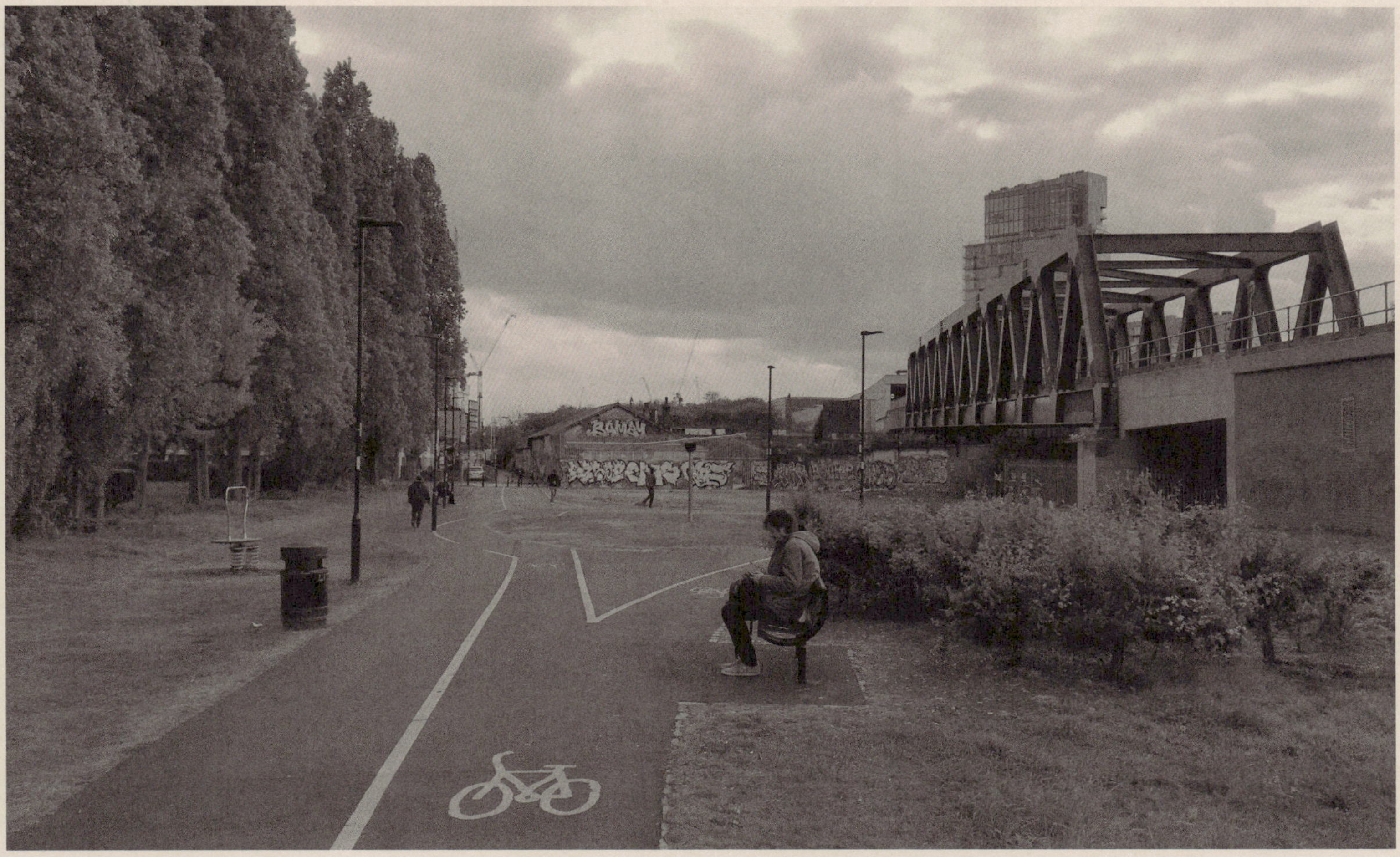

10

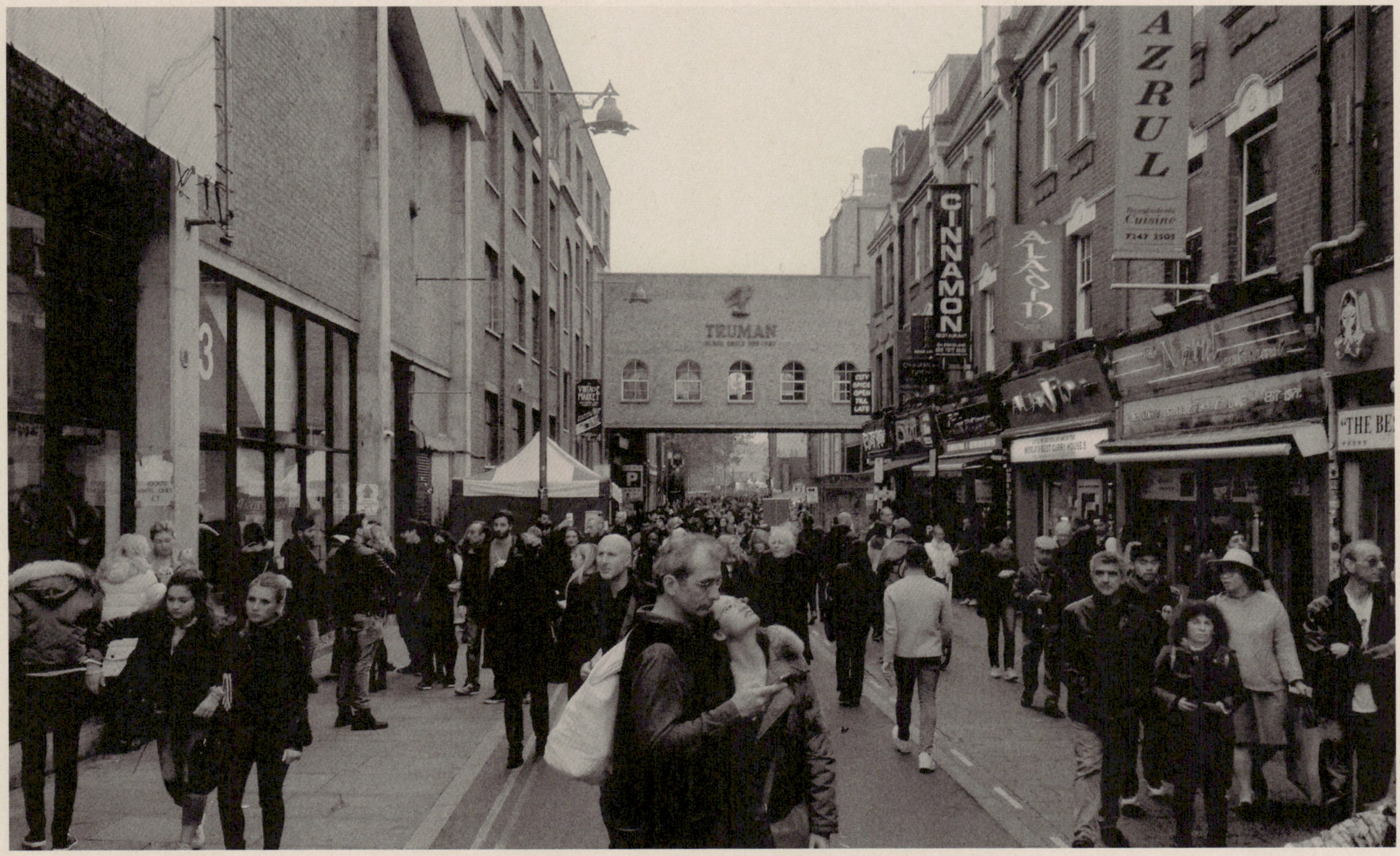

11

Additionally, however, the projects should not only test ideas and concepts, but also develop specific solutions for the goods yard site. The designs show possible and sometimes even impossible futures.[34] By visualising these futures, the projects stimulate our imagination, but also gauge the limits and conditions of the situation by experimentally testing them. This leads to new insights, provokes conflicts and highlights congruence. A vivid presentation enables the projects to spark public debate.

Designs are not inherently suited to foster or stimulate debate, however. If a project uses interpretation and manipulation as an end in itself to legitimise its own purpose, it does not contribute to a collective discourse. Only projects genuinely attempting to experimentally gain knowledge are of high value. Enquiry is at the core of an open test planning. Ideally, test planning is a 'discourse through design', methodically speaking.

From Urbanistic Thesis to Tangible Projects

In contrast to architectural or urban design competitions, in test planning, the goal of the process is to actually *define the design brief*. Through testing, relevant questions are asked and the major problems found before any final solutions are proposed. The aim is not to uncritically follow a predefined brief and solve its problems, but rather to define the brief by finding the relevant ones.

In the beginning, an *urban design hypothesis* is formulated in order to make a prediction about the future development of the site and its surroundings. Each hypothesis leads to different design decisions, and subsequently to different concepts. This includes the definition of the relevant context. Consequently, the perimeters of most project proposals differ from those set by Hammerson and Ballymore.

The *definition of the planning perimeter* is one of the main strategic decisions of a test planning process. If the planning perimeter is defined too narrowly and encompasses only a singular building site, many questions regarding the urban integration of the site into the city remain invisible and unanswered. If defined too loosely, challenges and potentials of the specific site get lost in the shuffle. Thus, the initial criteria at all relevant scales are to be set and put in relation. Only in this way can the full transscalar potential be tapped.

Urbanistic concepts but also architectural deliberations play a decisive role in the design process, especially in the case at hand, with a project of such high complexity yet relatively small size. Valuable heritage, whether listed or unlisted, the spatial quality of the access and public spaces, and the dimensions of the volumes, especially concerning light, have to be taken into consideration according to the requirements of each project approach. In order to ensure a certain degree of feasibility and provide realistic projects, the spatial constraints of the existing fabric and planning framework have to be taken into account. The partly listed remains of the goods yard on the southern half of the site and the encased Overground Line on the northern side severely limit any possible design, and both call for bespoke designs. While the ruin as an important piece of industrial heritage necessitates special programmatic and tectonic diligence (fig. 13), the concrete-boxed overground track needs to be integrated into the city's form (fig 14). Both parts of the project require creativity and courage for unconventional building types. The complexity

33 Scholl, B. (2017): 'Building Actor Relationships and Alliances for Complex Problem Solving in Spatial Planning'. In: *disP the Planning Review* 208 – Vol. 53.1 (1/2017). Special Edition: 'Assemblages for Innovative Planning: Shaping Processes of Transformation'. pp. 46–56.

34 See: Schön, D. (1983): *The Reflective Practitioner: How Professionals Think in Action*. New York: Basic.

of the goods yard is increased by other restrictions, such as the protected views on St. Paul's Cathedral and the limited space for foundations on the site due to the numerous tunnels (Central Line, Main Line open cut, Suburban Line, track reserve). For a design proposal to be concrete and potentially realisable, context-specific architectural solutions have to be found.

This situative design process metaphorically resembles an archaeological task: *unearthing the specific potentials and challenges of the site*. A generic top-down solution is bound to fail on this site, as simple diagrammatic schemes cannot cope with the complexities of the former goods yard. Therefore, the biggest challenge is to harmonise specific architectural solutions and the main urbanistic strategy. A general thesis without spatial evidence is as useless as a concrete project without urbanistic ideas. Therefore, tangible spatial design, along with its functional and architectonical requirements, must be integrated into an urbanistic vision that both anticipates the transformation of the immediate surroundings and further extends into the metropolitan scale. Only when both levels are forged into a coherent scheme can it become a valuable contribution to the test planning process. It is in this duality of urbanistic vision and tangible design proposal, between urban design and architecture, where the actual value of the projects lies.

From Tangible Projects to Reflections on Planning

The cognitive process of the method presented above can neither be categorised simply as a design exercise nor purely as reflection on planning. Settled somewhere between reflection and design, the test planning process can be seen as a guided urbanistic discourse, which addresses the development of the site at a very fundamental level. What is its historical identity, how can it be defined today and what kinds of imagined realities seem feasible for its future?

The nine projects attempt to launch the planning discourse by questioning the starting point of both Hammerson and Ballymore's and Hackney Council's proposals. They incorporate the sometimes harsh criticism by different stakeholders of Hammerson and Ballymore's high-rises as well as the problematic division between office and residence in Hackney's project – the offices on the western part cater to Hackney and link the site to the Central Business District (CBD) and the Tech City, while the residential homes on the eastern part fill a gap in Tower Hamlets' housing shortage. Both projects are characterised by a clear spatial division between living and working. The test planning proposals examine whether and how a genuine *mixed-use area* can be realised, in which living, working and public uses are integrated and which benefits from the *synergetic effect of the heterogeneous environment*. In this respect, and also by enlarging the planning perimeter and by their comparative and discursive nature, the approaches of the test projects not only cover a wide spectrum of possibilities, but they also diverge significantly from Hammerson and Ballymore's and Hackney's proposals. Nevertheless, the projects are also, and foremost, a presentation of a different planning approach – a critical reflection on current planning processes rather than a competing alternative to the Hammerson and Ballymore or Hackney proposals.

2000

2002

Braithwaite Viaduct listed as Grade II heritage, English Heritage

Small businesses and occupiers of the goods station issued with notices to leave on 9 May 2002

London Railway Heritage Society brought a judicial review against London Underground, who were about to demolish the unlisted parts of the goods yard

Acquisition of site by Hammerson and Ballymore Group

SOM commissioned to prepare site study

2003

The Court of Appeal decides in favour of London Underground and demolition begins to make way for the new 'Shoreditch High Street' station

2004–5

KCAP and Maccreanor Lavington start design process, partly based on SOM study

2005

Construction of East London Line extension begins, including the section running over the goods yard site (probably first planned in 1995)

2008

June: public consultation by boroughs for planning guidance

2009

10-week public consultation by boroughs

December: Bishopsgate Goods Yard Interim Planning

Guidance based on the plans of KCAP and Maccreanor Lavington approved by the Mayor of London

12 Timeline of the Bishopsgate goods yard planning process since 2000

2010

Interim Planning Guidance published

Overground railway and station completed

Developer design process started

2011, 2013

Selected public involvements by developers for several stages of the design process

2014

October: plans submitted by Hammerson and Ballymore for 30, 34, 42 and 49 storeys and a total of 1,500 homes, 19,000 sqm of retail space, 60,000 sqm office space as well as workshops

December: comments by Tower Hamlets and Hackney councils on the project

2015

July: amended application by Hammerson and Ballymore at Hackney and Tower Hamlets councils: towers to 26, 30, 38 and 46 storeys. The new proposals included 1,356 homes with 15.8 per cent classed as affordable, 78,000 sqm of office space as well as 18,500 sqm of retail and restaurant space

September: Mayor of London intervenes at request of developers despite the borough councils' complaints

November: local protests

December: despite the Mayor's decision, the councils hold meetings and reject the application

2016

January: developers hold a new 21-day public consultation

April: GLA planners publish report for public hearing, which recommends refusal

A public representation hearing was due to be held in the Chamber at City Hall on Monday 18 April 2016, but was deferred following a request from the applicant

Sadiq Khan succeeds Johnson as Mayor of London

2020

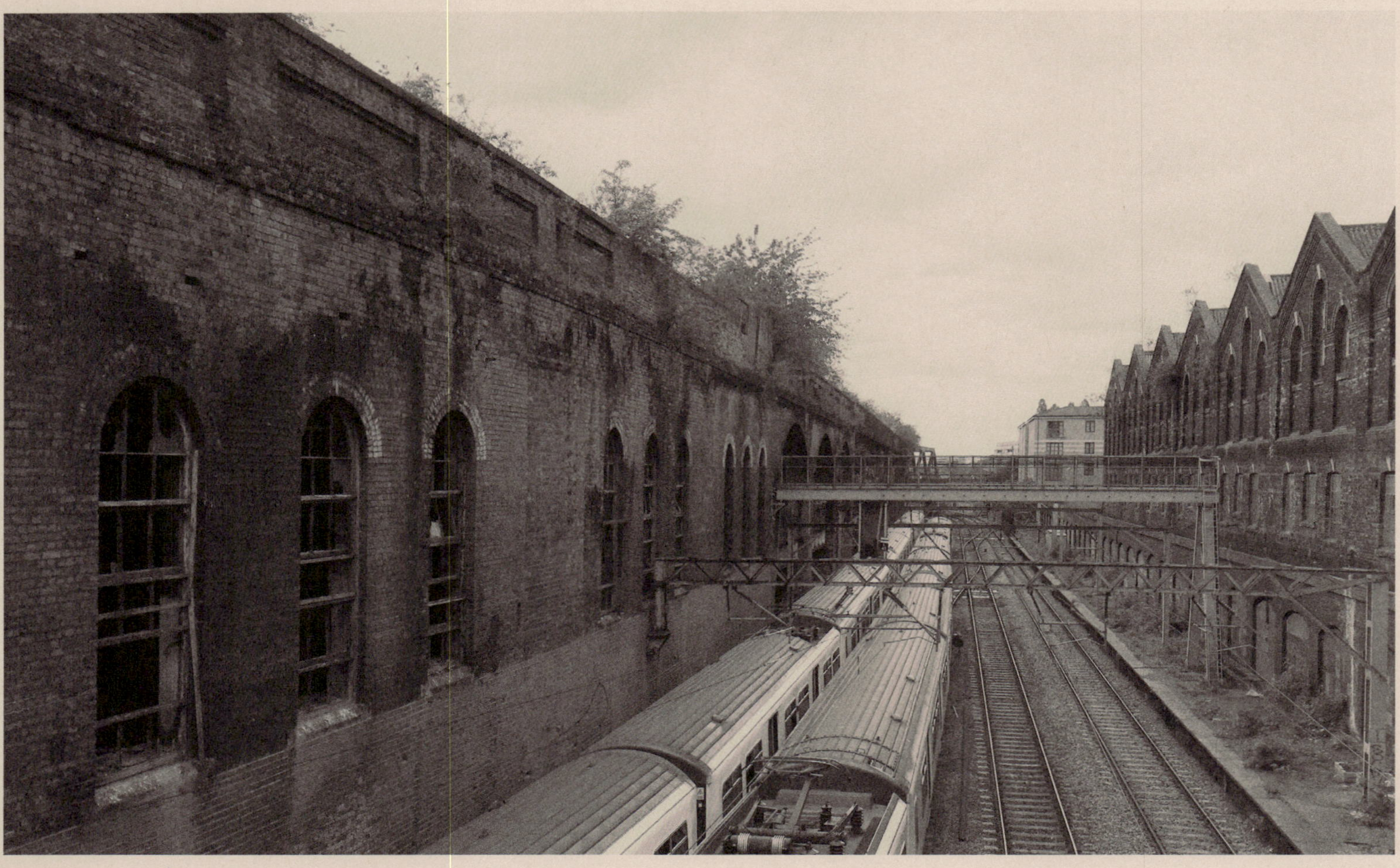
13

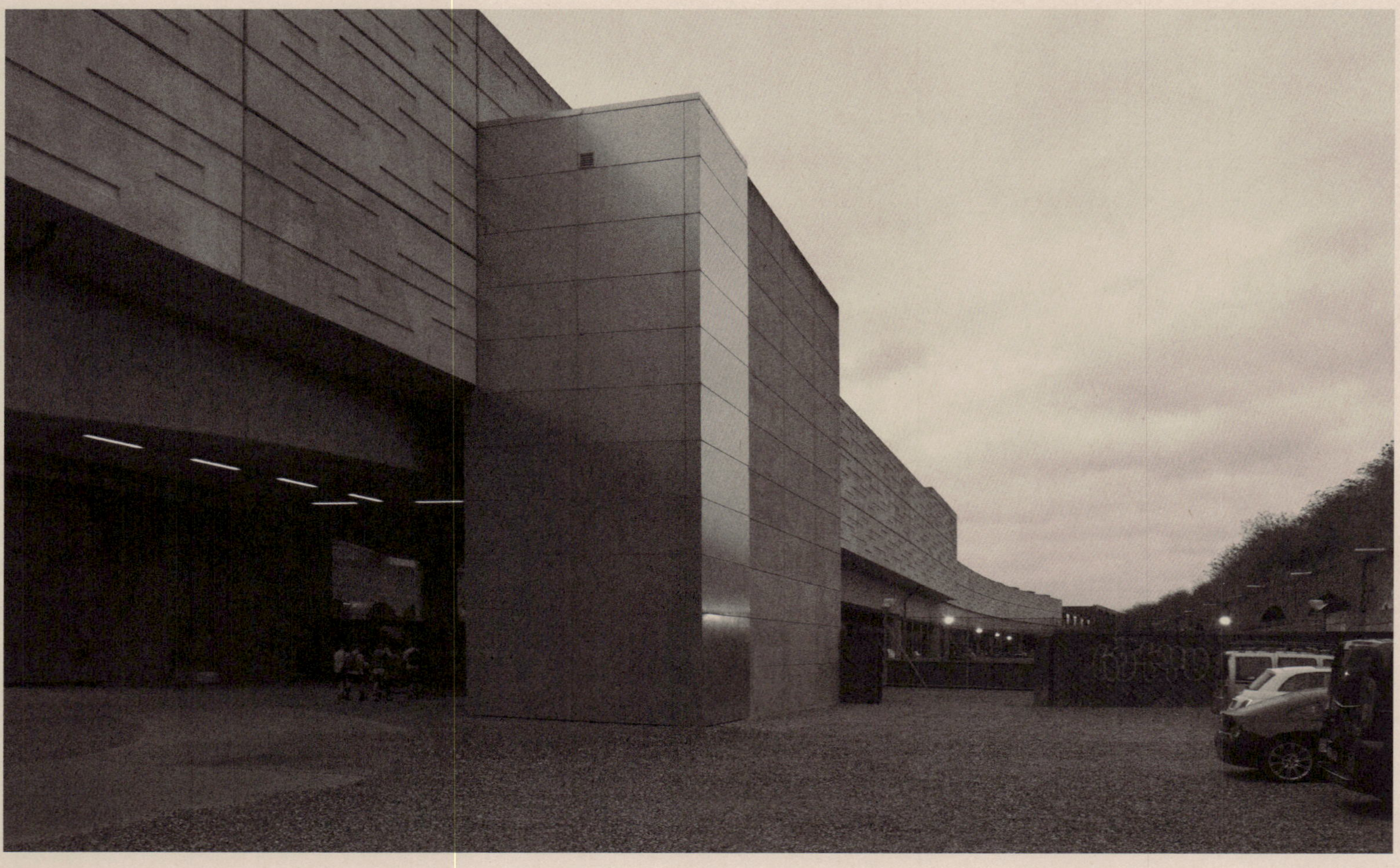
14

Towards Engagement

In order to rethink the future of the entire area, rather than just the site itself, several projects propose changes outside the goods yard such as programmatic switching (e.g. concerning public uses around Allens Gardens) or densification schemes for neighbouring sites (e.g. at the southern end of the tracks). The full potential of the test projects can only be unearthed by including the surroundings of the goods yard. This is meant both spatially and societally. Therefore, the concerns of different stakeholders within the planning process matter – the boroughs, the City, investors and developers, local enterprises and residents as well as their public institutions and clubs. Through the integration of a wider public, the political acceptance of a project can be fostered, but it also lays the foundations for designing a project with genuine urban qualities with a wide range of uses, reaching out to different user groups.
The essential idea of the test planning procedure can be seen as a professional shortcut within the discourse between stakeholders, since political processes are simulated to a certain extent. The simplistic dualism of project and alternative or 'developer' and 'public' is replaced by a more complex actor network and power geometry, and by a wide variety of proposals, which methodically leads to an urbanistic discourse. Only by presenting several proposals as a spectrum of possibilities is the involvement understood as a discourse. Applied early in the planning process, test planning can act in five ways:

1. Raise public awareness of the specific challenges and complexities of the site.
2. Rule out spatial, social or economic concepts that are unrealistic or one-dimensional.
3. Identify dissent and conflicts as well as consent and synergies of different stakeholder groups.
4. Unearth specific potentials of a place.
5. 'Break the ice' to spark a public debate on a positive note and to find surprising solutions, rather than triggering public anger after revealing a fixed solution.

In the following chapters, the test projects are presented and compared, alongside the proposals of the developer and Hackney (chapter 3.2), while the most important resulting insights are synthesised in a separate chapter (chapter 3.3).

3.2 Case Study Bishopsgate Goods Yard Test Projects

This chapter presents and discusses eleven projects as thought experiments. Nine projects were developed in partnership with the Institute for Urban Design at ETH Zurich in the Spring Semester 2017.

In addition, two previously developed projects are included in this text as discussion points: the developer-led project by Hammerson and The Ballymore Group (H&B), submitted in 2014 and resubmitted and withdrawn in 2016; the other commissioned by Hackney Council. Both projects focus on the developers' site and do not actively intervene or explicitly anticipate future changes of the surroundings. In contrast, the nine design tests had the freedom to redefine the design perimeter and envision site-related changes on a larger scale. Another important factor is the definition of the density, usually measured by the Floor Area Ratio (FAR). Since not clearly defined in London's zoning plan, the FAR is part of the negotiations between the public authority and the proprietor. The project by H&B proposes a FAR of 5.13, the project by Hackney Council 3.23. This is a substantial difference of more than 80,000 square metres and obviously has a great impact on the physical design scheme. In order to identify more precisely the appropriate density for the Bishopsgate goods yard site, all nine test project densities came in at various points between these two, searching for the optimal density.

Developers' Project: Hammerson and Ballymore (2016)

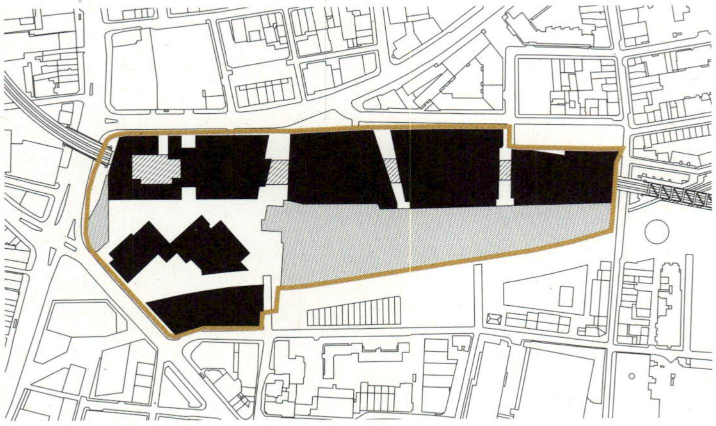

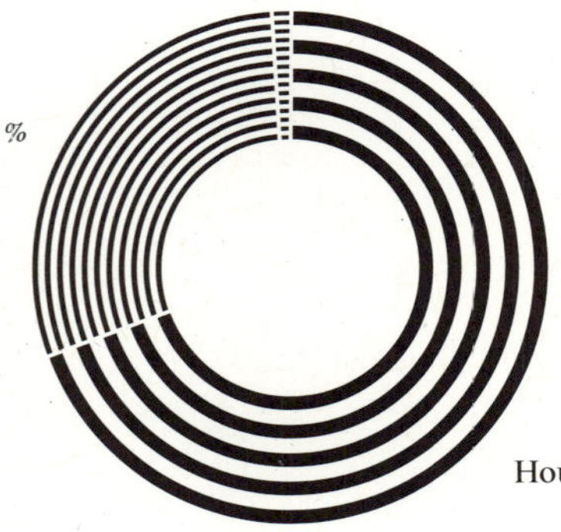

Site Area		43,700 m²	
Floor Area		224,200 m²	100 %
	Housing	156,000 m²	69.6 %
	Offices	66,000 m²	29.4 %
	Commerce	2,200 m²	1.0 %
	Public	0 m²	0 %
Density (FAR)		5.13	

The project led by the developers Hammerson and Ballymore (H&B) is based on a very basic idea. The south-eastern part of the site has two major constraints, one being that a significant area of this part contains listed buildings making it difficult to build on. The second issue is that the site is used by different underground infrastructures such as railway tunnels, meaning it is very difficult to pile or to use as foundations. Thereafter, the project consequently proposes not to build on this part of the site. Instead, the historic brick vaults are refurbished and used as retail spaces, as a sort of semi-outdoor shopping complex. A publicly accessible park six metres above street level crowns the historic structure. To compensate, high-rise buildings of up to 166 metres in height are placed in the northern and western part of the site (fig. 16). The higher towers are close to the City of London in the west, the lower towers facing Brick Lane in the east. The height of the proposed scheme is therefore determined by the numerous constraints on the site and allows for a relatively high Floor Area Ratio (FAR) of 5.13 and a high percentage of marketable appartments in the higher price range. This conceptual decision to cluster building mass on two thirds of the site in order to create an open public park that generously connects Bishopsgate and Brick Lane is based on a masterplan by KCAP Architects and Planners and Maccreanor Lavington Architects of 2004. This masterplan was used as the basis of the Initial Planning Guidance (IPG) in 2009.

Even though most volumetric decisions of the masterplan were preserved in the following design process by H&B, other relevant aspects were fundamentally altered (fig. 15).

Firstly, the elevated park does not serve as a connecting device in the pedestrian network anymore. Since the diagonal connection at the south-western corner towards Liverpool Street Station and the generous vertical connections between the park and Brick Lane in the east have been given up in the design process, the park creates neither a connection to important locations on a larger scale nor a continuous green network along the railway tracks to the east. In addition to the lack of a clear and visible vertical connection at the eastern end, the residential spaces bordering the park at the northern edge turn it into a leisure space for residents, while the cul-de-sac access to the park makes it useful mostly for shopping complex users (fig. 19). The concept of the park has been changed completely. The truly public gesture of the park as a connector for the city with important public uses is undermined; the space becomes functionally intimate (fig. 17). Its balancing role as a transscalar and highly public device in the design scheme and the associated compensation for the high-rise residential buildings loses its legitimation, and the logic of the set-up threatens to fall apart. As a park without core public functions, it is questionable whether this elevated green surface is of public value at all – especially since Allens Gardens, a park with similar dimensions, on street level and without towering high-rises at its immediate borders, is adjacent to the site, opposite Brick Lane. Would it not be more efficient and socially productive to invest in the beauty and urbanity of Allens Gardens, and to better connect it to its surroundings, including the Bishopsgate goods yard?

Secondly, the close-meshed pedestrian network proposed in the masterplan has been turned into a much wider grid, resulting in a single east-west passage and one north-south connection (fig. 18). For a site of nearly 45,000 square metres in the middle of a historic city fabric with traditionally small plot sizes, the lack of porosity is significant, its urban integration

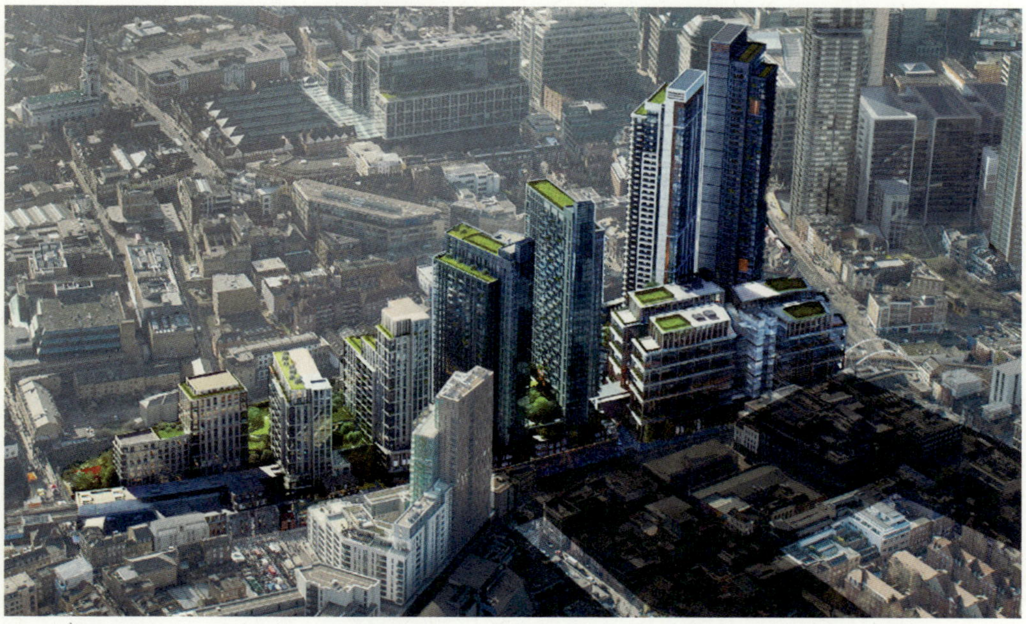

15 Visualisation

critical. In addition to the many retail surfaces with extensive service spaces, the towers create a sum of logistical spaces and escape routes at ground level. The conglomeration of all these technical spaces leads to highly determined floor plans, large building footprints and consequently to a wide-meshed pedestrian network lacking porosity. This forces people to move in only a few predefined ways, which may be economically profitable, though urbanistically highly problematic. Additionally, the entrances to the site are gates rather than open street connections. Combined with the retail-optimised and meandrous form of the pedestrian network, the project creates a very intimate atmosphere that lacks public character. Its quasi-privacy seems to alter the masterplan's idea of a well-connected open quarter in London's east into a semi-outdoor shopping complex with housing slabs. These two fundamental modifications, and the building height of the skyscrapers, led the boroughs of Hackney and Tower Hamlets and the Greater London Authority (GLA) to oppose the proposal. The GLA states that 'the potential public benefits are to be delivered in a way that would result in unacceptable and avoidable significant negative impacts'. The boroughs opposed the application on various grounds: its visual impact and loss of light for nearby homes, businesses, and conservation areas and heritage sites; its lack of affordable homes – only 10% was proposed; its lack of appropriate business space for the local creative and tech sector – the site is supposed to be earmarked for a business / jobs-driven development; its poor quality of architectural design; and finally its negative impact on air quality.[1] Jules Pipe, the mayor of Hackney at the time commented that the project of H&B was 'out of scale' and 'completely unsuitable for this part of Shoreditch. [...] The towers are on a vast scale and would damage the whole local environment. The housing provided would be luxury accommodation, to be bought mostly by overseas investors, and would do nothing to alleviate London's housing crisis. The scheme does not provide enough, or the right kind of employment space.'[2] The scheme would lead small and medium enterprises (SME) to abandon the area's tech cluster. The opposition is based on a handful of different reasons, but shares a common ground: the feeling that the initial vision of an open and adaptable city[3] has somehow been abandoned in the planning process, the over-specification of form and function making the proposed project brittle.[4]

1 hackney.gov.uk / bgy#bg3, accessed 25.11.2017.
2 Hayman, A. (2015): 'Hackney explores "tech cluster" plan for Bishopsgate Goodsyard'. In: *Property Week* 20.2.2015.
3 See: Rieniets, T.; Sigler, J.; Christiaanse, K. (2009): *Open City. Designing Coexistence*. Amsterdam: SUN.
4 Sennett, R. (2006): *The Open City*. downloads.lsecities.net/0_downloads/Berlin_Richard_Sennett_2006-The_Open_City.pdf, accessed 25.11.2017.

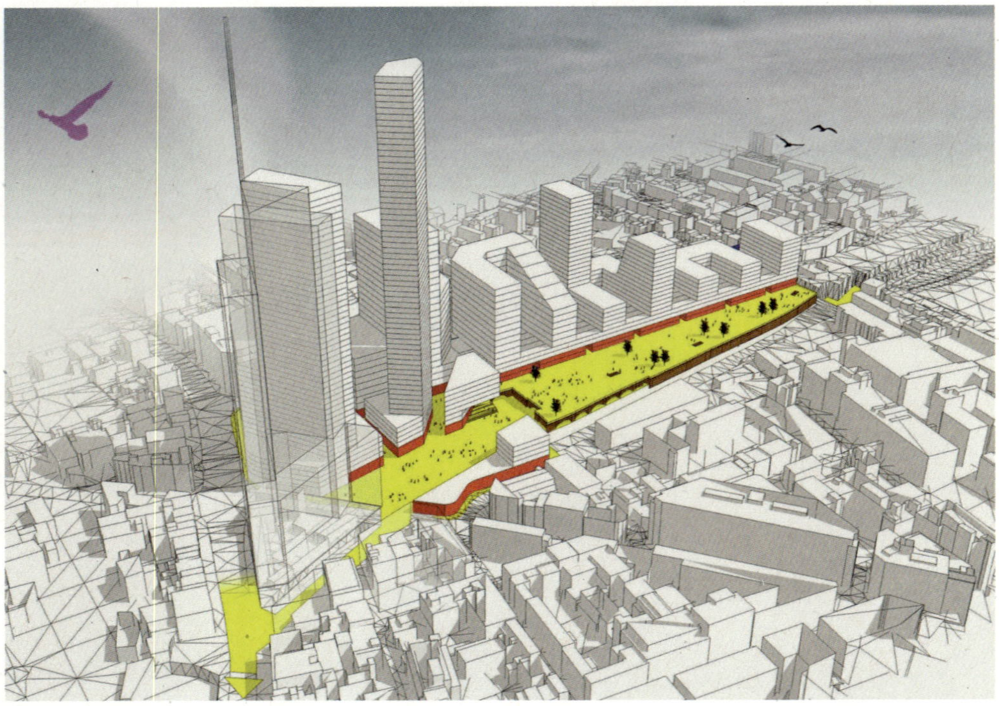

16 Visualisation of the spatial concept by KCAP Architects and Planners and Maccreanor Lavington Architects

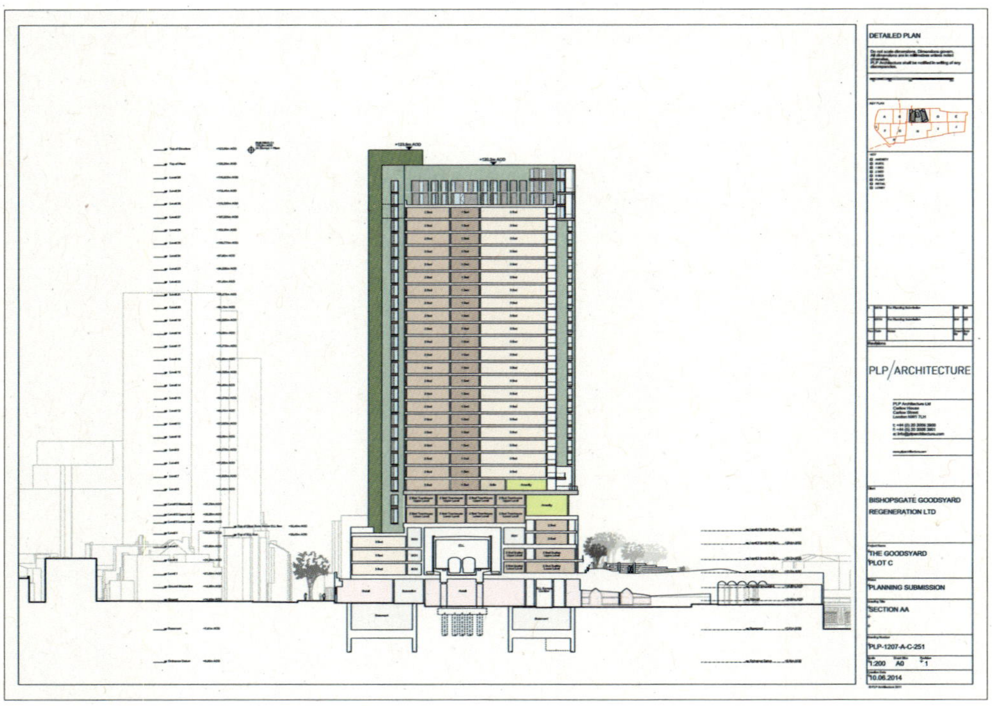

17 North-south section

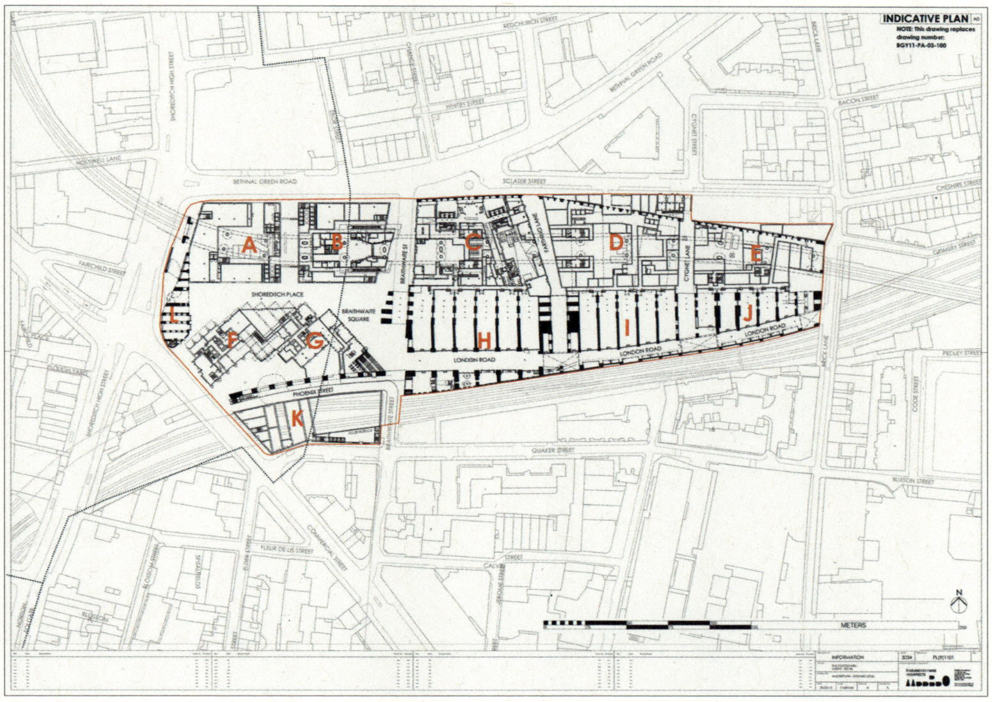

18 Ground level floor plan

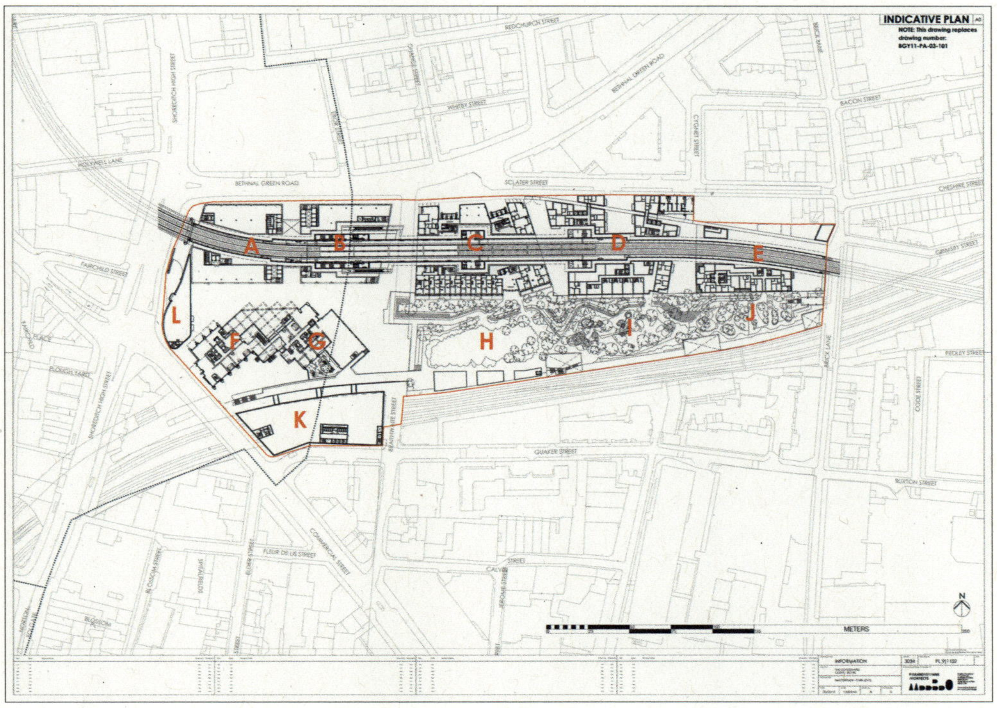

19 Second level floor plan

Alternative Project: Hackney Council (2015)

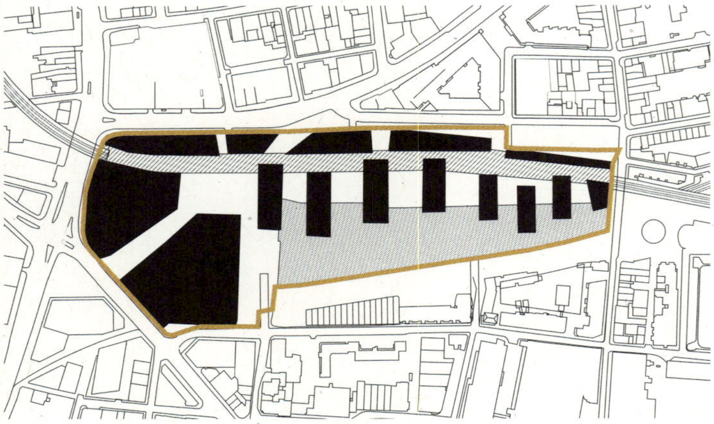

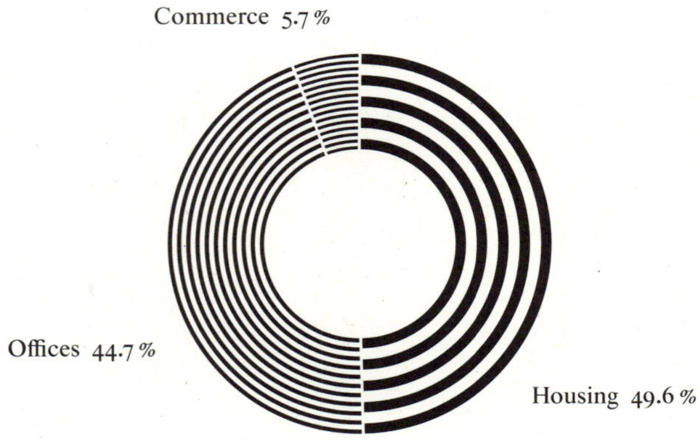

Site Area		43,700 m²	
Floor Area		141,000 m²	100 %
	Housing	70,000 m²	49.6 %
	Offices	63,000 m²	44.7 %
	Commerce	8,000 m²	5.7 %
	Public	0 m²	0 %
Density (FAR)		3.23	

In 2014, Hackney Council commissioned a study to develop plans for an employment-led scheme for the site to work out an alternative low-to-medium rise development for the site (fig. 20). Scaling down density, massing and the height of the buildings, this alternative can be read as a direct critique of the H&B project. The study, undertaken by Lambert Smith Hampton and a range of consultants including global design practice Gensler, includes 961 homes – fewer than the 1,461 proposed in H&B's plans.[1] This alternative scheme would still be mixed-use, with retail and residential elements, but it would provide more employment space, including more space for SMEs. Hackney commissioned the study because an employment-led scheme was not considered viable in 2010, when the IPG was approved. When the IPG was prepared, the area was seen as a marginal employment location and a popular residential location. Between 2010 and 2015, however, the employment growth in Shoreditch was significant, with predominantly technological enterprises having clustered in the area. The present scheme is therefore more focused on employment. Furthermore, the massing of the volumes is more moderate, the density lower, and the focus is shifted from retail and expensive housing to SMEs and affordable family housing. The urban layout is very diagrammatic: large office buildings for SMEs in the western part and slender terraced housing slabs for families in the east, mirroring the different political agendas of Hackney and Tower Hamlets. A conference centre is located at the western tip of the site, highlighting the potential for functions that surpass the local sphere of influence and operate on a citywide scale. The conference centre should become the social centrepiece of Shoreditch's rising tech cluster. The viaduct is treated similarly to the H&B project, except that the large surface on the roof of the viaduct is purely a residential garden. While the programmatic statement of the proposal is clearly presented, the layout of the public spaces is chaotic. The scheme is spatially labyrinthine and confusing. It does provide a clear vision of how The Goodsyard could contribute to the surroundings and London's East in terms of the programmatic mix and the moderate skyline, but not regarding the spatial layout of the public space, nor the scheme's potential to adapt for future and yet unknown uses. Just as the neighbourhood's soaring demand for office space within the last decade has clearly shown, focusing on a very narrow user profile can prove highly risky, both economically and socially.

1 Hayman, A. (2015): 'Revealed: Hackney's rival Bishopsgate Goodsyard plan'. In: *Property Week* 27.2.2015.

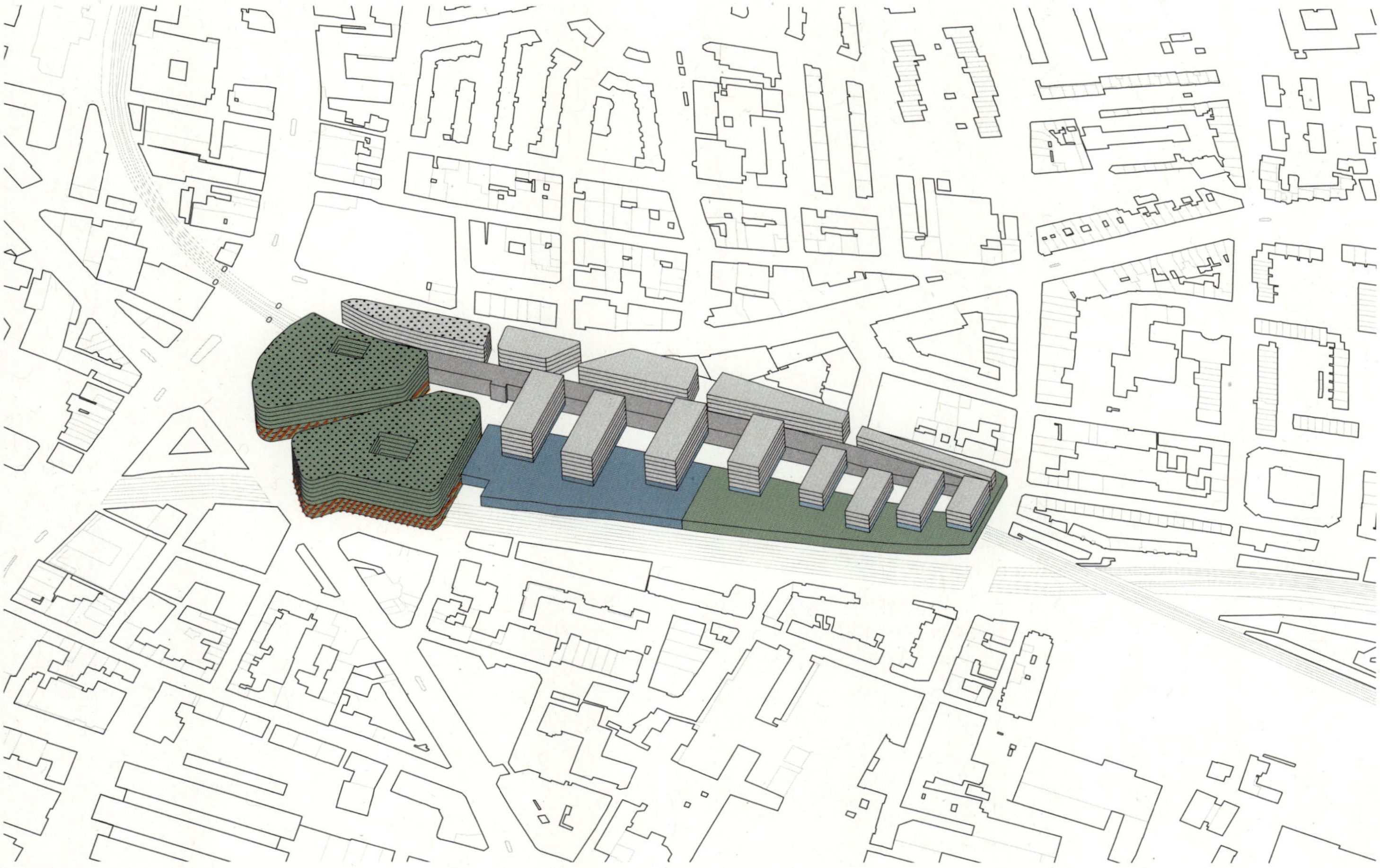

20 Visualisation of the spatial concept

- Housing
- Commerce / New Warehouse
- Kindergarden / Doctor
- Office
- Public (Optional)
- Public Roof
- Concrete Boxed Overground Track

I Eastward Bound

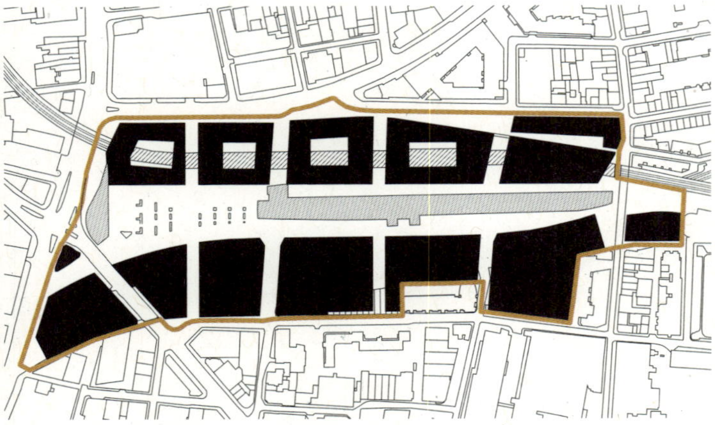

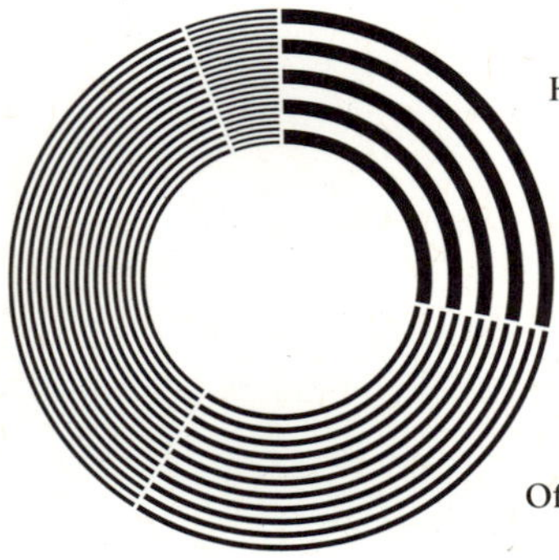

Site Area		65,515 m²	
Floor Area		233,057 m²	100 %
	Housing	65,911 m²	28.3 %
	Offices	72,502 m²	31.1 %
	Commerce	81,290 m²	34.9 %
	Public	13,353 m²	5.7 %
Density (FAR)		3.56	

The project defines a transformation area that stretches between Bethnal Green Road and Whitechapel Road, starting at the Bishopsgate goods yard and leading eastward towards Mile End Park, and eventually even further east. The train viaduct is the designated spine of this linear project and its main public space. By interpreting the Bishopsgate goods yard as a gateway both for the development corridor and its central pedestrian and bicycle line, the project uses the goods yard as a catalyst for a metropolitan-scale strategy. The strategic focus of this new corridor not only propels the urban densification process of the underused low-density areas adjacent to the train tracks, but also defines the project's role for the transformation of London's East (fig. 25). Additionally, a handful of new north-south connections between Bishopsgate and Mile End Park resolve the fragmented street network. These new connections link both sides of the corridor and rework the area between the two historic roads, transforming it from an infrastructural backwater between two main roads into an attractive greenway with new uses for old viaducts.

Consequently the site of the Bishopsgate goods yard is structured around a large square, designed as a publicly accessible entrance gate (fig. 23). The listed fragments of the viaduct are treated as ruins. They are not only material witness of the goods yard's history, but also spatially and atmospherically define the central public space. The solid construction and robust spatial framework of the viaduct mean that it can be filled with a variety of public functions relating to the neighbouring districts, such as community centres or educational and cultural programmes (fig. 22).

The buildings bridging the train tracks at the southern edge of the goods yard form the conceptual backbone of this layout (fig. 24). This strategic move allows the creation of a large public space for London's East, while still keeping a reasonably high density. Furthermore, it offers the possibility of integrating the project into the fine-meshed urban tissue of the Spitalfields area by completing both the existing street network and its block sizes (fig. 26). Therefore, the project almost self-evidently integrates itself into its urban context (fig. 21). Due to its block structure, the project allows for a high process flexibility, ranging from one large development unit encompassing the whole goods yard up to eleven smaller units. In contrast to the privately owned blocks, the viaduct functions as both central and public device, and is therefore publicly owned. The gentle shape of the facades facing this main public space originates in the fixed position of the train tracks. It is based on structural considerations and gives the design its character and unique appeal. Foremost, however, the slightly curved urban form leads the way to London's new East.

The project's fundamental goal is not to densify the Bishopsgate goods yard as much as possible, but to use the strategically important site as a tool both to create a metropolitan-scale public space and to start a densification process of a much larger transformation area.

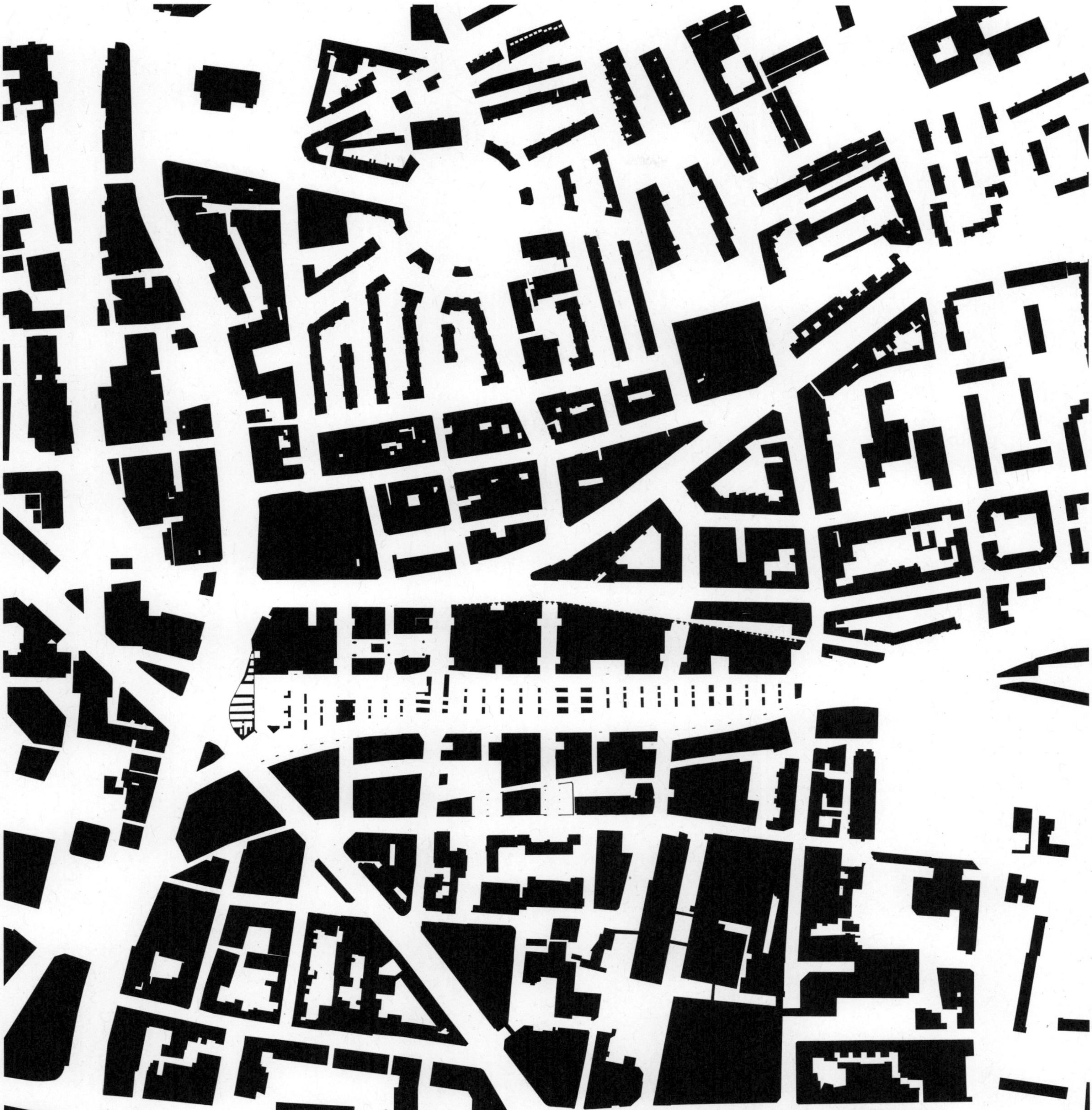
21 Urban layout

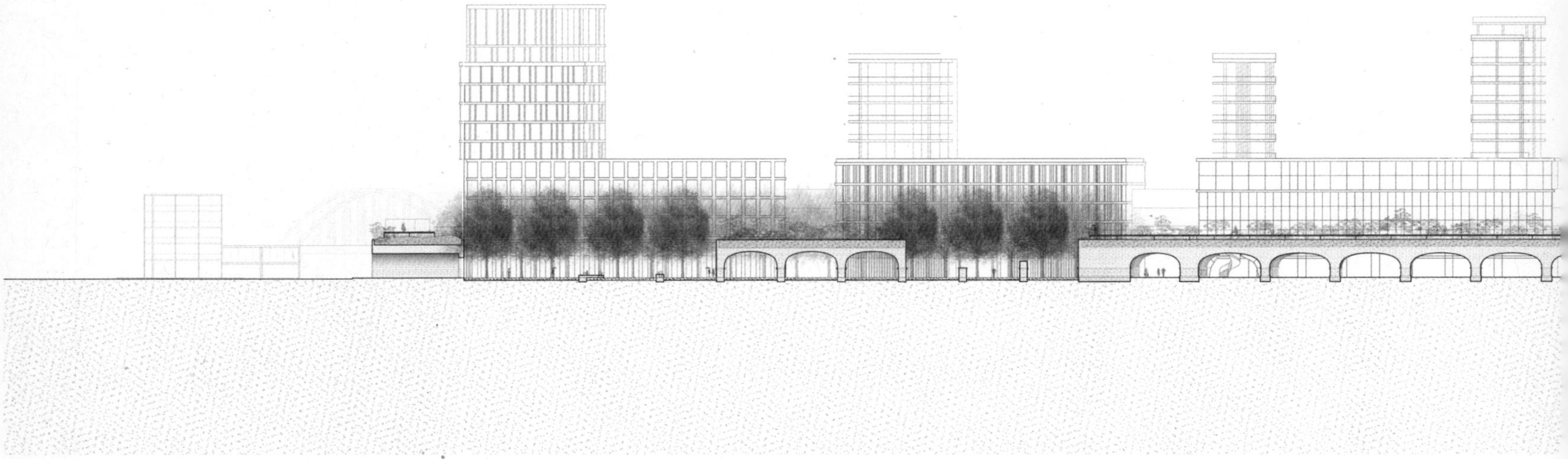

22 West-east elevation

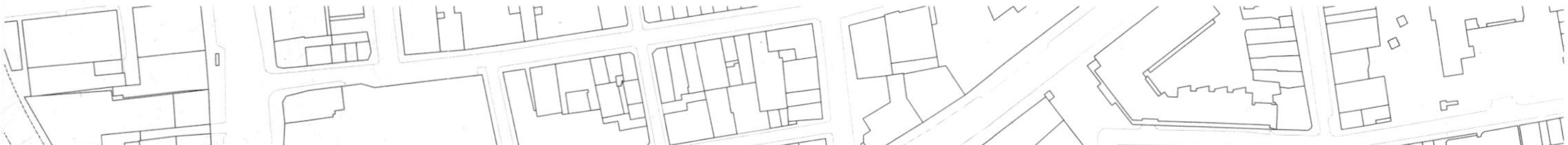

23 Ground level floor plan

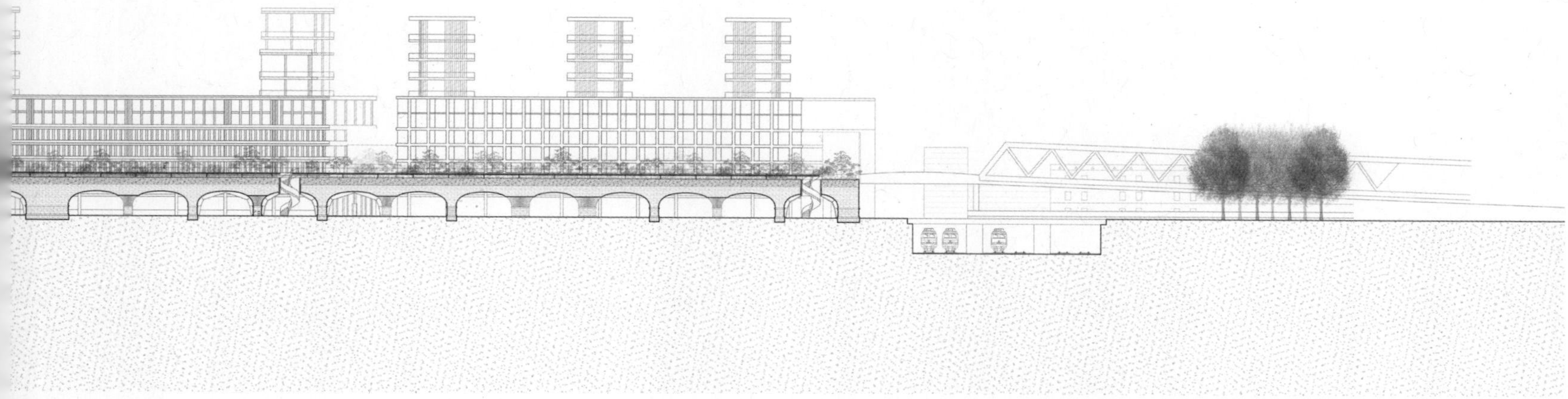

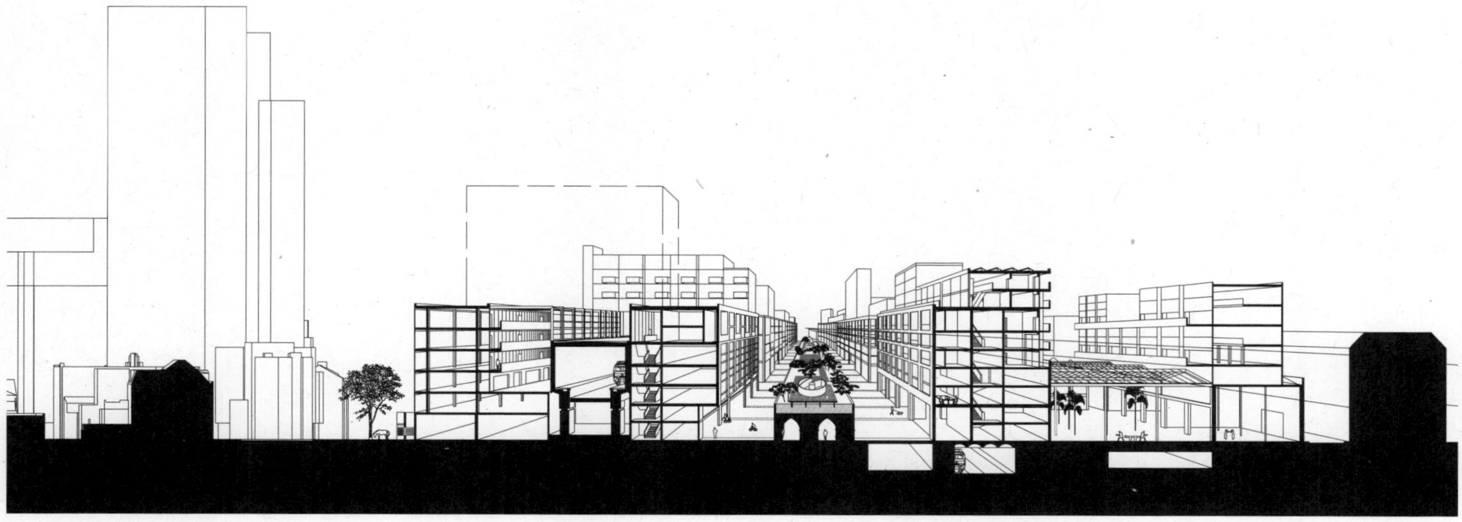

24 North-south section

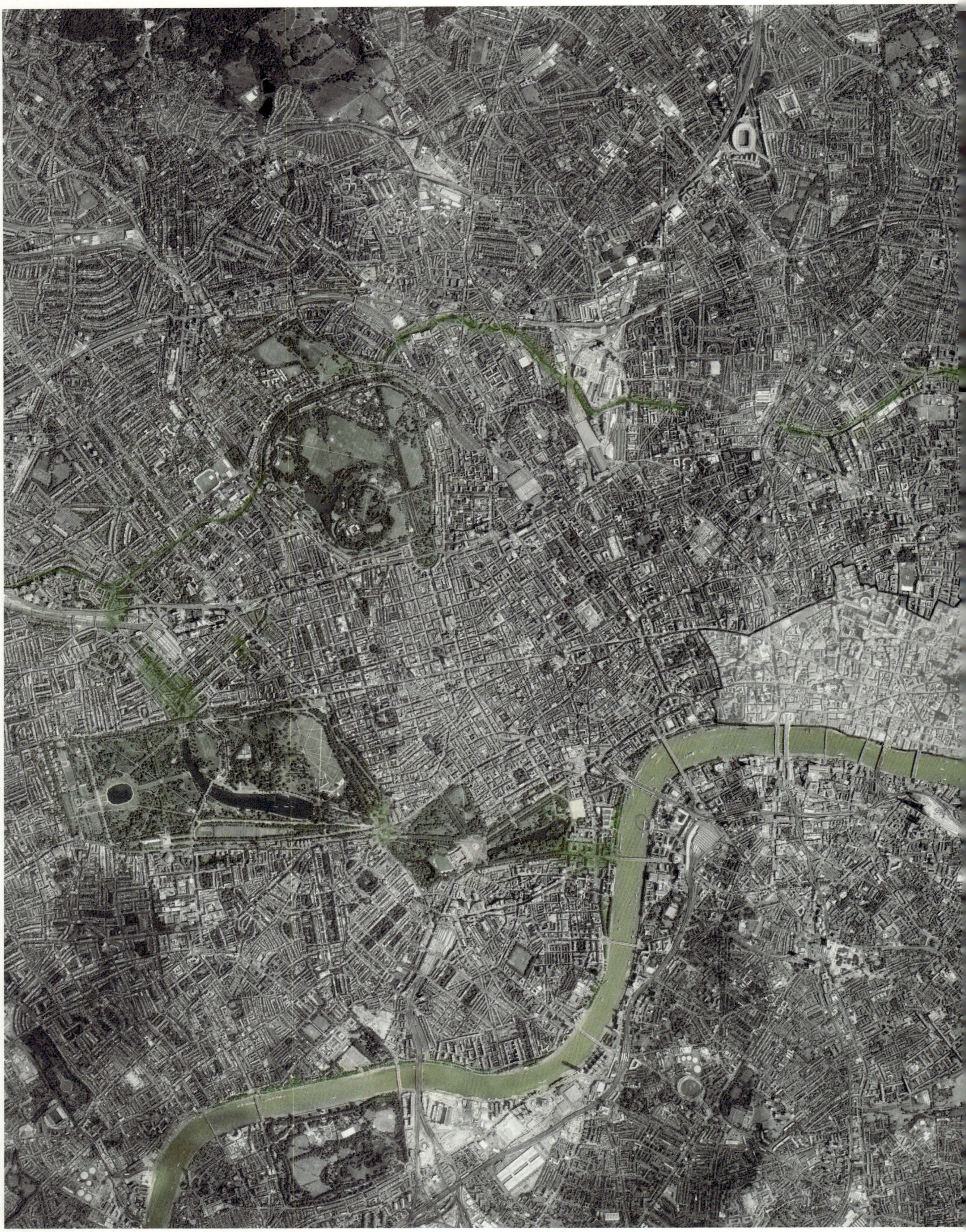

25 Concept drawing of the large-scale transformation scheme

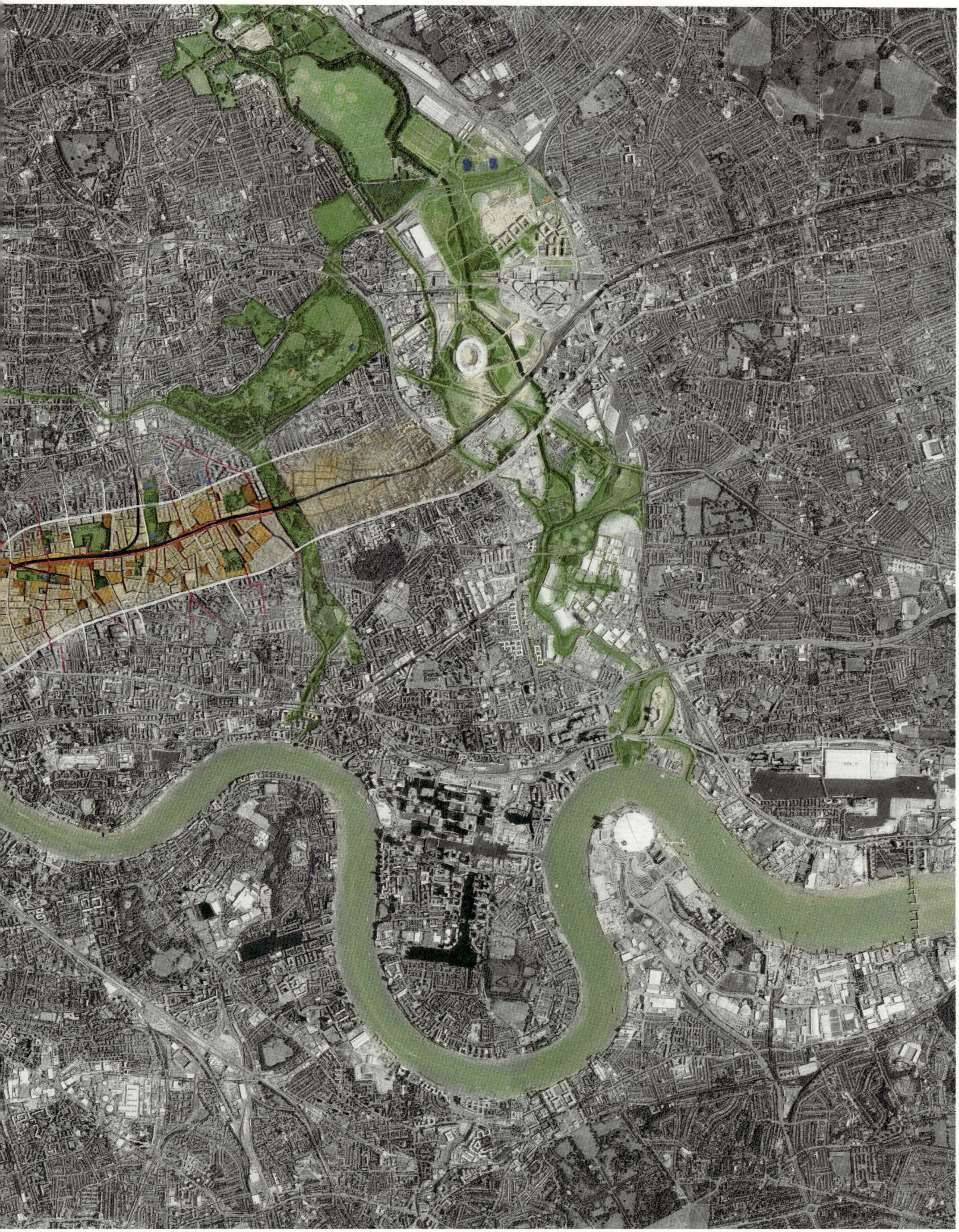

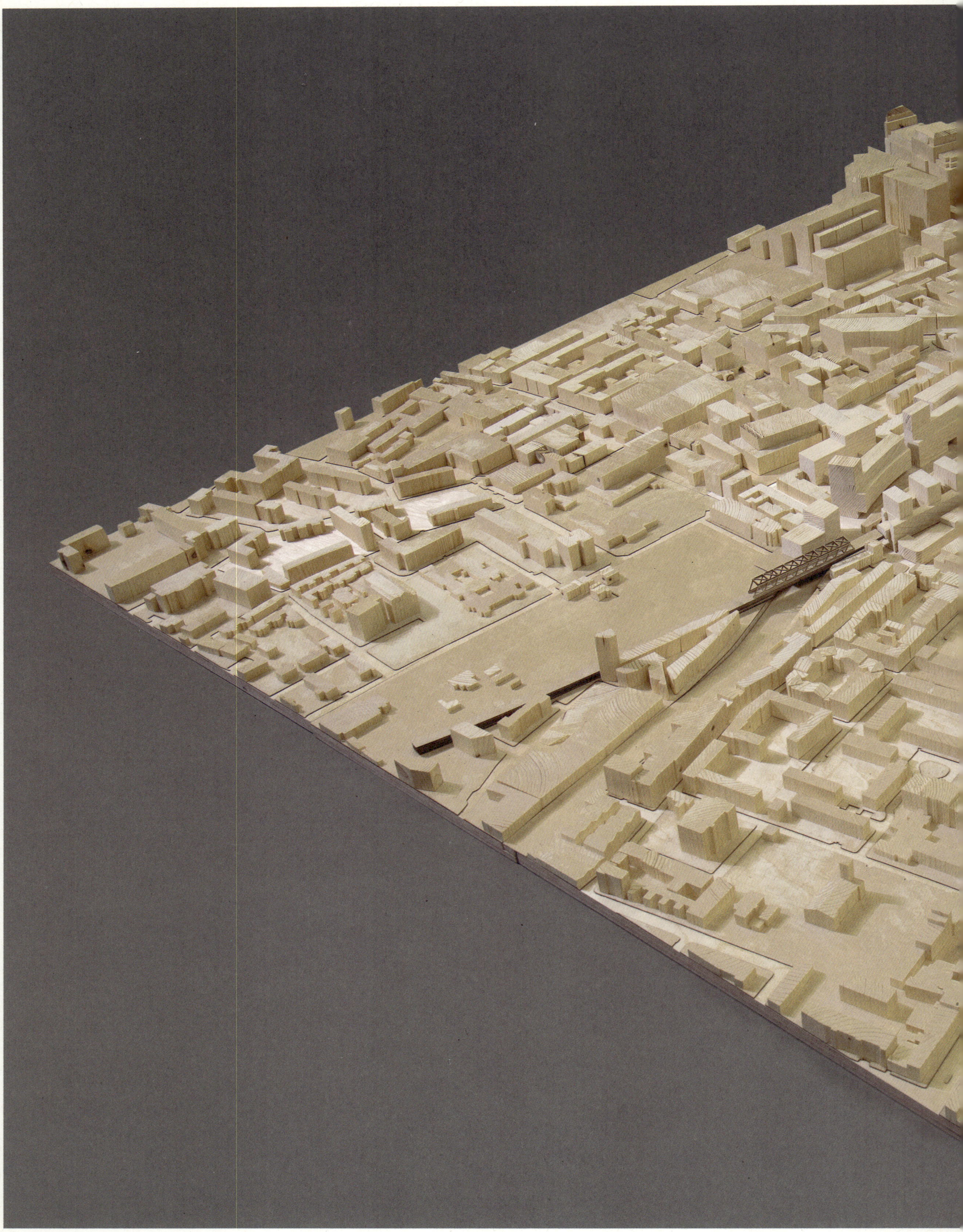

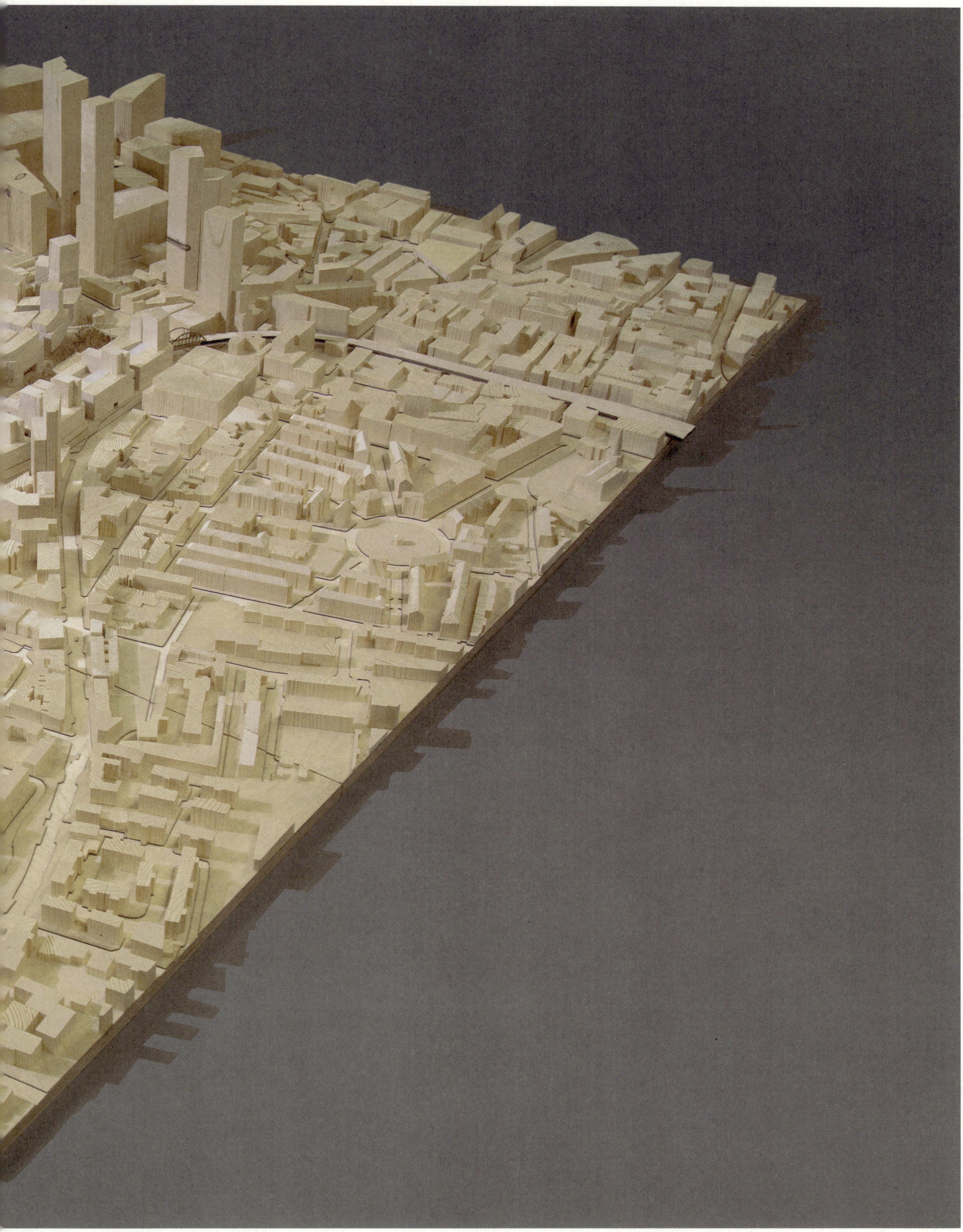

II Urban Catalyst

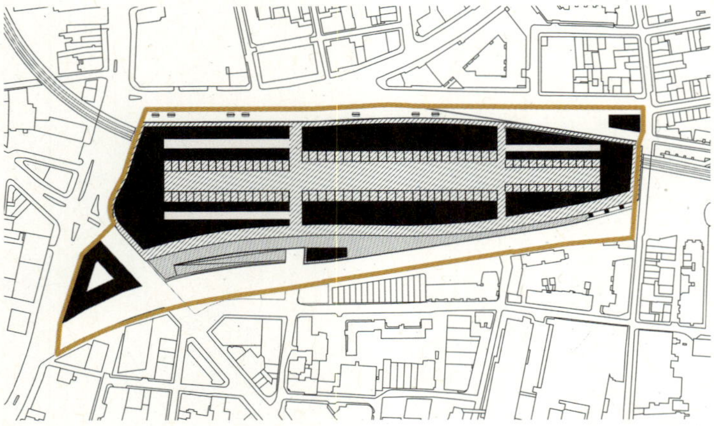

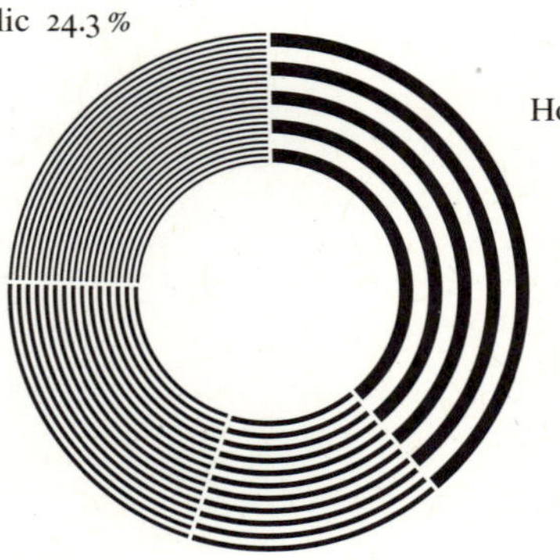

Site Area		52,200 m²	
Floor Area		175,322 m²	100 %
	Housing	68,308 m²	39.9 %
	Offices	28,324 m²	16.1 %
	Commerce	36,089 m²	20.6 %
	Public	42,601 m²	24.3 %
Density (FAR)		3.36	

In an urban context of extreme contrasts, the project provides a surprising answer to the task of an integrative urban project. Rather than continuing the East's finely spun street network, it proposes a single large structure (fig. 34). Like a sponge, it absorbs uses from the neighbourhood, but remains permeable and transparent (fig. 28). A sequence of public spaces and manifold uses connects Shoreditch High Street with Brick Lane, keeping the borders between indoor and outdoor spaces blurred. The porosity of the public ground floor guarantees the integration of the project into the neighbourhood, despite the project's monolithic appearance. This project unlocks the full potential and strength of a big building rising from both the physical and functional legacy of the goods yard as an infrastructural and economic centre, and catalyst of neighbourhood development (fig. 33). Atop the covered railway, along its sunny southern facade, runs a linear park that connects the City to Allens Gardens and the outer east. The park is doubled by vineyard-like public terraces, overlooking the historic fabric of Spitalfields (figs. 27–29). Together, a park as well as terraces create a unique new space for the neighbourhood. The vitality of the neighbourhood is ensured not only by the many public uses and the existing Shoreditch High Street station, but also by a new proposed Underground stop for the Central Line (fig. 31) and several large-scale public uses, such as a theatre, a library or sports facilities, which make use of the depth of the building.

The horizontal configuration is mirrored in the upper storeys, where mostly residential units are planned (fig. 30). Different types of stacked row houses are allotted around a semi-private courtyard. These are sized according to the goods yard's structural grid. The proposal convinces by its coherent structure, which is well integrated into the surroundings despite its large dimensions. It has the potential to become a technological hub and a social incubator for London's East, the iconic start of a greenway to the east and a horizontal counterweight to the forest of high-rises that is growing on the eastern fringe of the City of London (fig. 32).

The concept of a big building can also be problematic, however. Dividing the project into smaller investment units needs an innovative business concept, and the unavoidable depth of the building requires a proportion of uses that are not in need of much daylight: this part would thus be suited to cultural uses, a congress centre, retail or offices, as opposed to residential use where more daylight is needed.

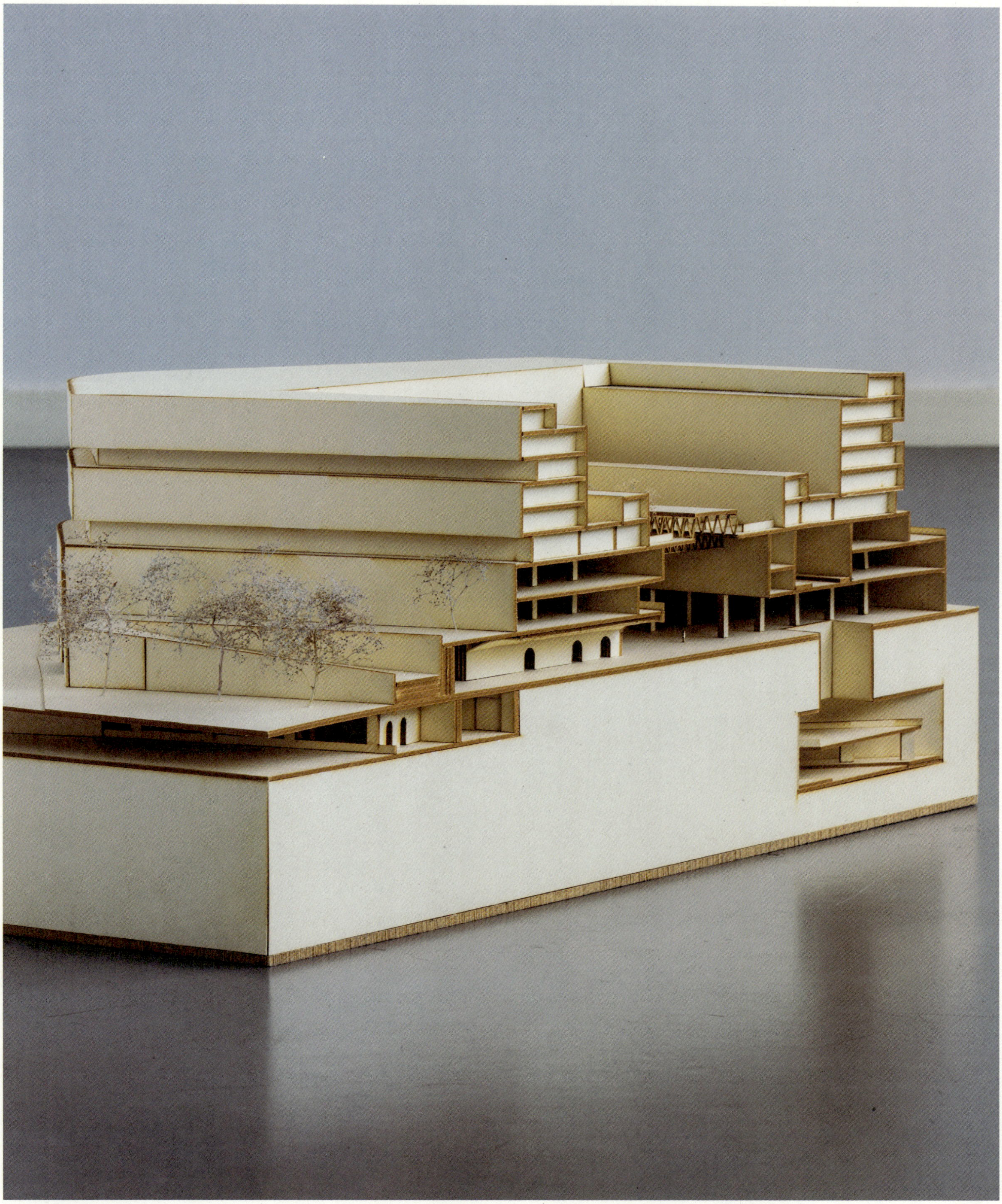

27 Model 1:200

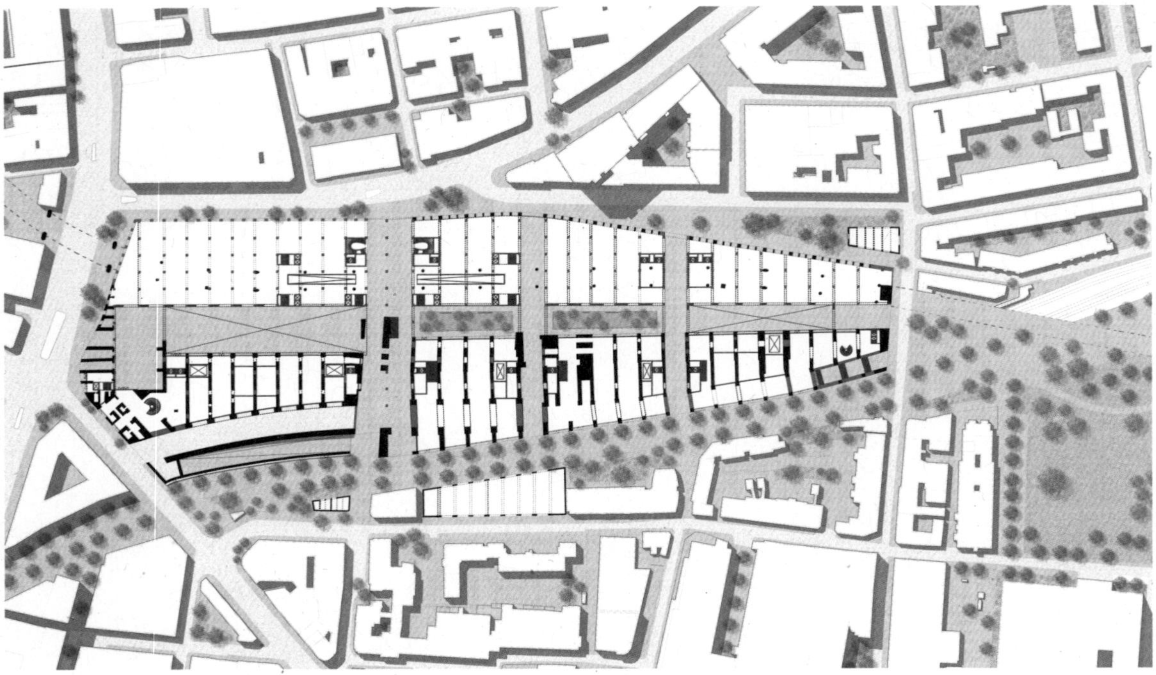

28 Ground level floor plan

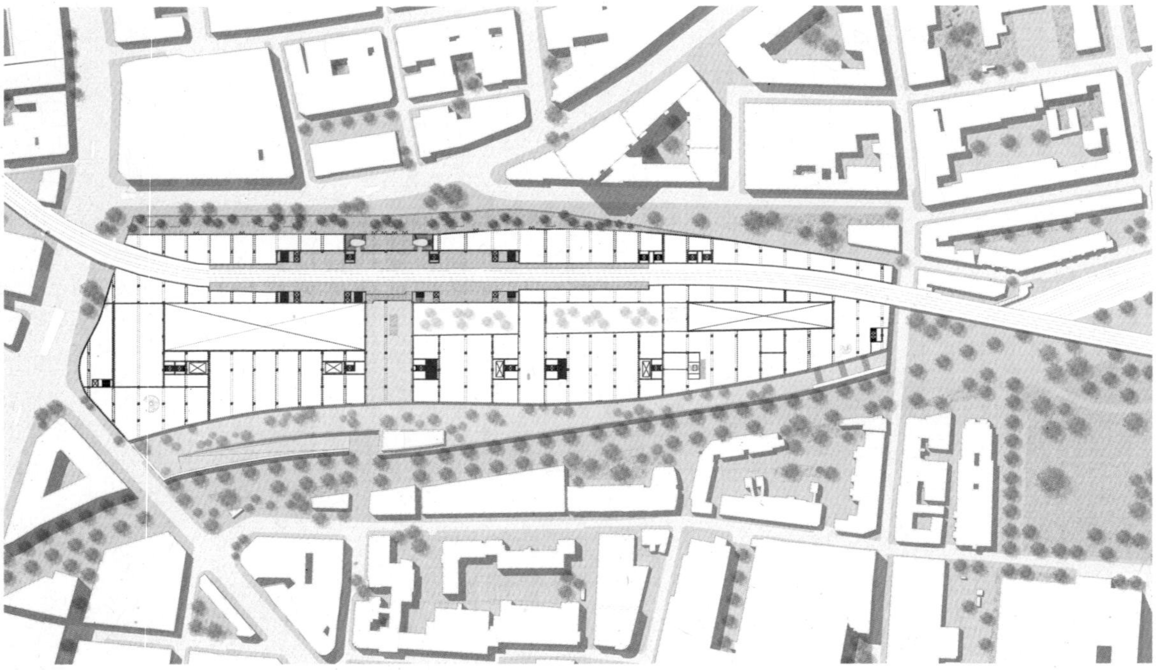

29 First level floor plan

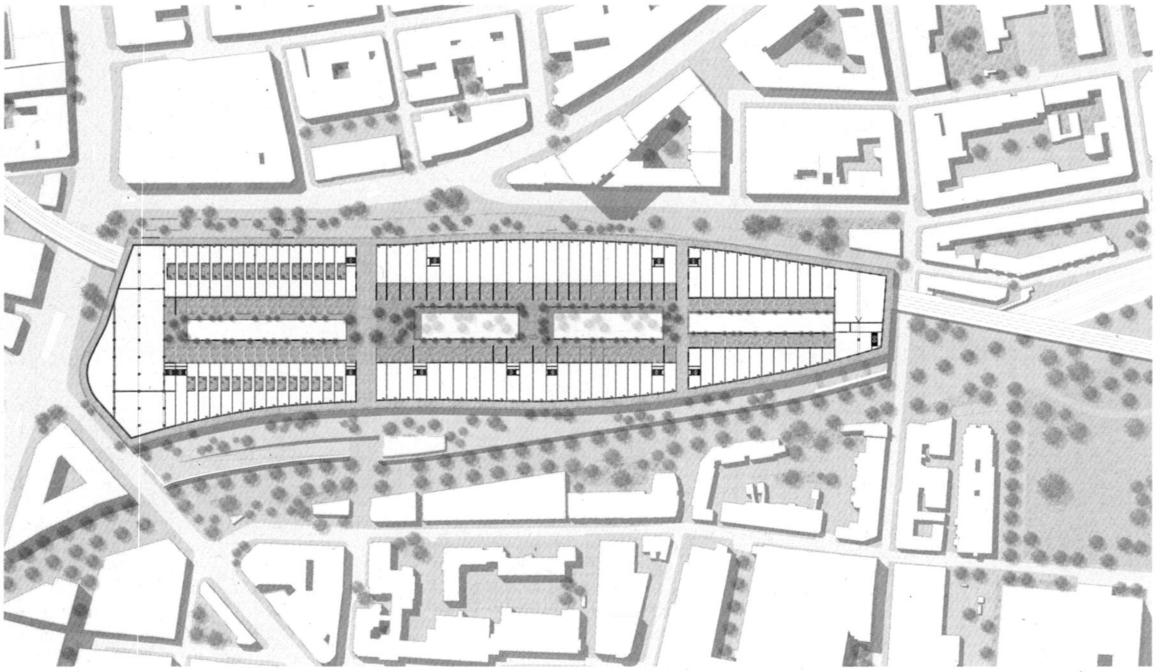

30 Third level floor plan

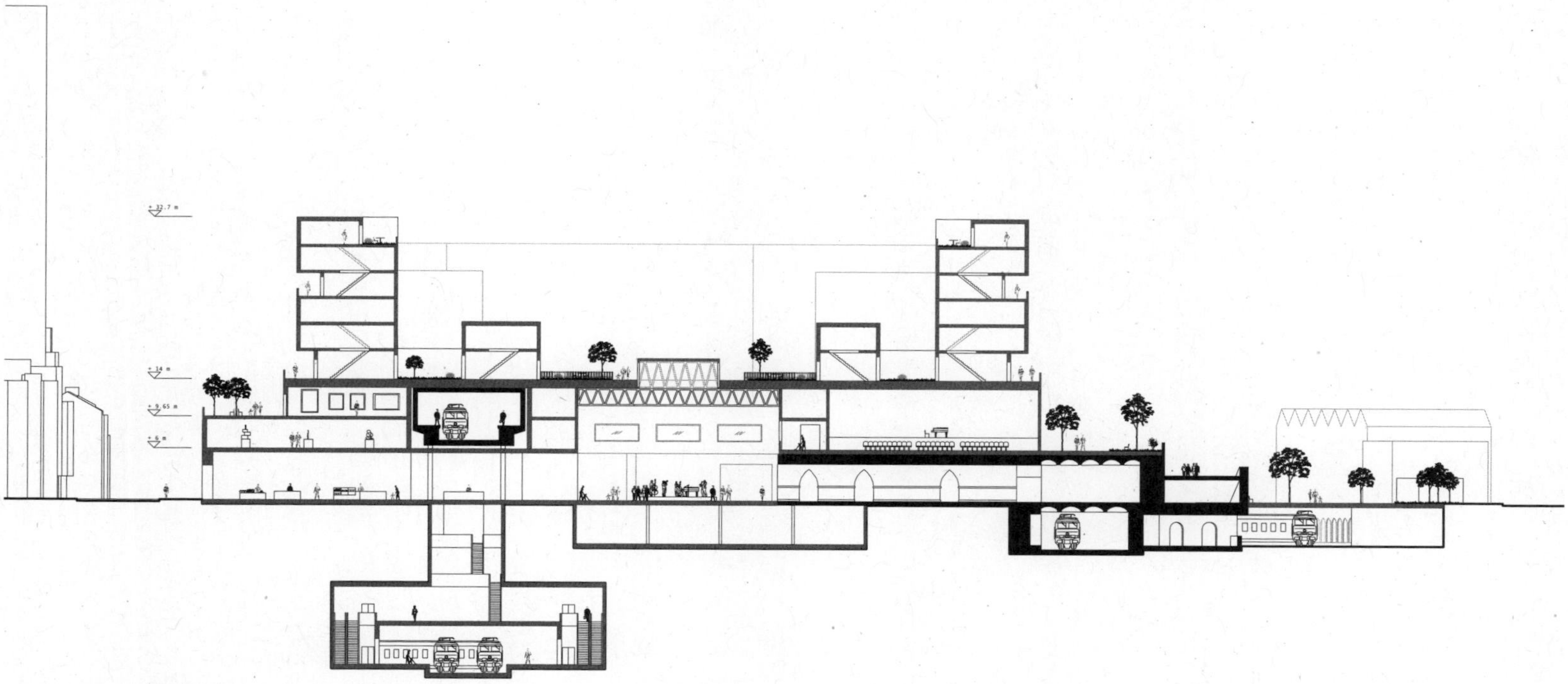

31 North-south section

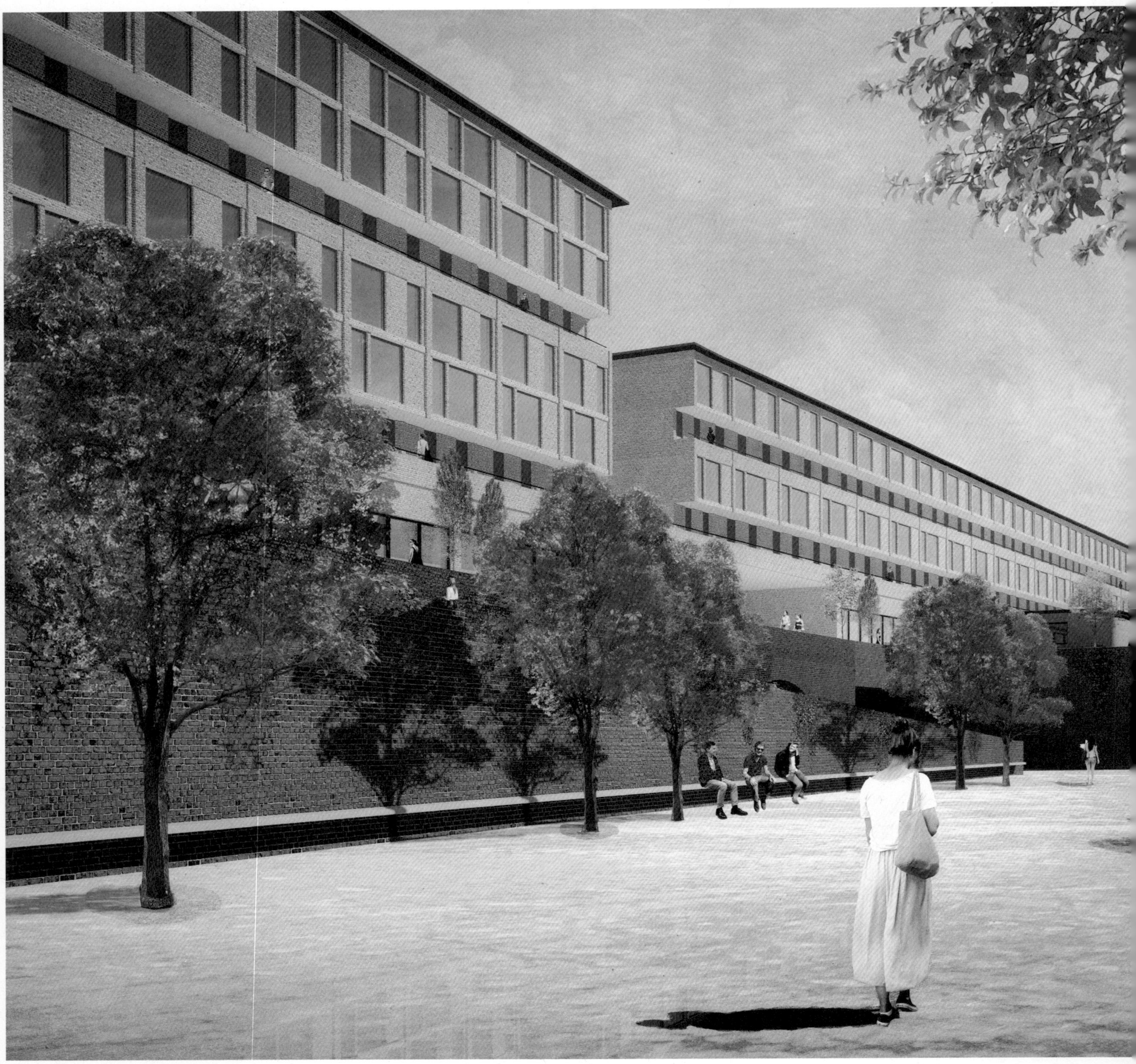

32 Visualisation of the greenway on covered tracks

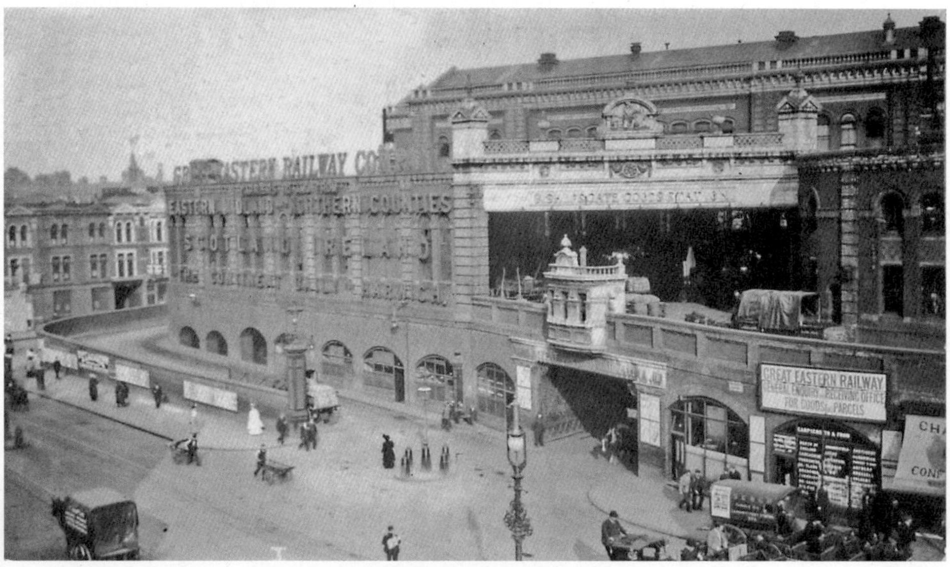

33 Bishopsgate goods station in the first decade of the twentieth century

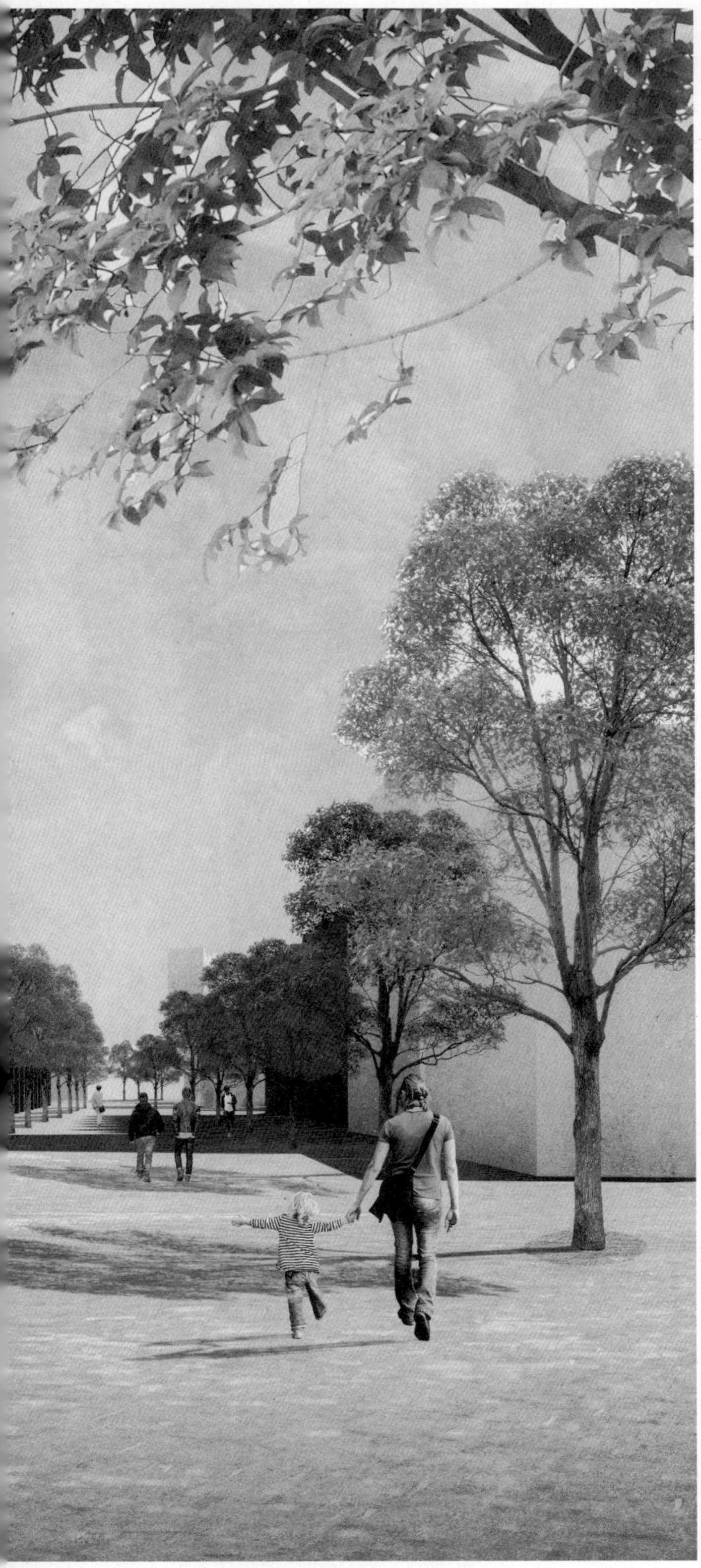

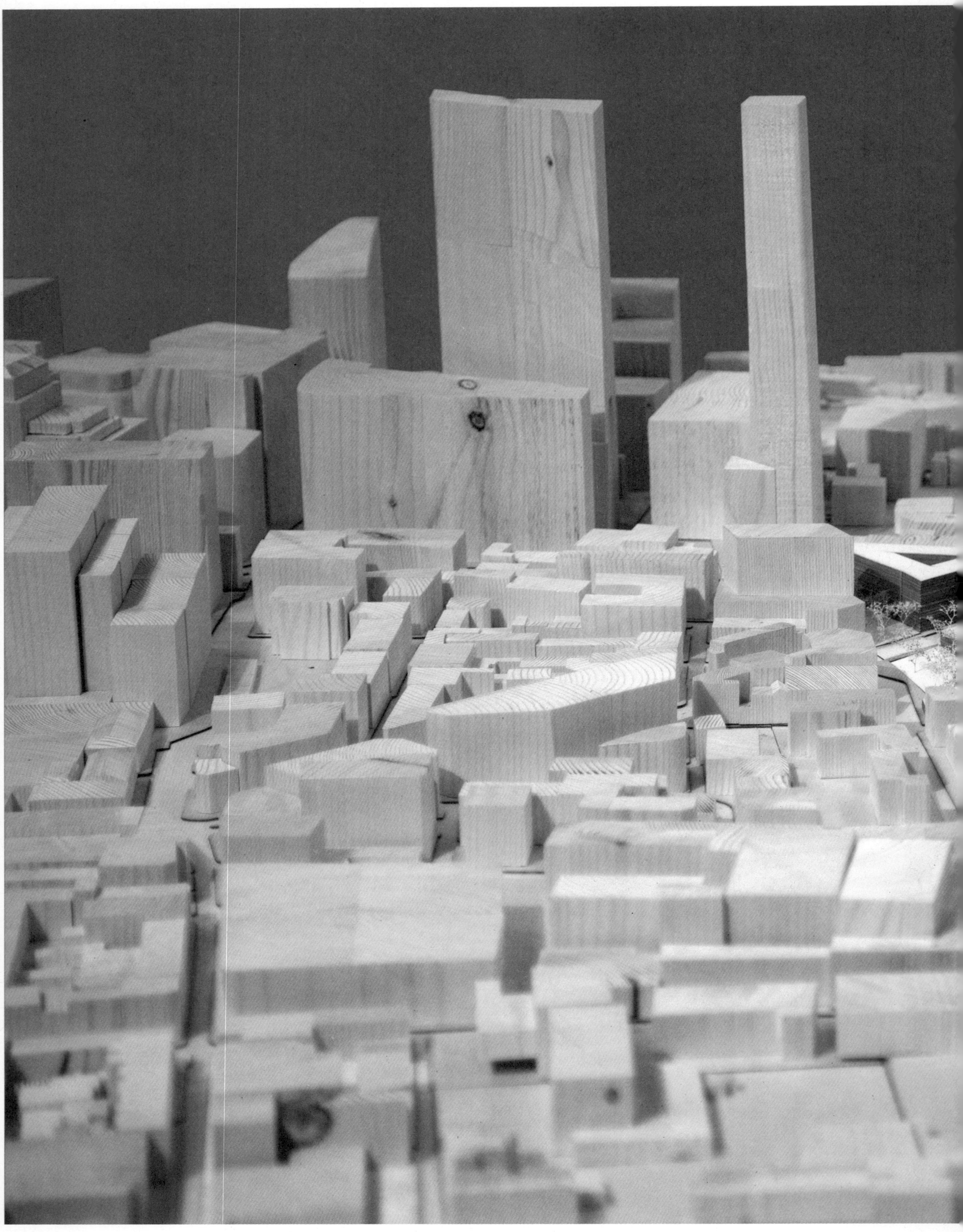

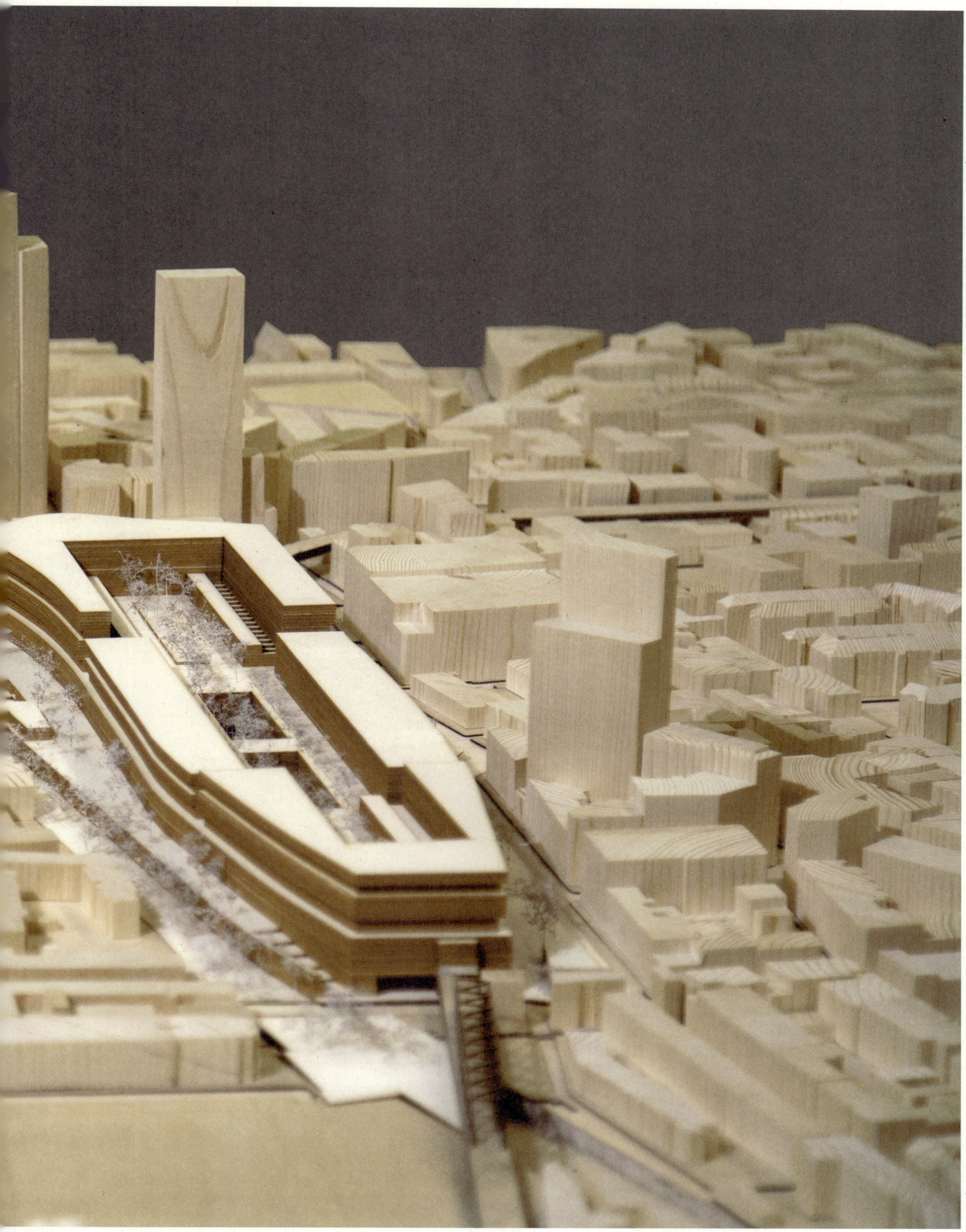

III Towards Ownership Diversity

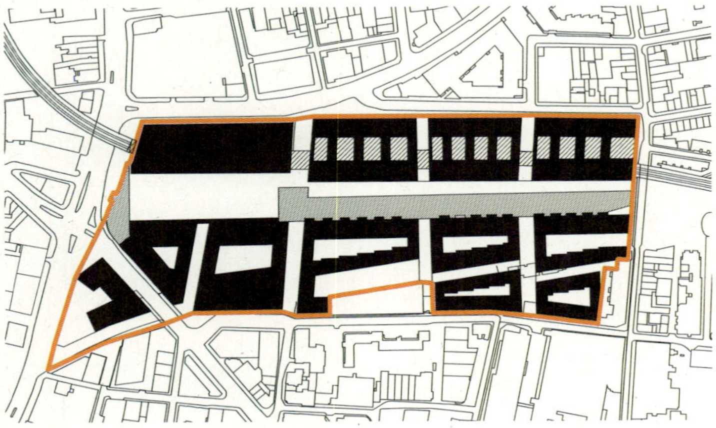

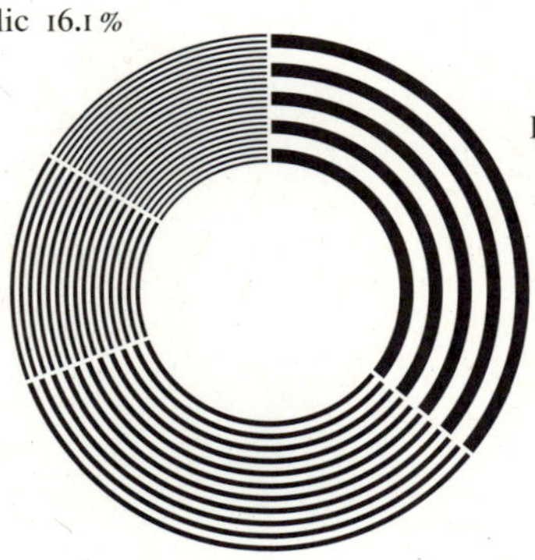

Site Area		59,190 m²	
Floor Area		216,360 m²	100 %
	Housing	77,862 m²	36.0 %
	Offices	72,698 m²	33.6 %
	Commerce	31,035 m²	14.3 %
	Public	34,765 m²	16.1 %
Density (FAR)		3.66	

This project is based on the ambition to create an urban fabric that grows out of the neighbouring structures, while fulfilling the economic requirements of higher density (fig. 39). To this end, the project is an adaption of a typical London typology: the terraced house.

The framework of the urban design is simple. The site is divided into a northern and a southern half, which are subdivided into four and five blocks respectively. In between is a central public space. It opens onto Shoreditch High Street station as a square and to the east widens into the Allens Gardens as a park, making use of the covered railway tracks (fig. 36).

The design's distinctive features are to be found at a small scale. Except for the plot north of the square, the lots are narrow and long. The rigid block structure is filled with numerous plots. On the ground floor, this creates a similar rhythm and vibrancy to Brick Lane, Bethnal Green or Spitalfields (fig. 35). The richness of the chosen typology is highlighted in the cross-section (fig. 38). As a reaction to the physical context and led by the restrictions of the existing underground infrastructures, alleys and courtyards with different qualities are formed. The typical London mews are reinterpreted, and their potential as domestic and intimate urban spaces is fully tapped. The extant fragments of the viaduct are neatly integrated. Its distinctive arches are turned into shop entrances. On its roof, a park-like green space is created. The entrances to the apartments are dotted along this linear space (fig. 37).

The project proves that by using a well-tried typology, even when adapted in dimension, a dense low-rise neighbourhood composed of small units with sophisticated open spaces can be created. A prerequisite for the success of the scheme, however, is an uncompromising implementation of small investment units.

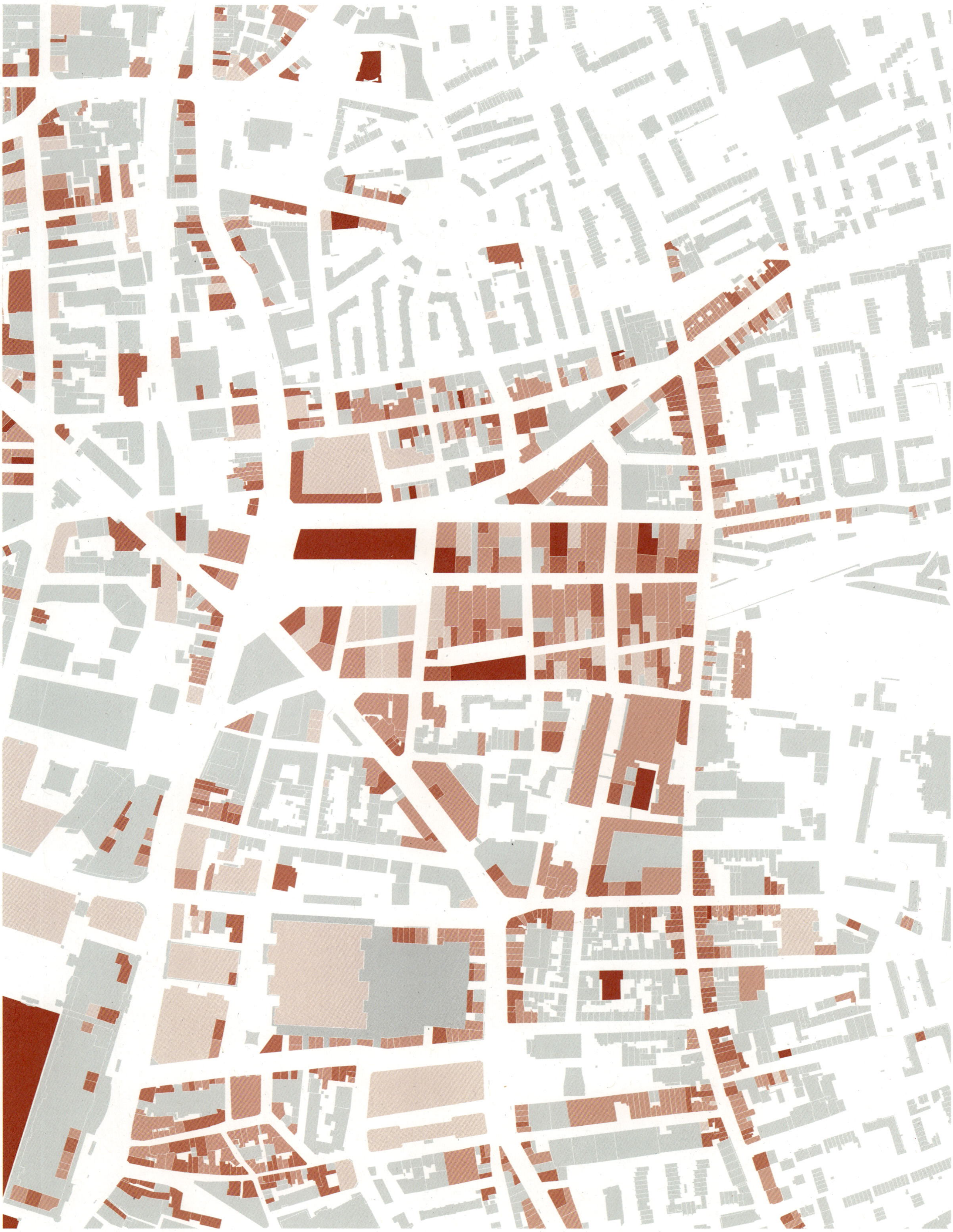

35 Ground level uses in the neighbourhood

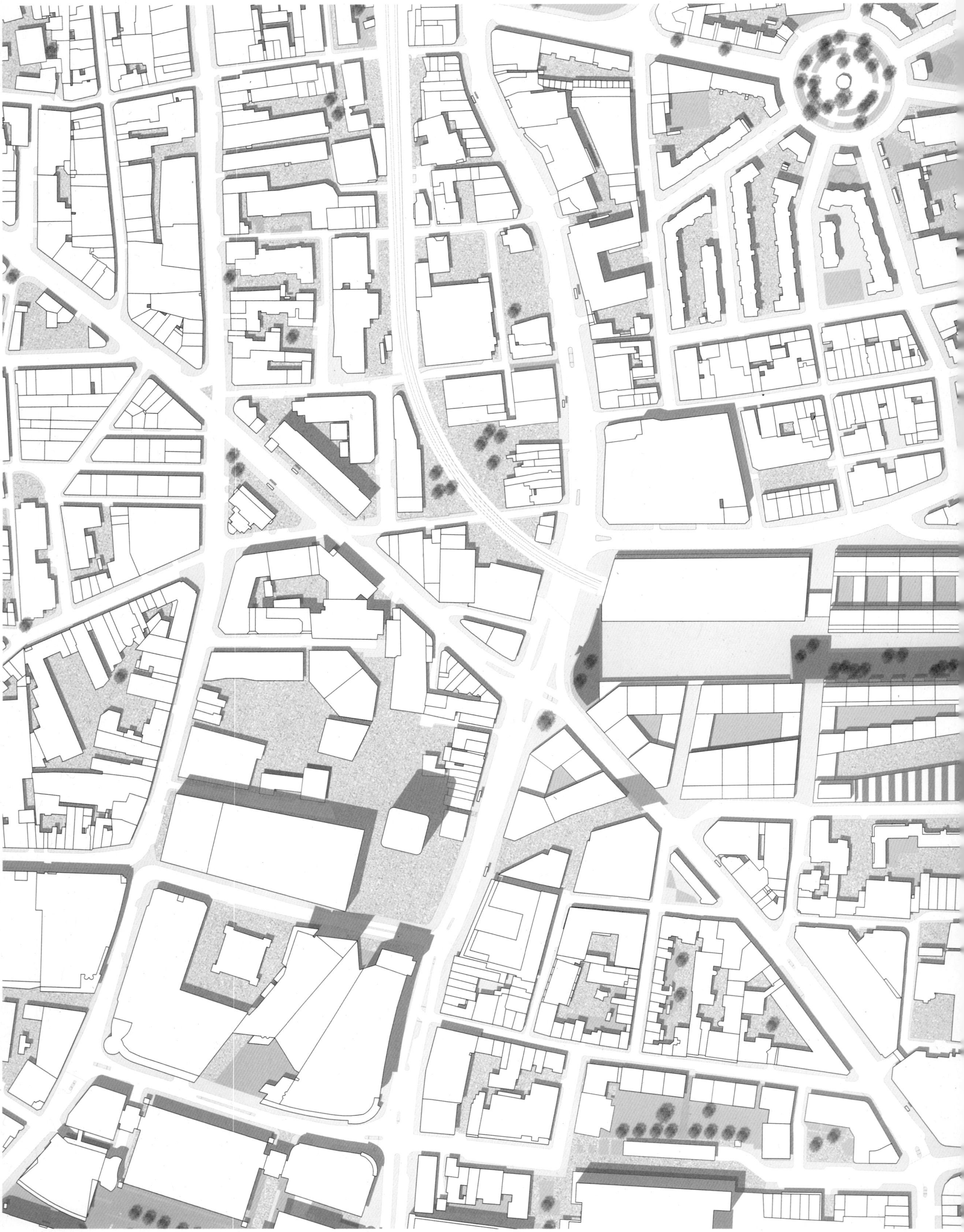

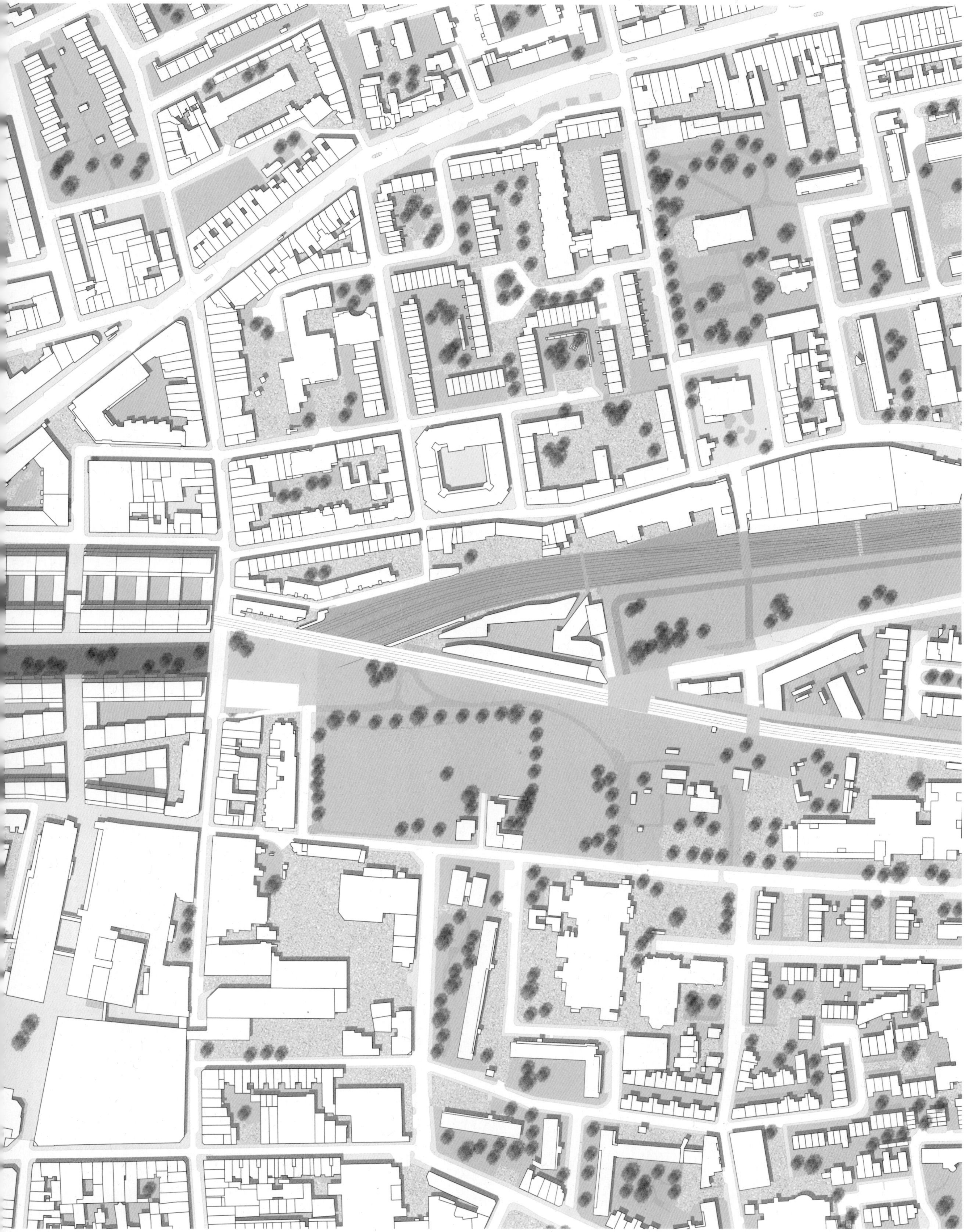

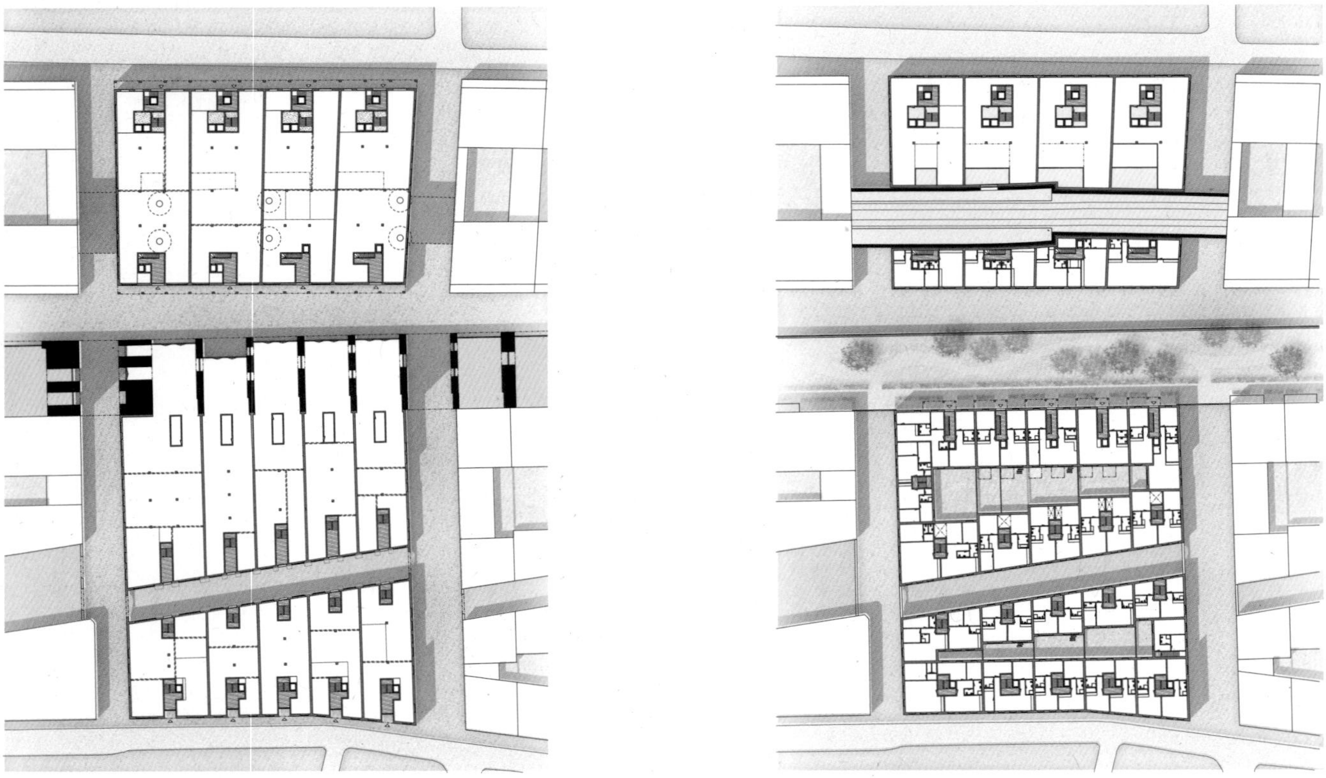

37 Floor plans: ground level, third level and fifth level

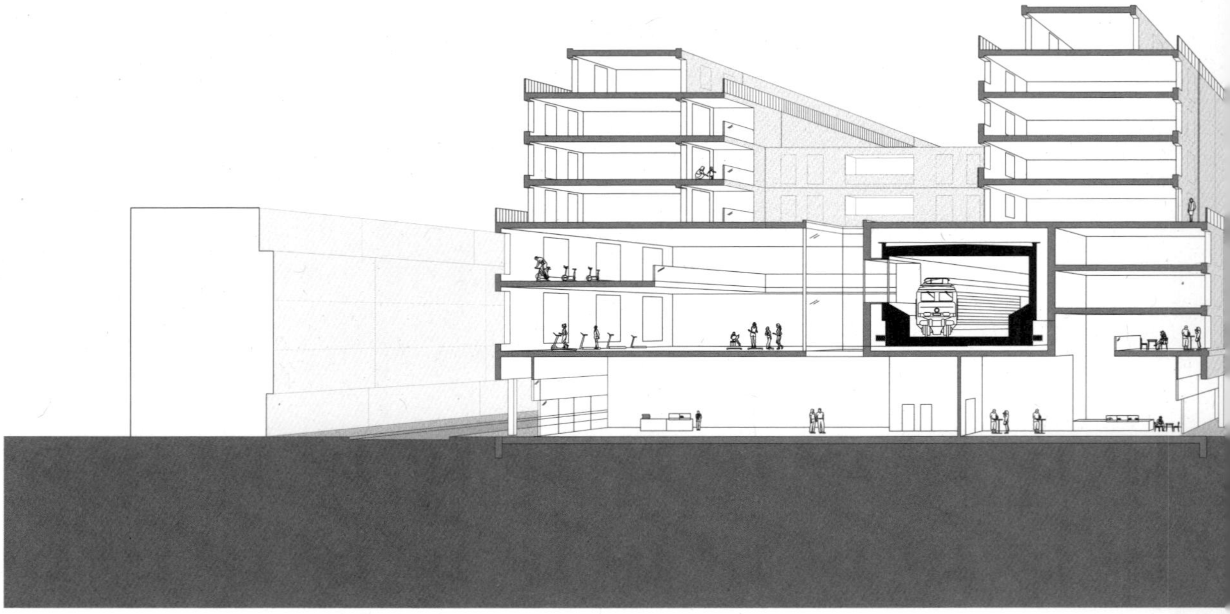

38 North-south section

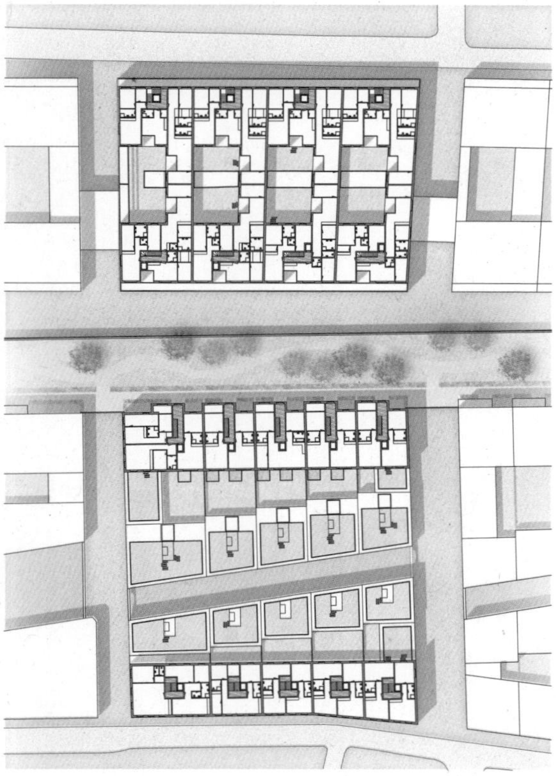

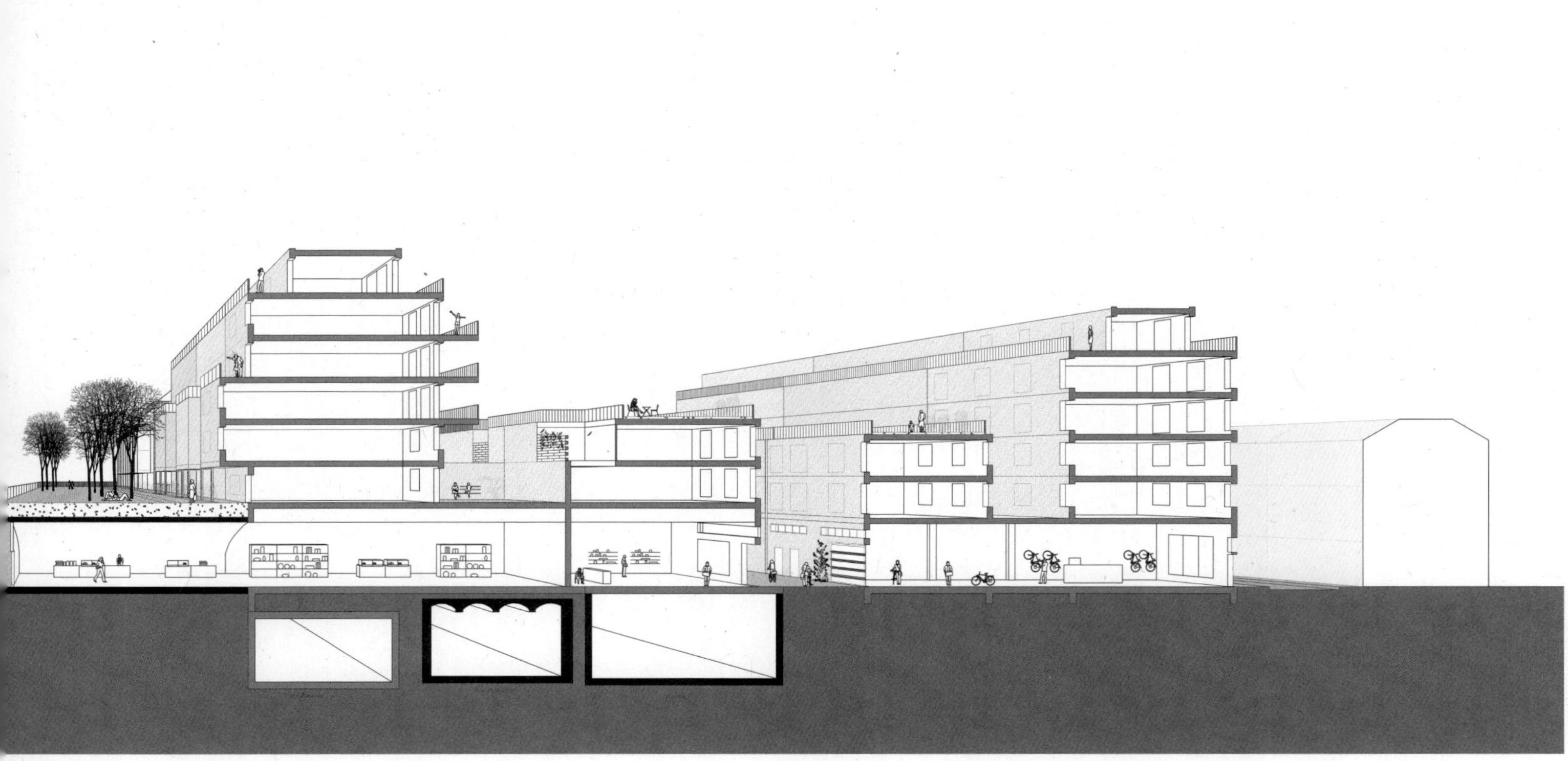

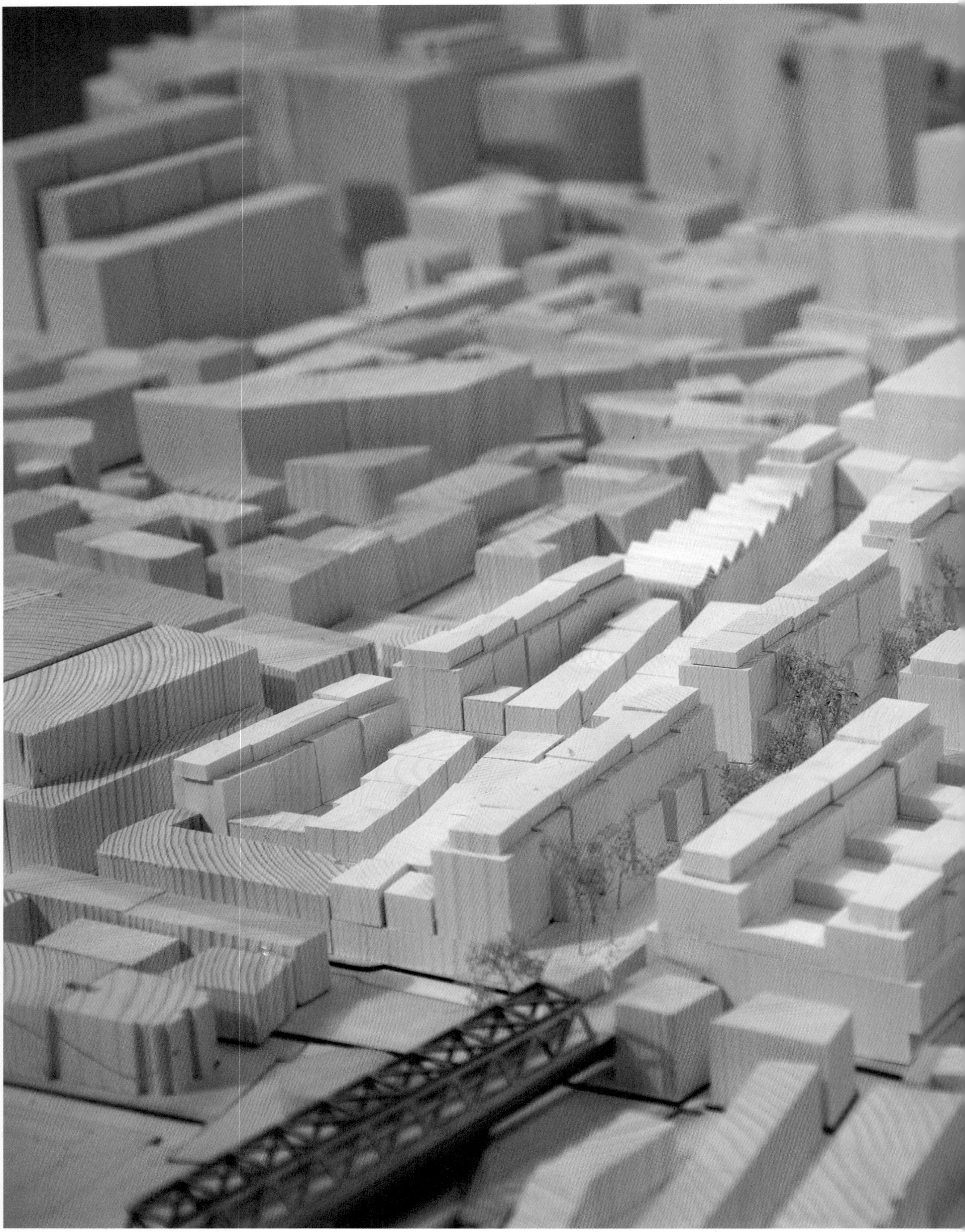

39 Model 1:500

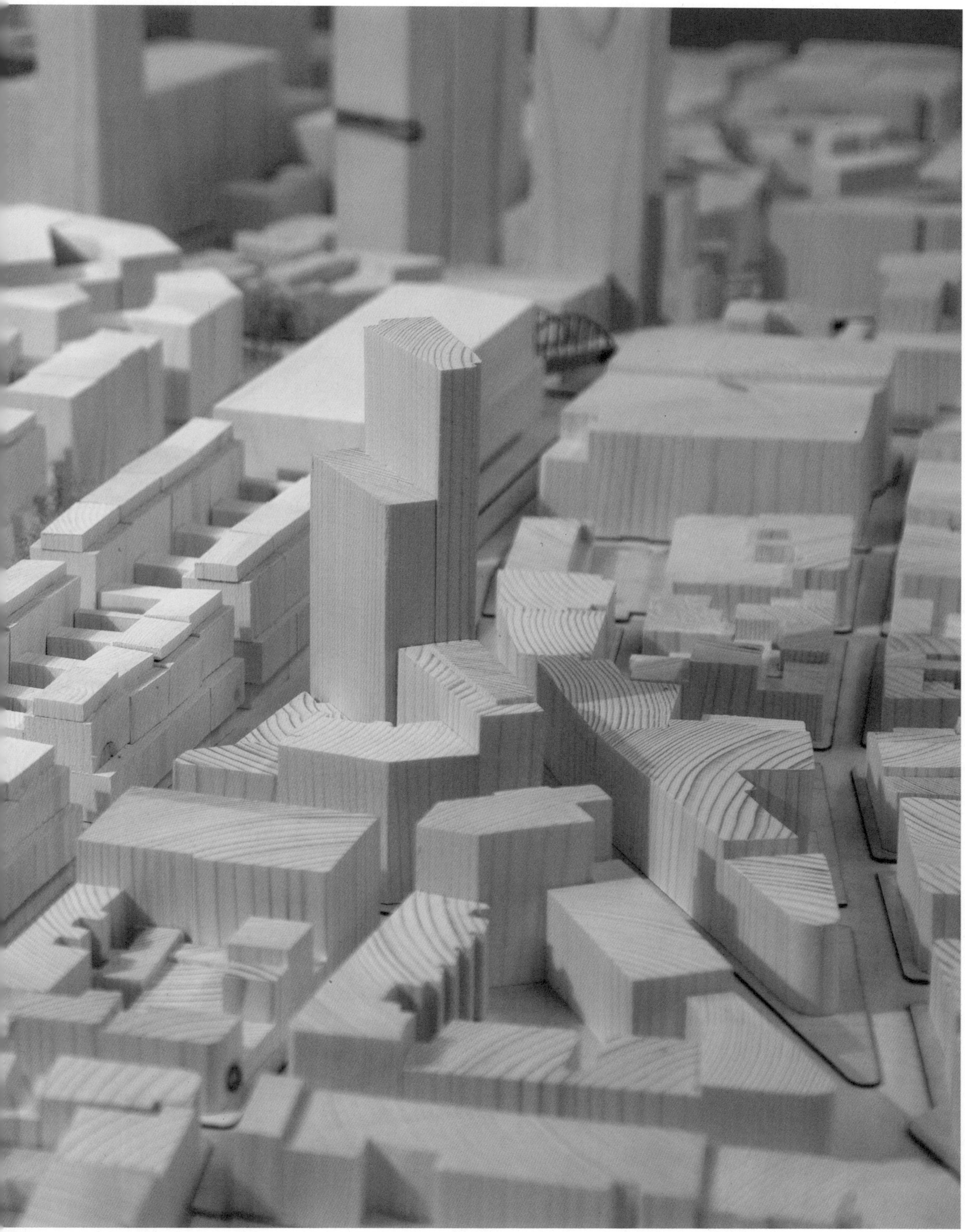

IV Vertical Zoning

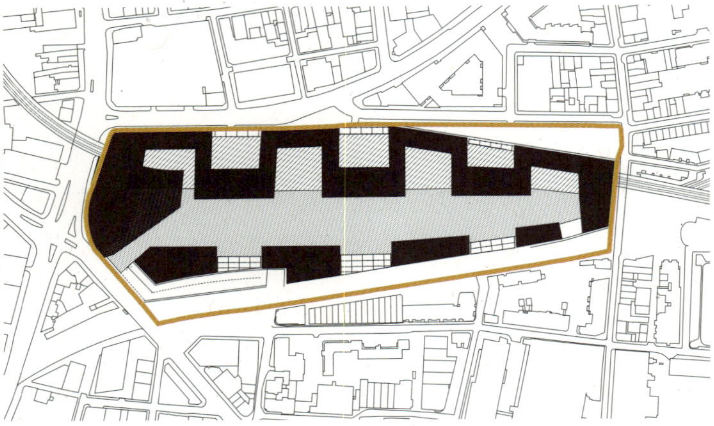

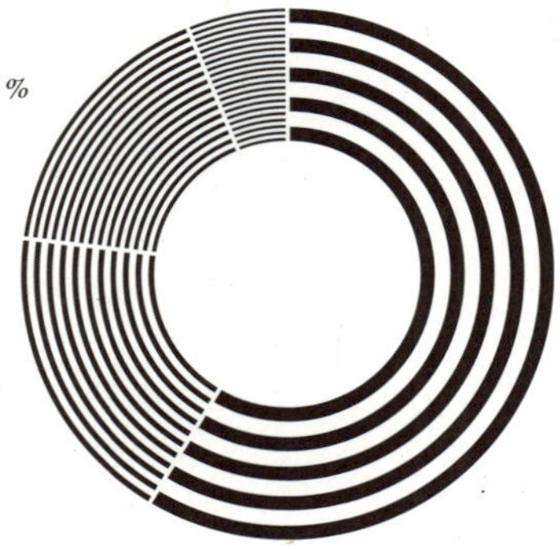

Site Area		44,700 m²	
Floor Area		172,094 m²	100 %
	Housing	101,298 m²	58.9 %
	Offices	31,870 m²	18.5 %
	Commerce	28,879 m²	16.8 %
	Public	10,047 m²	5.8 %
Density (FAR)		3.85	

The guiding principle of this project is the extension of the existing viaduct in order to create a continuous pedestal – similar to the former goods yard. Following this decision, two complementary worlds are created: the pedestal itself, made up of large spaces for public uses, and the residential spaces on its top (fig. 46).

The advantage of the concept is that both the demand for an urban centre of metropolitan import and the need for high-quality living space can be met. Because of its porosity and appeal, the pedestal facilitates integration into the surrounding fabric at ground level. Its presence and large-scale uses lend it regional significance, but are also woven into the surroundings (fig. 41). The distance between the public uses and the apartments on the upper floors follows from the conceptual design and is harnessed by the designers. Different residential typologies are scattered around a park that spreads over several levels, creating diverse open spaces similar to a hanging garden (figs. 40, 42–45). The introvert upper part is counter-balanced by a new pedestrian-only street connecting west and east by using the covered railway tracks, creating a 'Gate to the East' (fig. 47). Thereby, public accessibility to the Allens Gardens is improved considerably. The proposal seizes the opportunity to reorganise the Gardens and densify its surrounding area.

The quality of the project lies in its fusion of seemingly conflicting requirements into a symbiotic system, justifying the preservation of the viaduct and its extension. The stacking of very different urban realms – a housing development surrounding a park that sits on a public plinth – questions classic zoning policies. The radical structure of the project also leads to problematic lighting situations in the pedestal, however, and renders the project's realisation process extremely rigid. A development in multiple steps seems hardly possible.

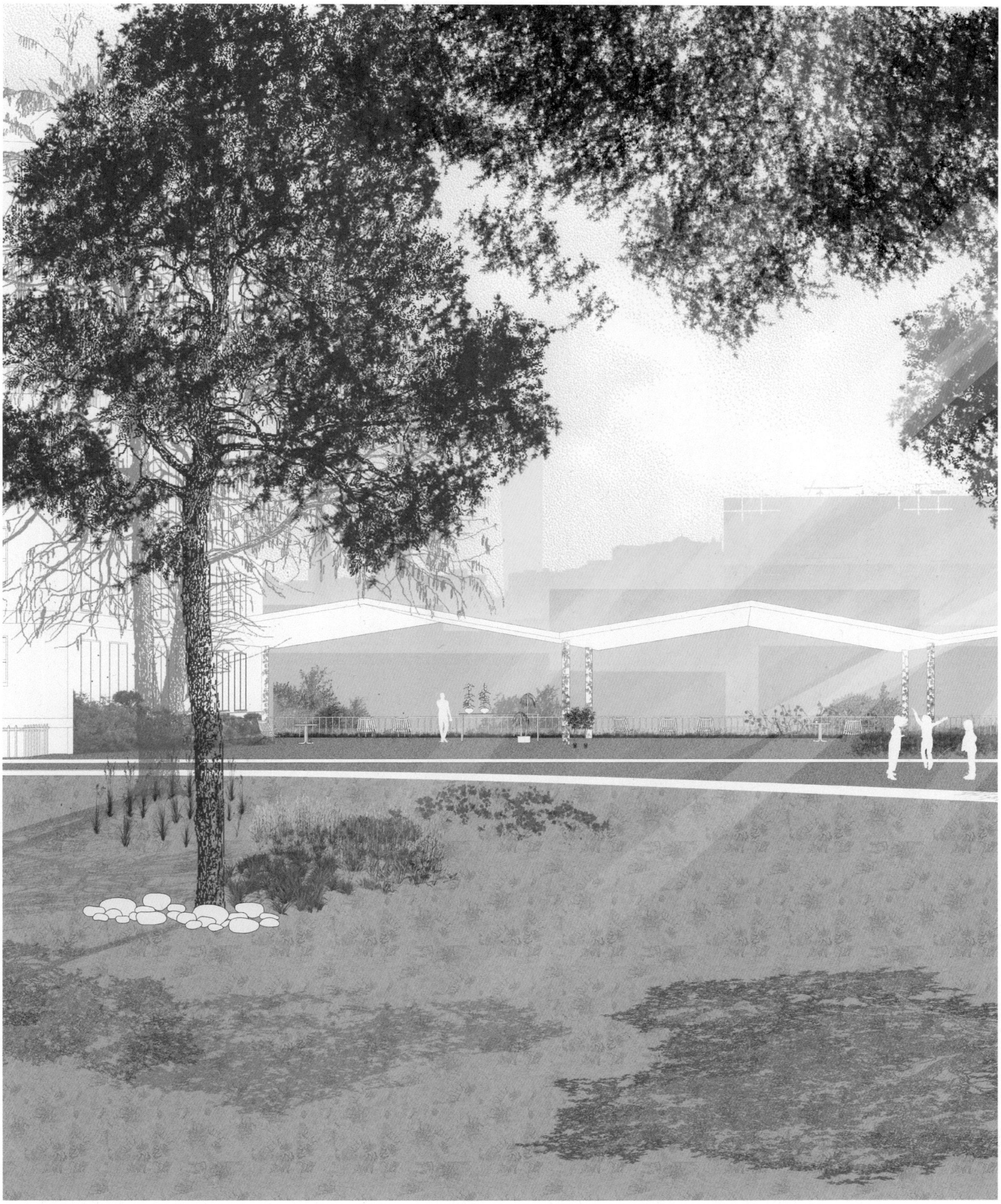

40 Visualisation of the park level

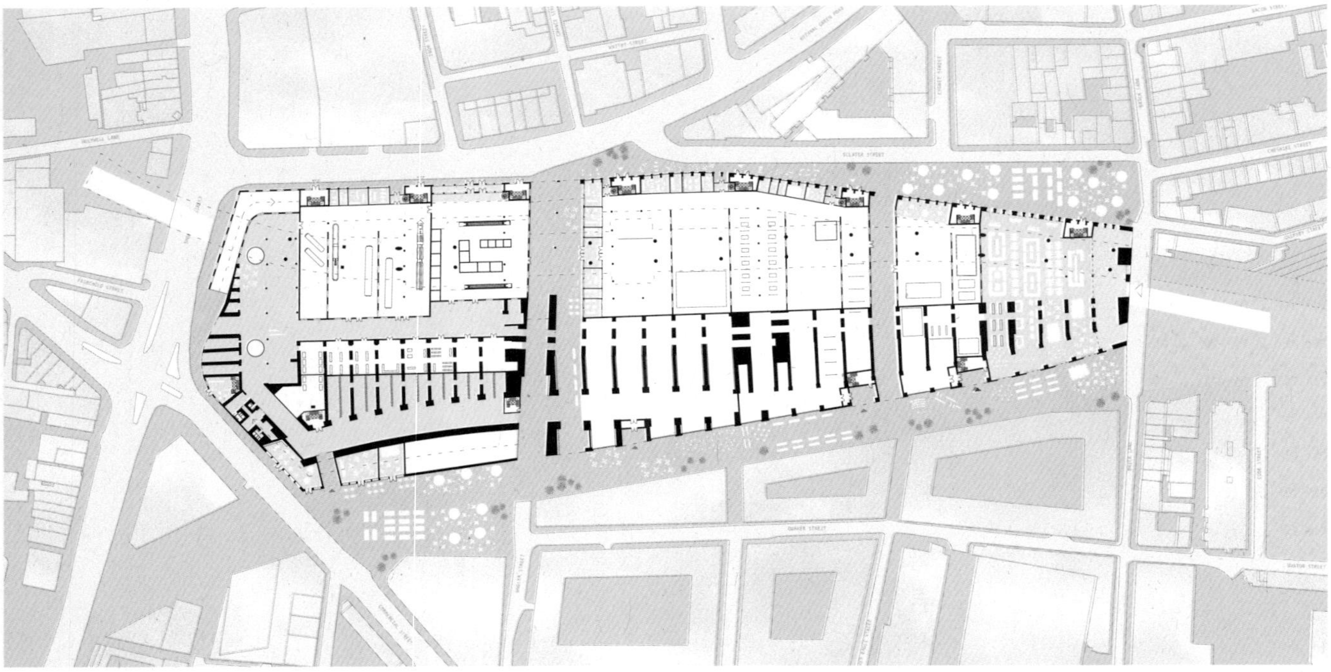

41 Ground level floor plan

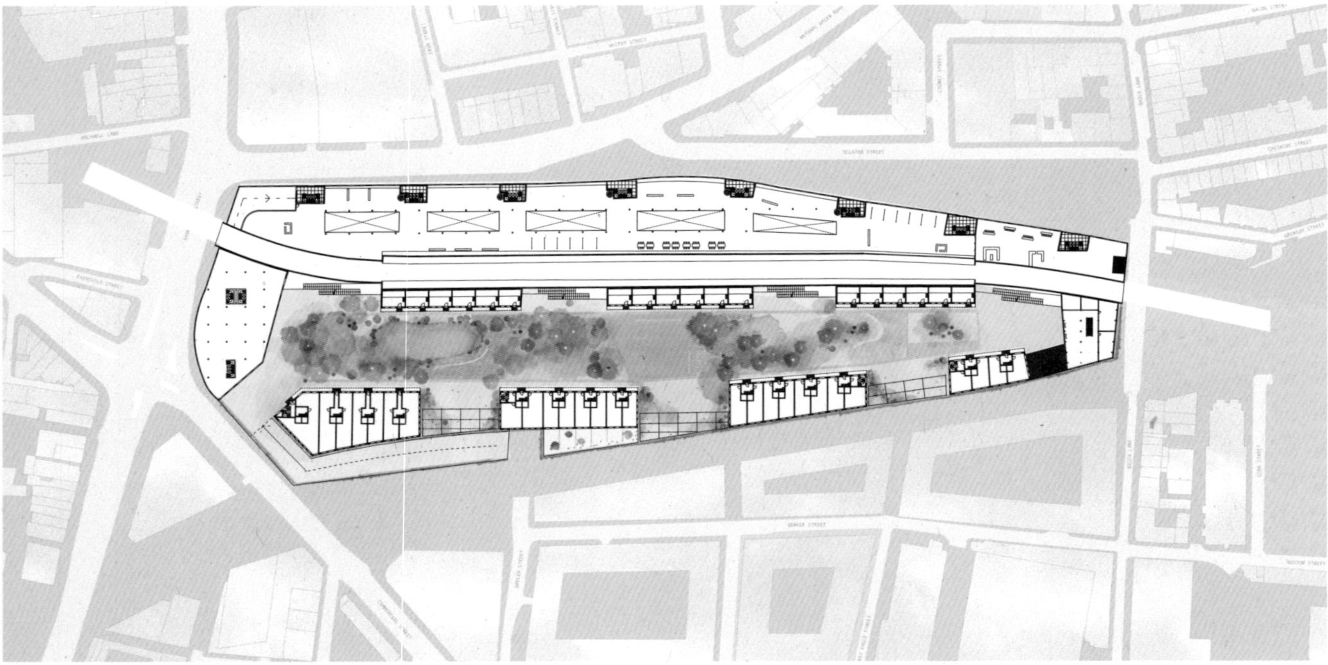

42 Third level floor plan

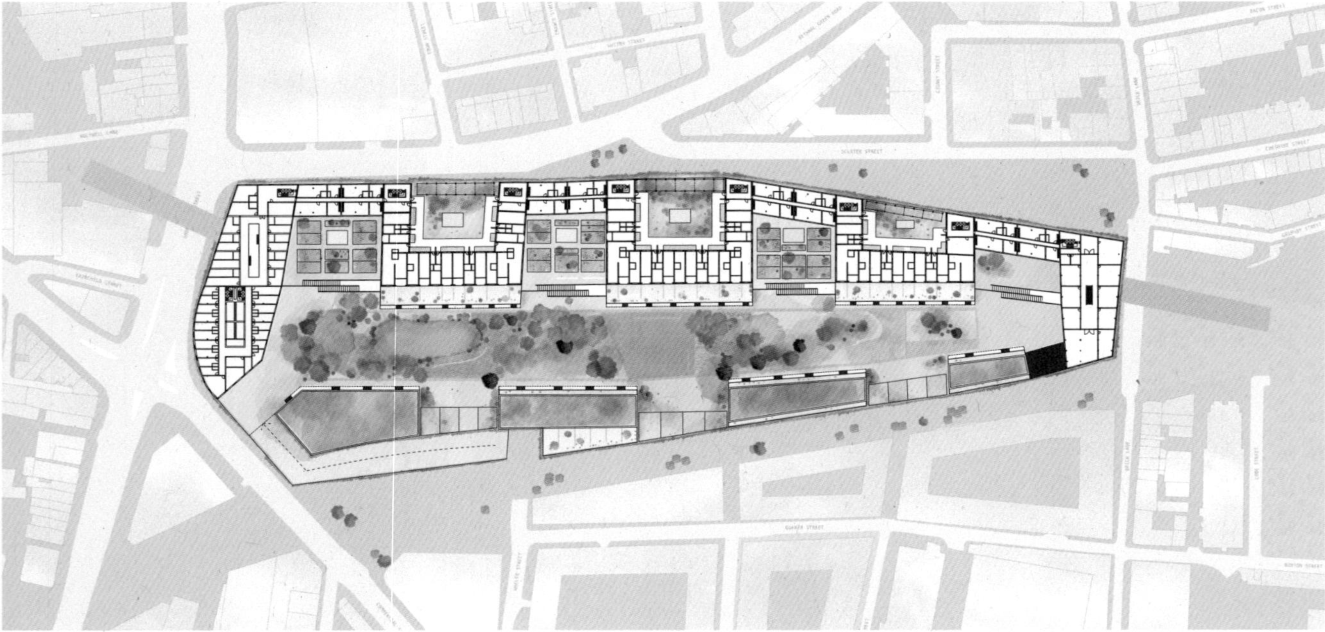

43 Fifth level floor plan

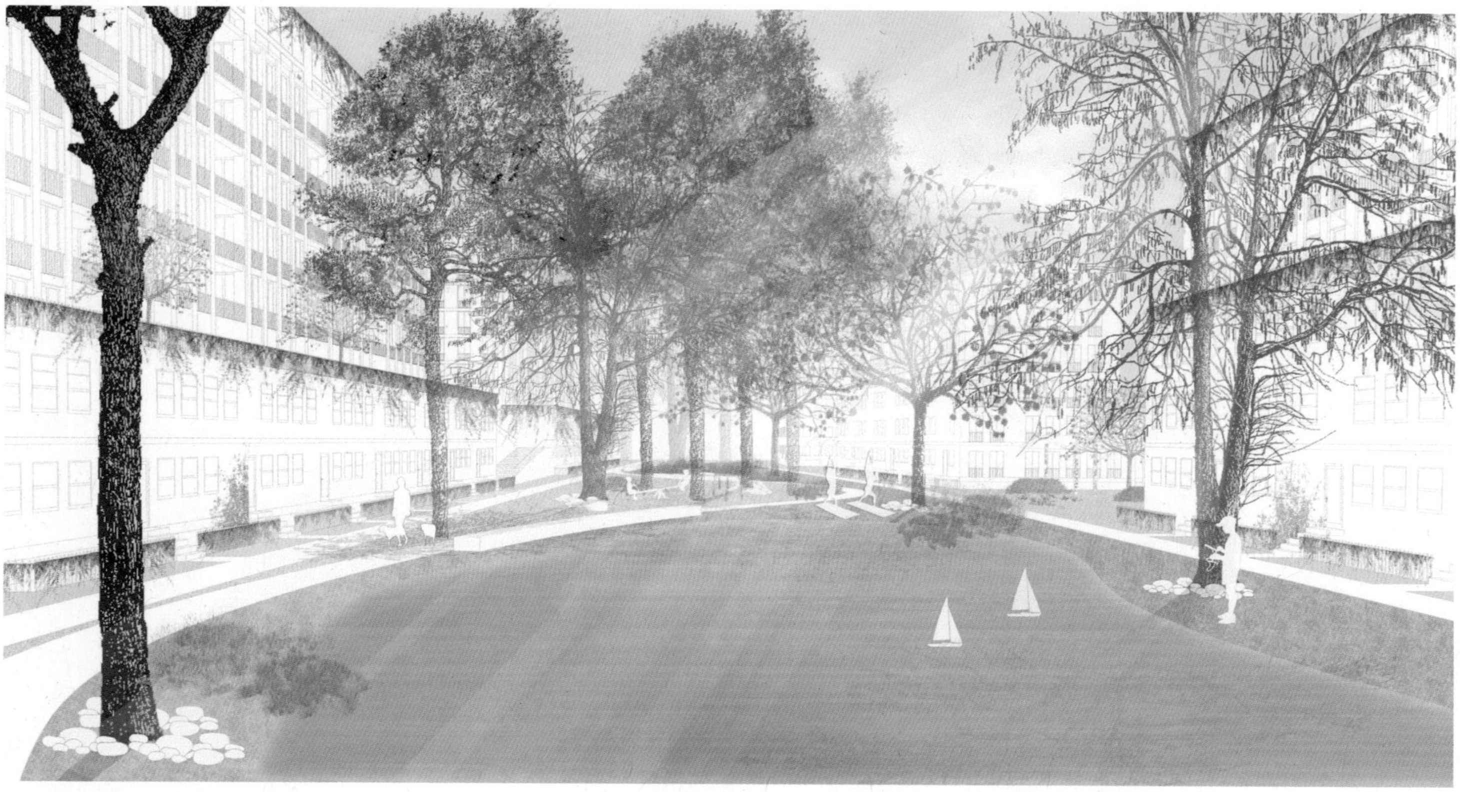

44 Visualisation of the park level

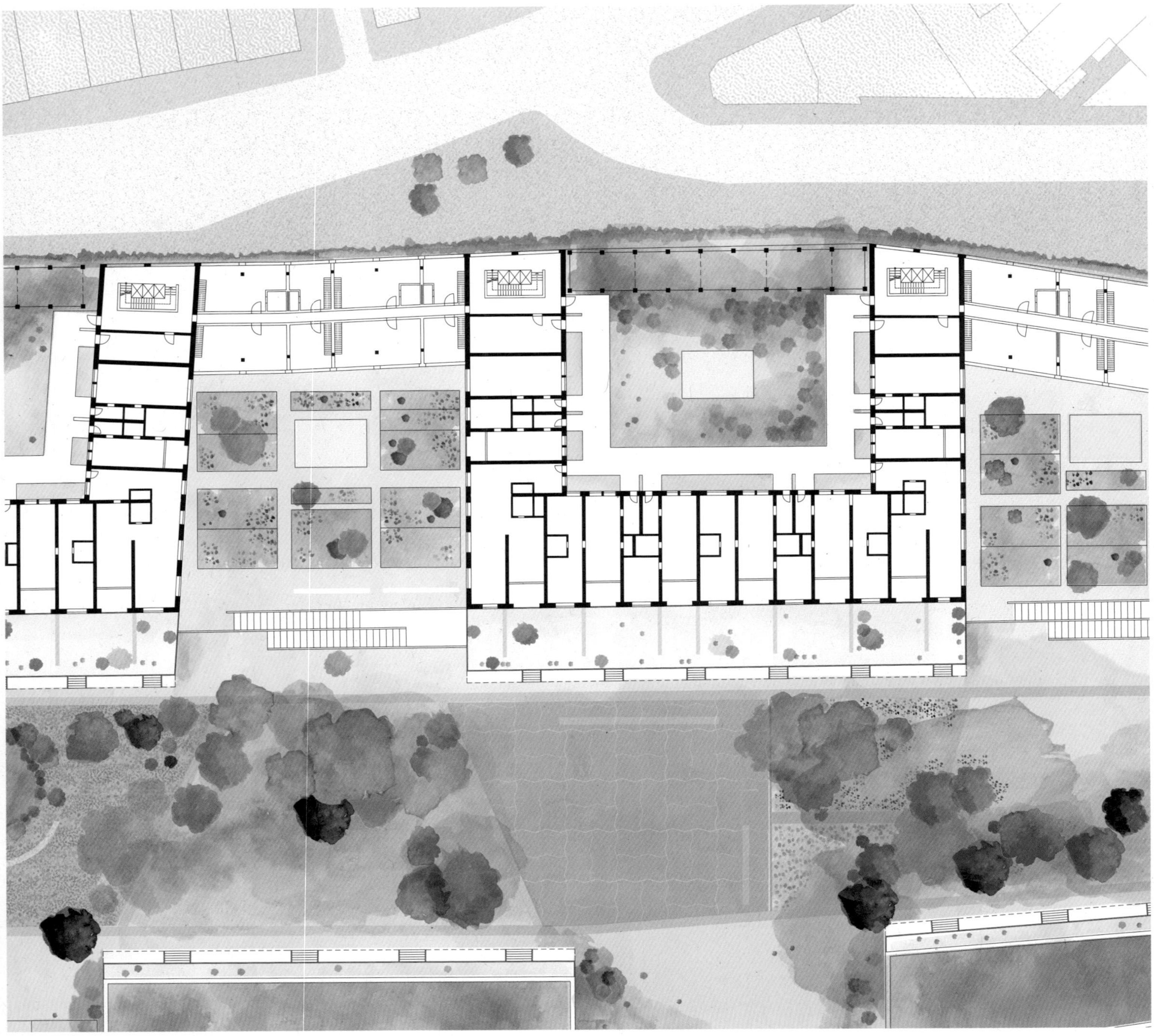

45 Floor plan detail, fifth level

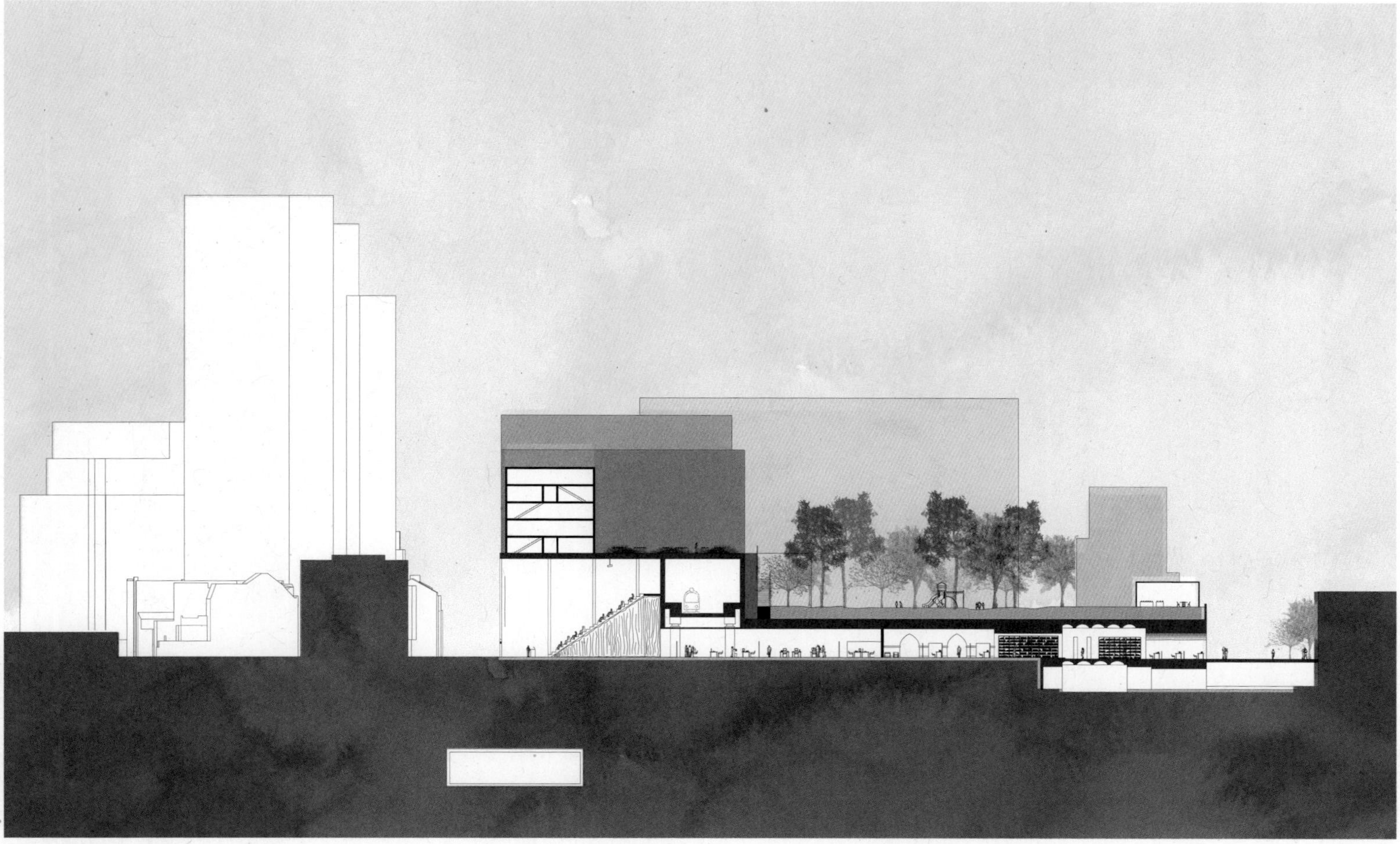

46 North-south section

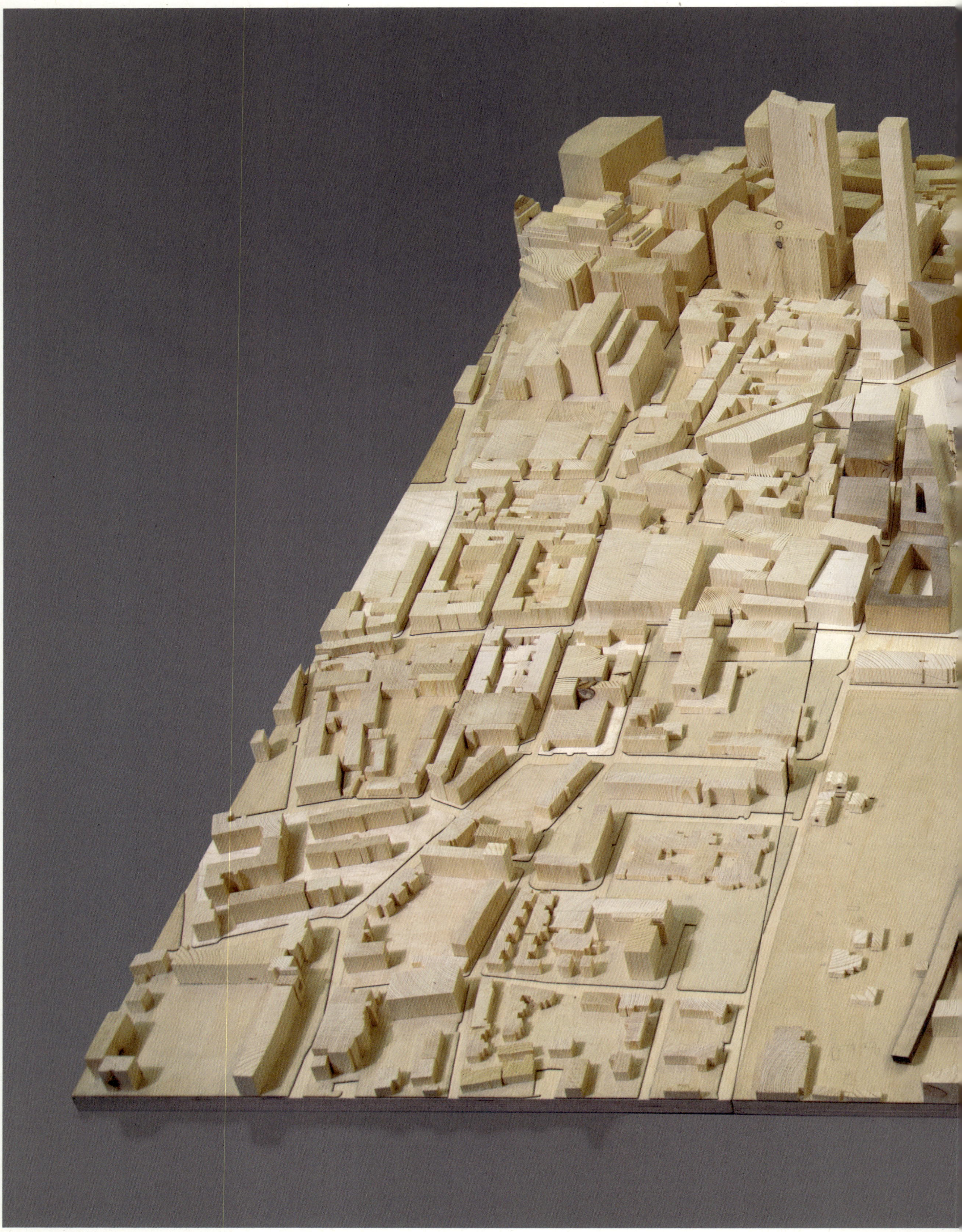

47 Model 1:500

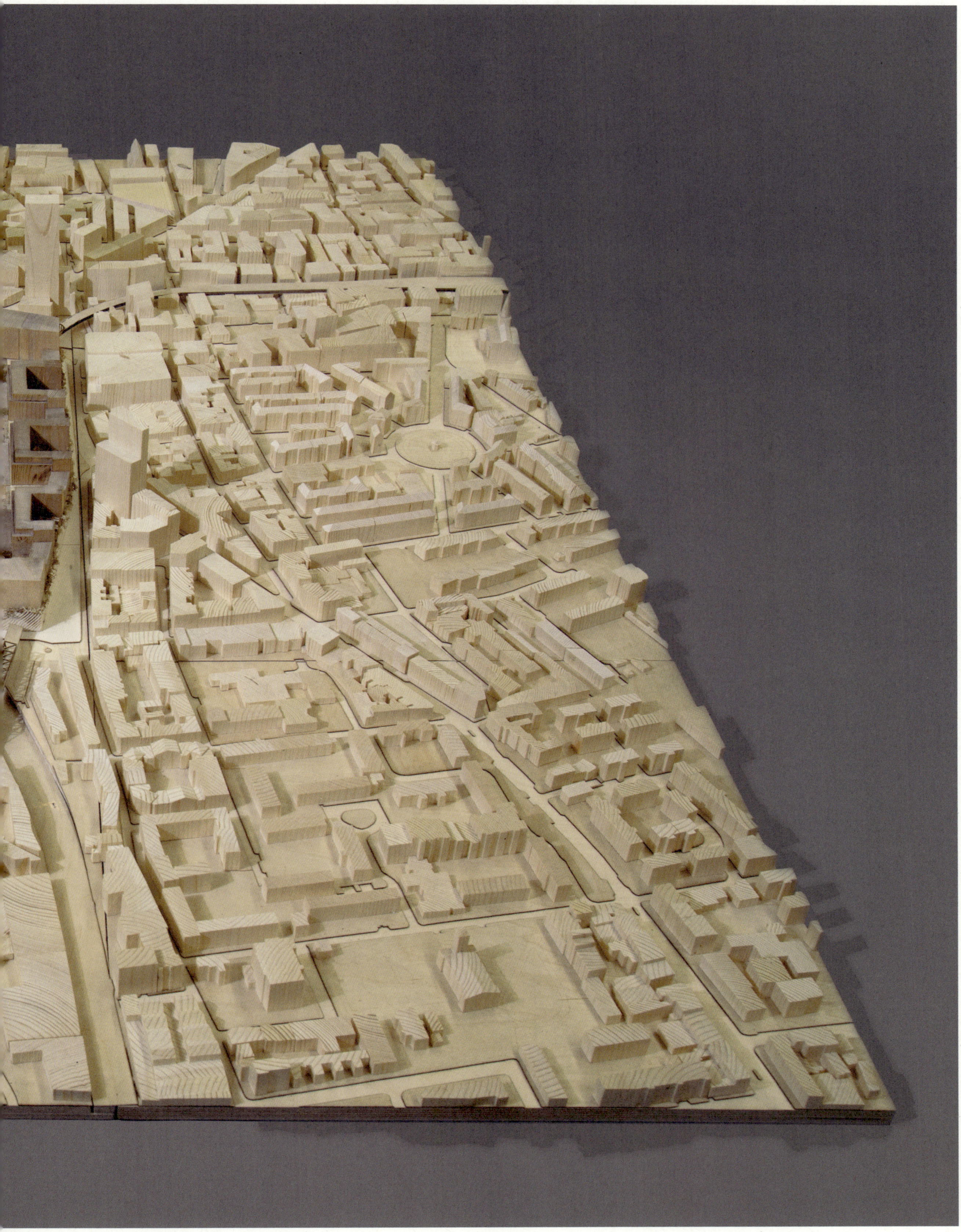

V Neighbourhood Centre

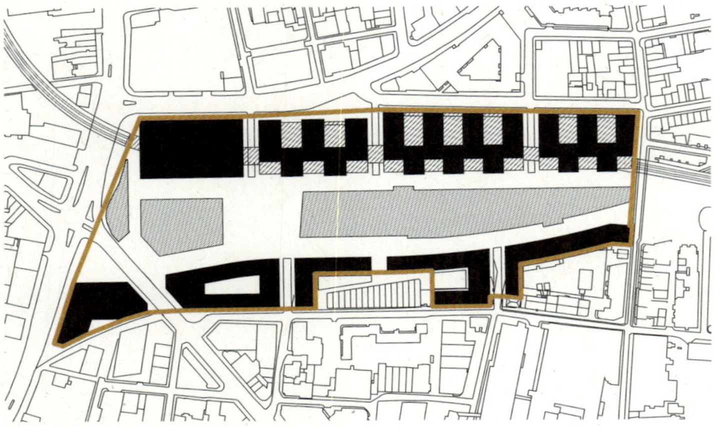

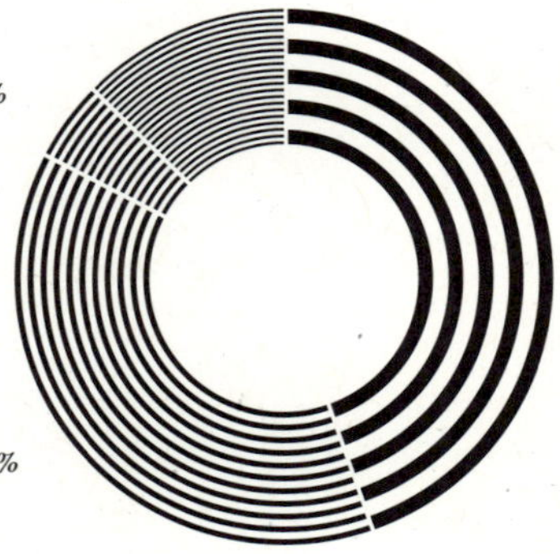

Site Area		54,670 m²	
Floor Area		202,300 m²	100 %
	Housing	90,680 m²	44.8 %
	Offices	76,800 m²	38.0 %
	Commerce	9,790 m²	4.8 %
	Public	25,030 m²	12.4 %
Density (FAR)		3.70	

This urbanistic proposal aims to establish a new centrality for the surrounding neighbourhoods. The extant viaduct forms the project's core. Partly preserved and partly extended, it creates a lively strip featuring public, collective and neighbourhood-related uses (fig. 50). In order to make the new centre accessible, the borders isolating the viaduct today are removed. The existing trench containing the train tracks is replaced by a representative facade (fig. 49), and accessibility is fostered by the creation of a public space communicating between the City of London and the new neighbourhood centre (fig. 48). To the east of the site, a new square links a sequence of public spaces to the Allens Gardens. In the long term, the existing buildings surrounding the open spaces will be densified (fig. 51).

The southern connection to Spitalfields is more difficult to establish. By covering the rail tracks, however, the two neighbourhoods can be neatly integrated. Similarly, the northern border between site and neighbourhood is bridged by continuity of the street grid. Thus, the urban pattern of both the southern and northern neighbourhoods is linked to the project, opening new urban spaces on the historic, albeit newly interpreted, centre (fig. 53). Therefore, the entrances to the station are placed at the project's most public location.

The complex demand for building types is exemplified by the area north of the new centre, where office spaces and apartments have to be reconciled with the London Overground rails crossing the building plots. A meandering framework allows sufficient daylight and provides the apartments with private terraces (fig. 52). The space below the London Overground is used as a 'rue intérieure' to access the apartments and separates residential units from office spaces and retail.

Implementing the urbanistic concept requires that the tracks, which cut along the southern edge of the site, be covered. The proposal can easily be divided into separate investment and construction units. By eliminating barriers and thus establishing better connectivity between neighbourhoods, the project manages to invert the current situation from a closed site separating neighbourhoods to a new centre. The project stands out, both because of its successful integration into the existing fabric and the creation of a new public centrality for Shoreditch.

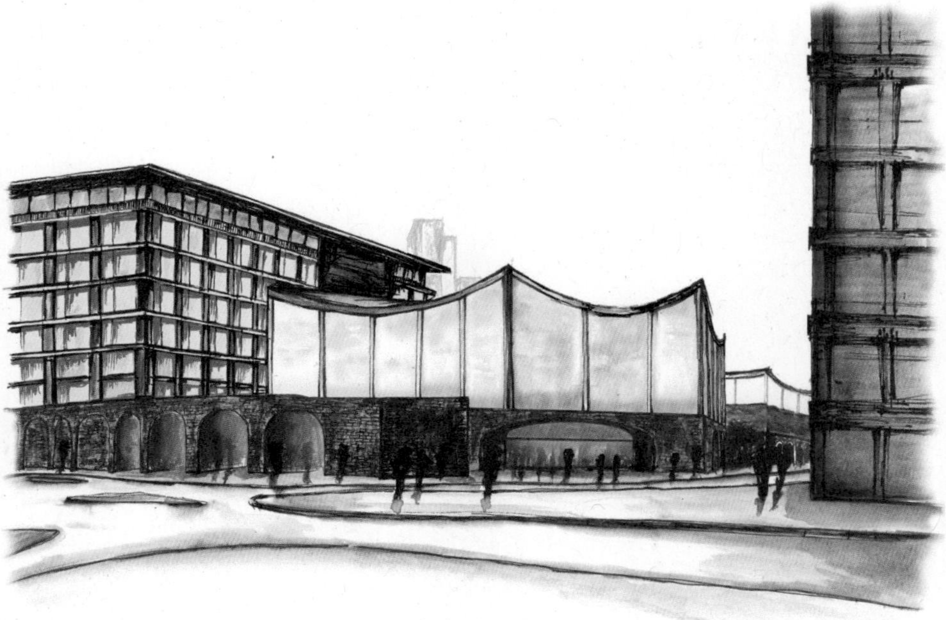

48 Visualisation of the south-western tip of the goods yard

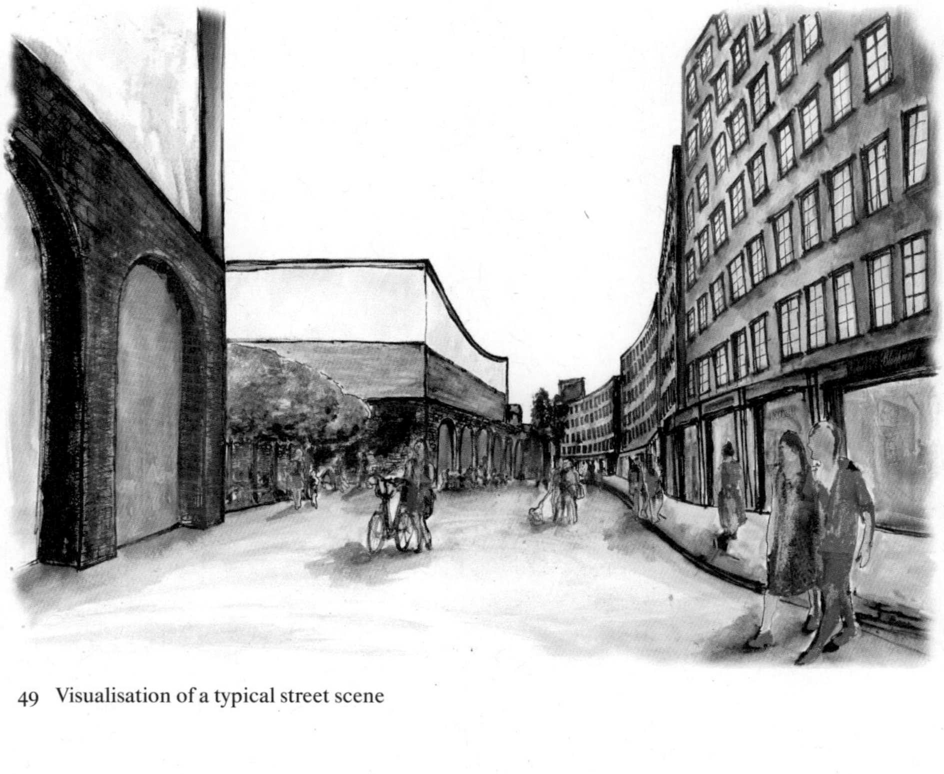

49 Visualisation of a typical street scene

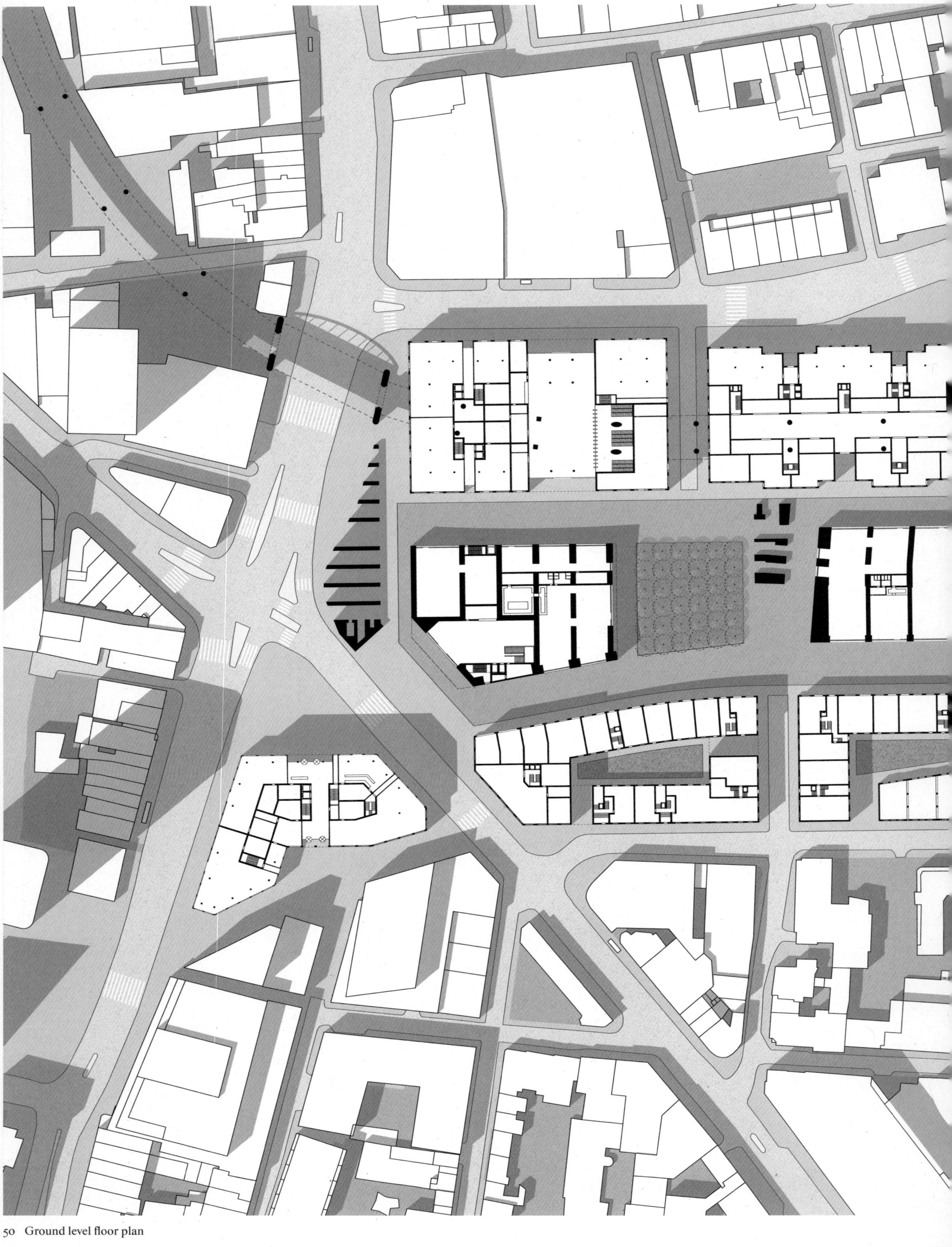

 Ground level floor plan

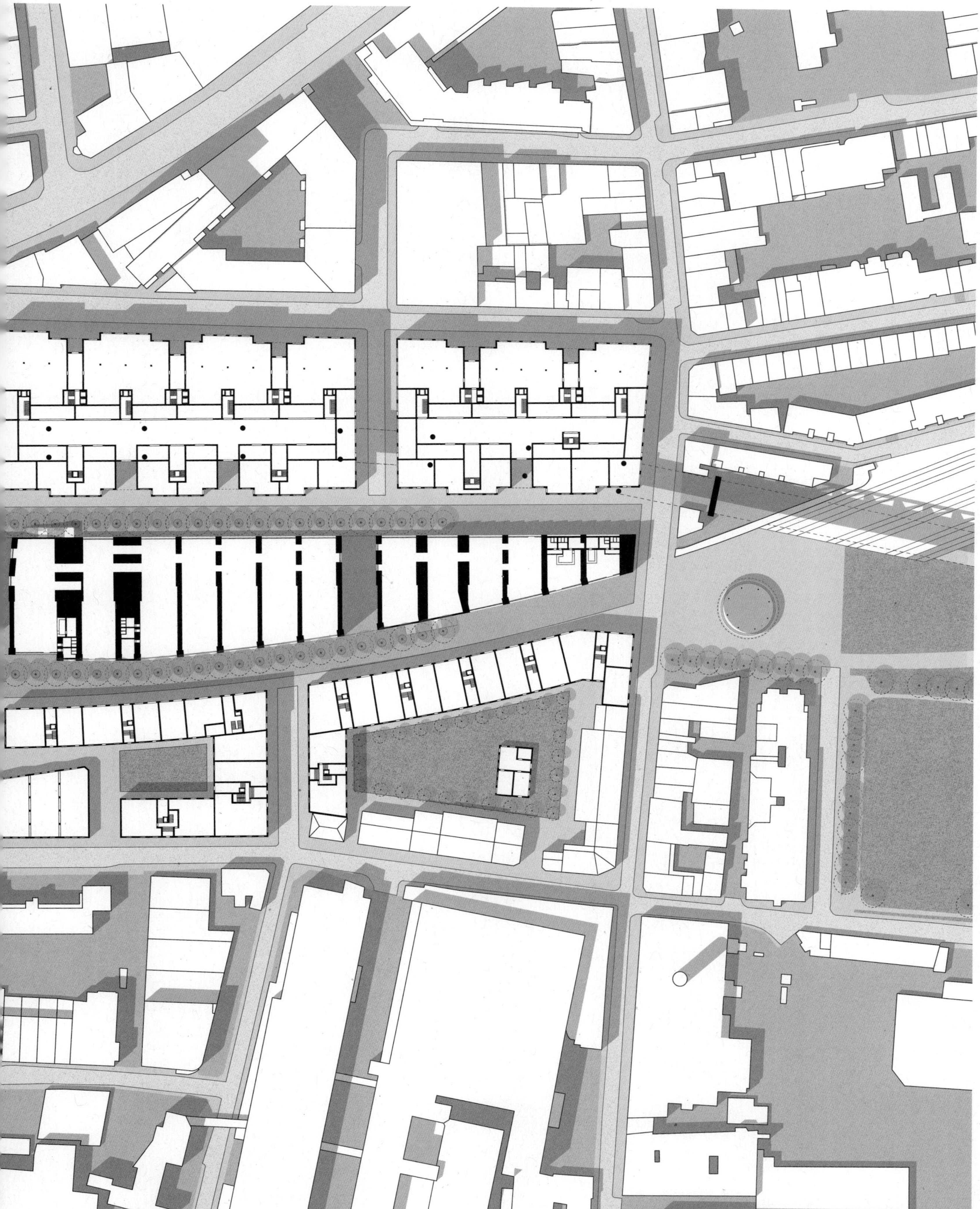

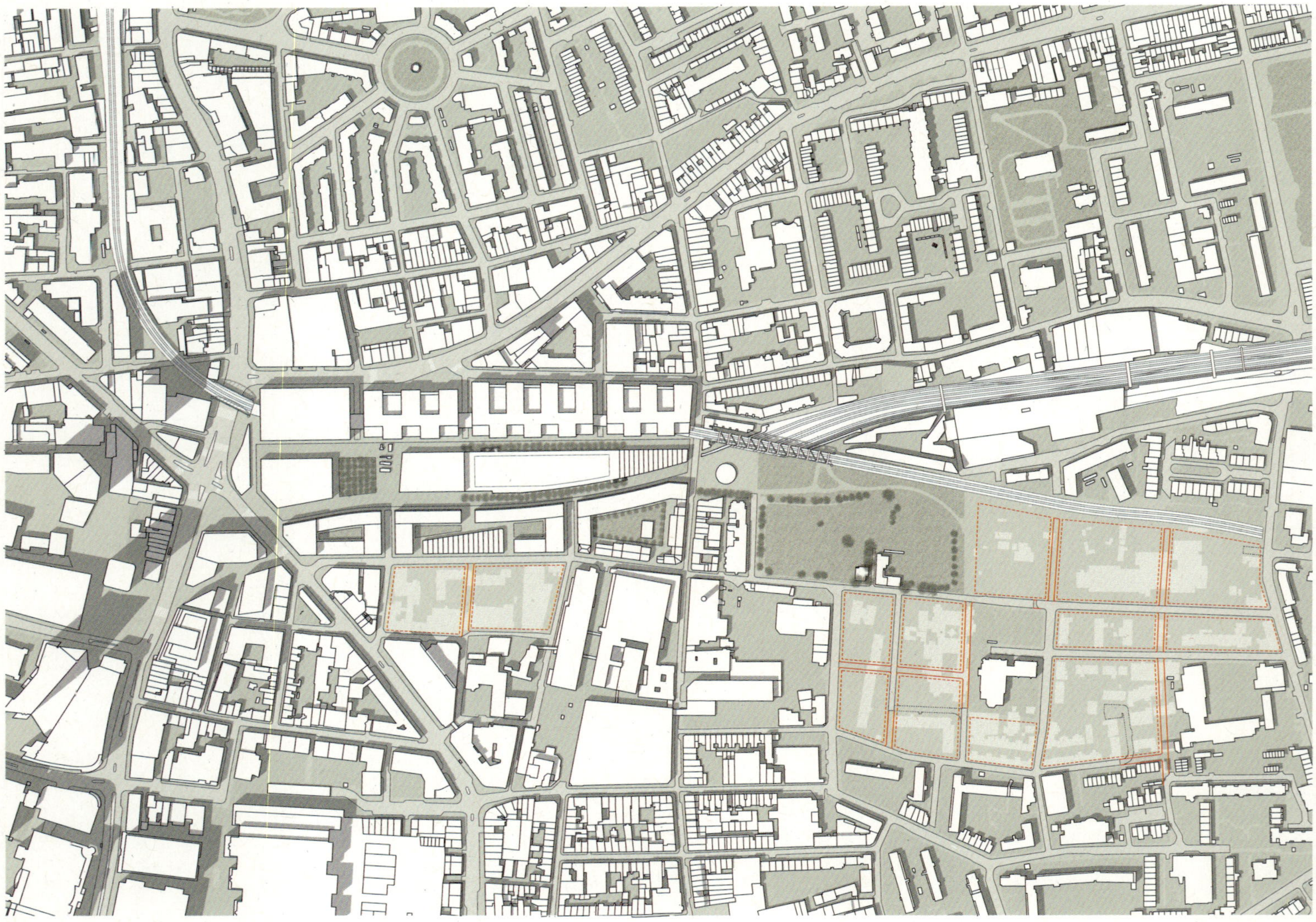

51 Masterplan

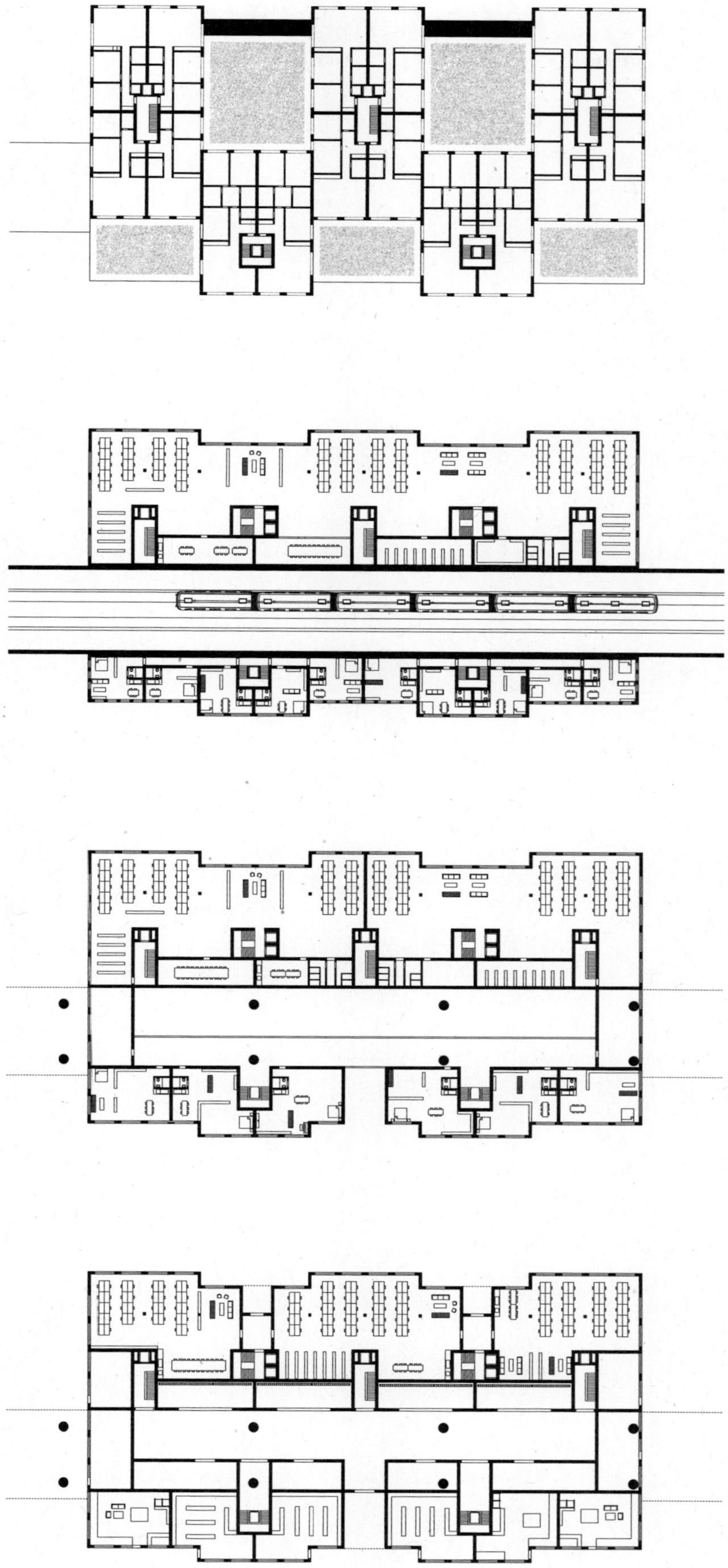

52 Floor plans: ground level, first level, third level and fifth level

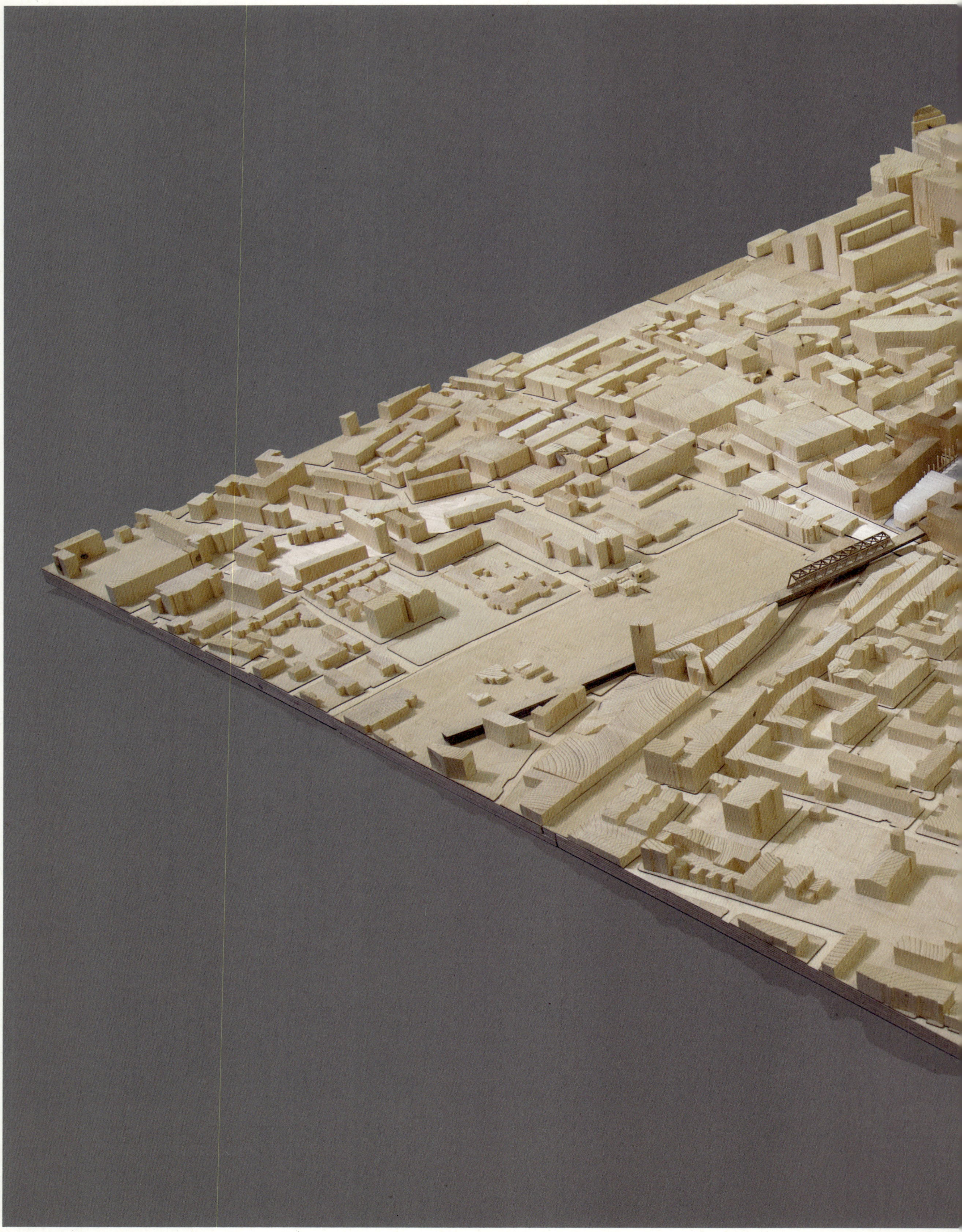

 Model 1:500

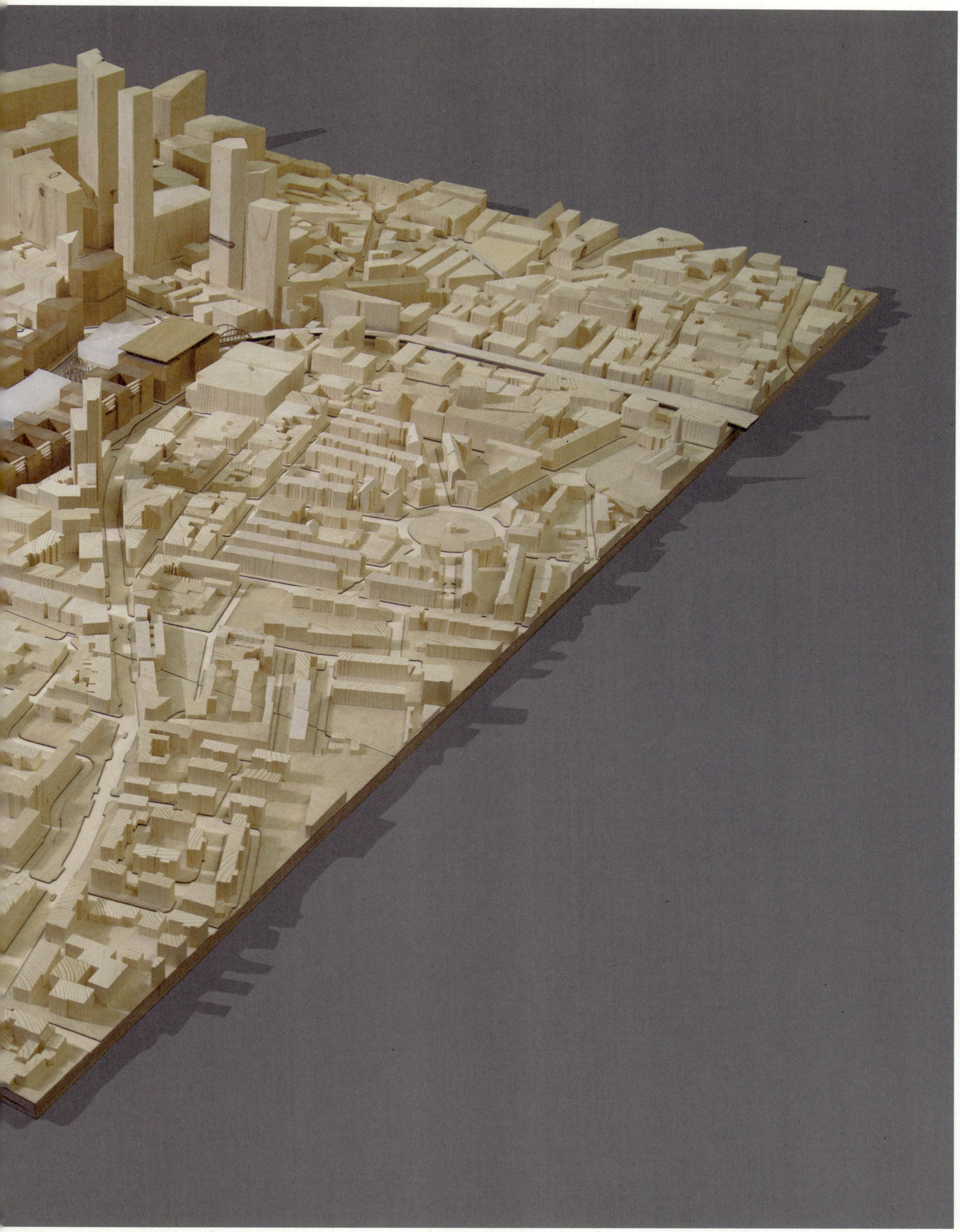

VI Metropolitan Park

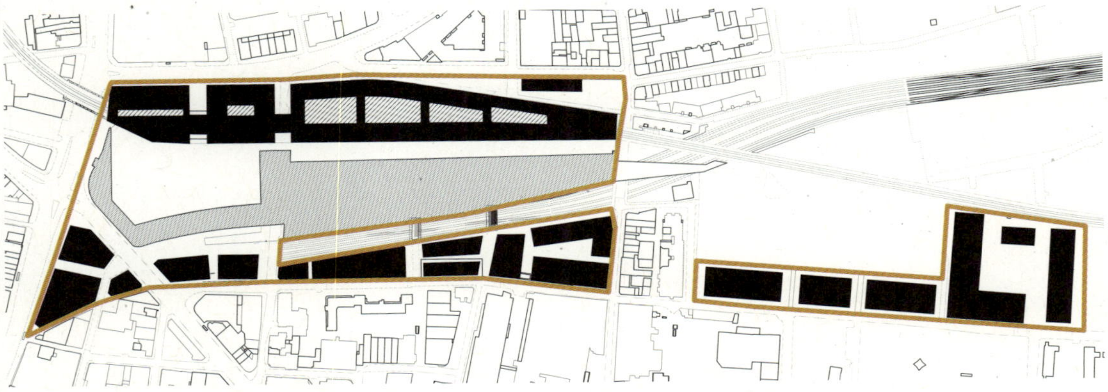

Site Area		74,540 m²	
Floor Area		332,000 m²	100 %
	Housing	194,000 m²	58.4 %
	Offices	93,000 m²	28.0 %
	Commerce	11,300 m²	3.4 %
	Public	33,700 m²	10.2 %
Density (FAR)		4.45	

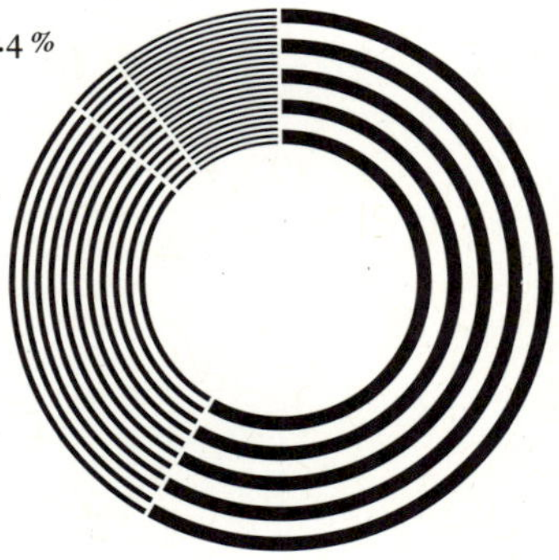

At first glance, this proposal bears resemblance to the Hammerson and Ballymore project: buildings are concentrated on a thirty-five-metre-wide strip on the northern half of the site, cleared of all historical remains for the construction of the London Overground. This allows the southern part to be transformed into a public park (fig. 54). Upon closer inspection, however, what this proposal demonstrates is that with seemingly minor tweaks, the much-criticised H&B project could easily be urbanistically successful. (See: Developers' Project: Hammerson and Ballymore 2016). In contrast to the developers' proposal, this project is better integrated into the local and metropolitan context.

In the photograph of the model, the project's ability to connect at both the local and the metropolitan scale becomes apparent (fig. 58). As a new link in the city, it connects Allens Gardens and the City of London, closing a gap in the current fabric. At a larger scale, the proposed elevated park, envisaged to evolve from the current overgrown state of the goods yard ruin with simple landscape interventions, could be the starting point for a network of paths and neighbourhood parks that appropriate under-utilised parts of the railway infrastructure towards the east.

At street level, the duality of employing multi-scalar interventions is smoothly resolved (fig. 57). The western part of the site features a large public square, enclosed by parts of the goods yard ruin, a modern public arena in direct connection with the park on the upper level. The ground floor of the goods yard, reused as gallery space, connects well to the lively streets of the neighbourhood such as Brick Lane. Newly added alleys connect the site with the surrounding fabric and bridge the existing infrastructural barriers. A significant proportion of the site hosts a wide range of public uses. The building masses in the northern part of the site, with their monolithic simplicity, are conceived as multifunctional units; shops and public uses line their facade overlooking the square and goods yard, while neighbourhood uses such as a public library occupy a second layer of floors. This fosters a visual relationship with the elevated park. Residences or offices occupy the rest of the building floors up from this base, breaking the monolithic structure into smaller groups of units.

The integral approach of the project unifies complementary elements, the park and the buildings, into a single system, wherein they mutually stimulate each other. The large area of the park justifies the high density of built surface in the other parts, while the buildings activate the open space (fig. 56). Further, by enabling the connection to the east, the project becomes the key trigger for developing the rest of the areas east of the goods yard. The reorganisation of Allens Gardens is just one example, illustrating the massive potential for densification along the new eastern corridor from the City of London towards Victoria Park (fig. 55).

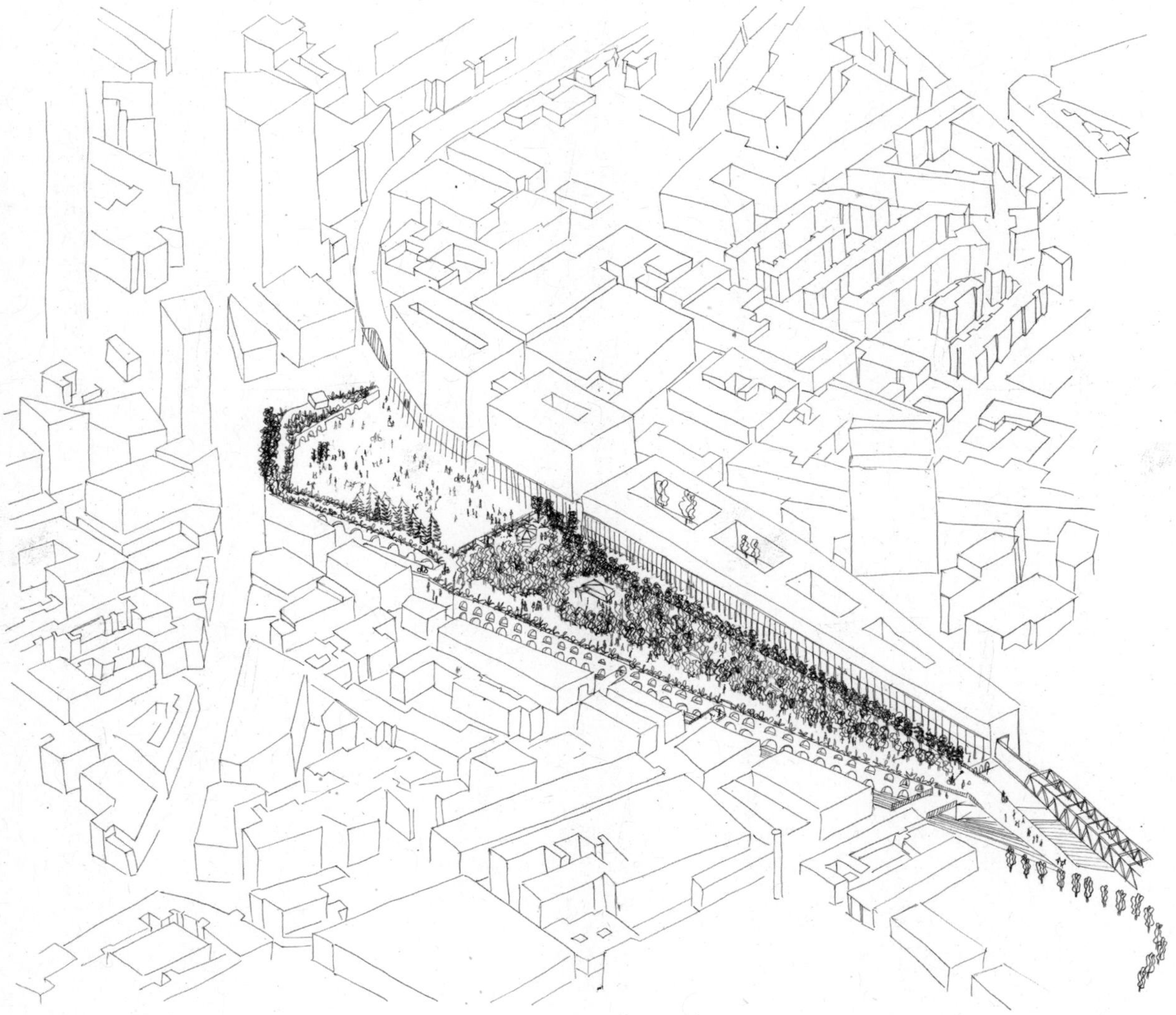

54 Visualisation of the spatial concept

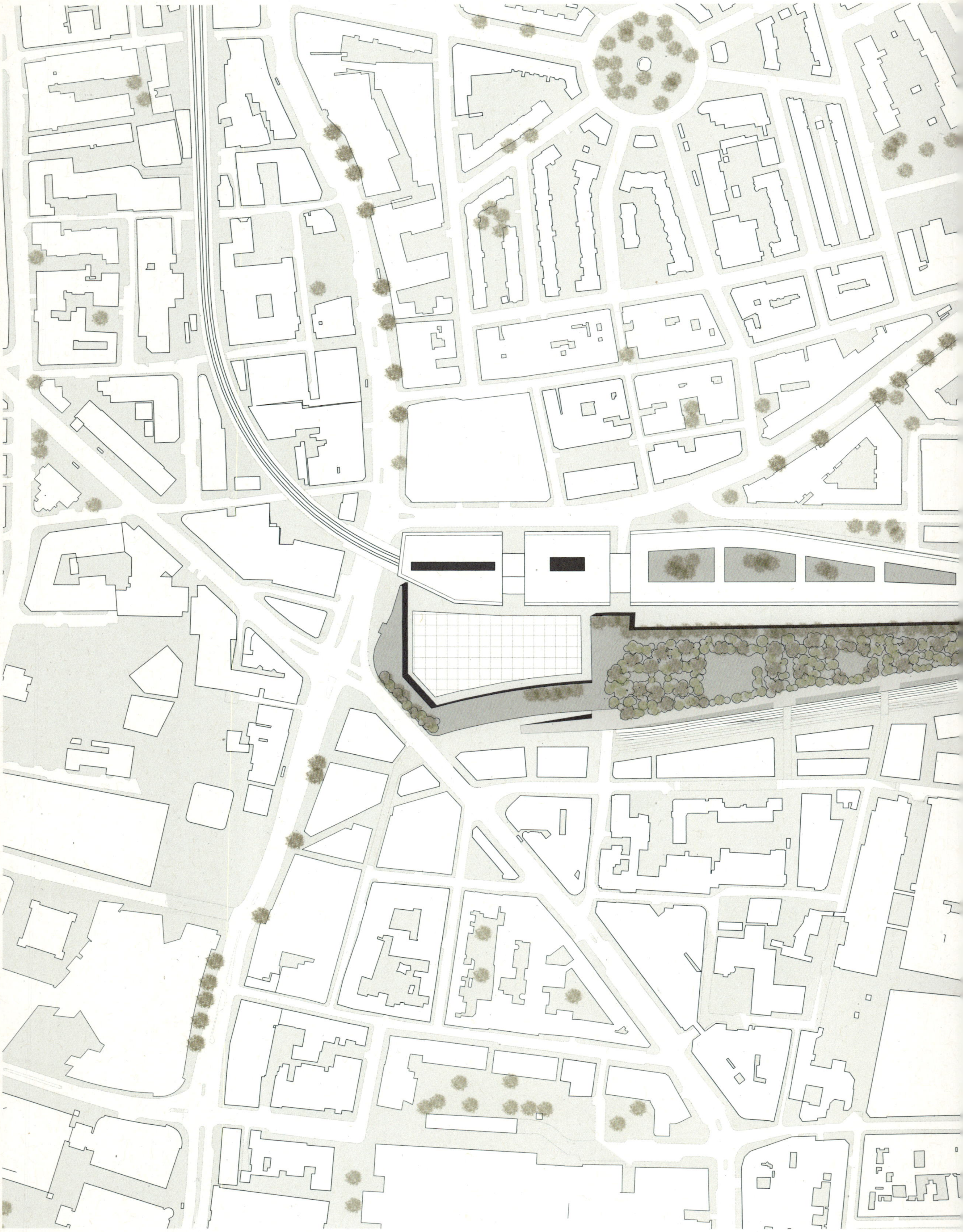

 Masterplan

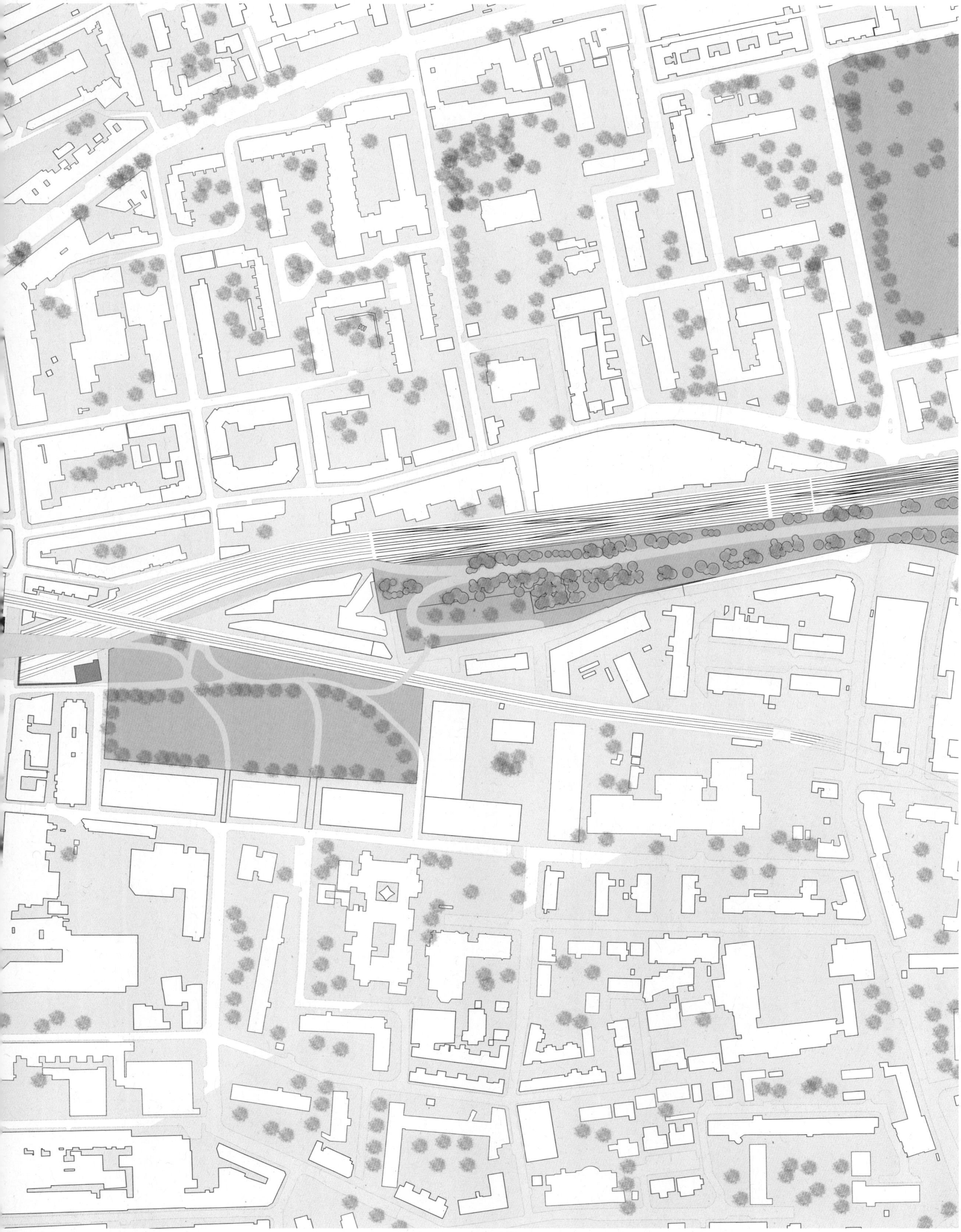

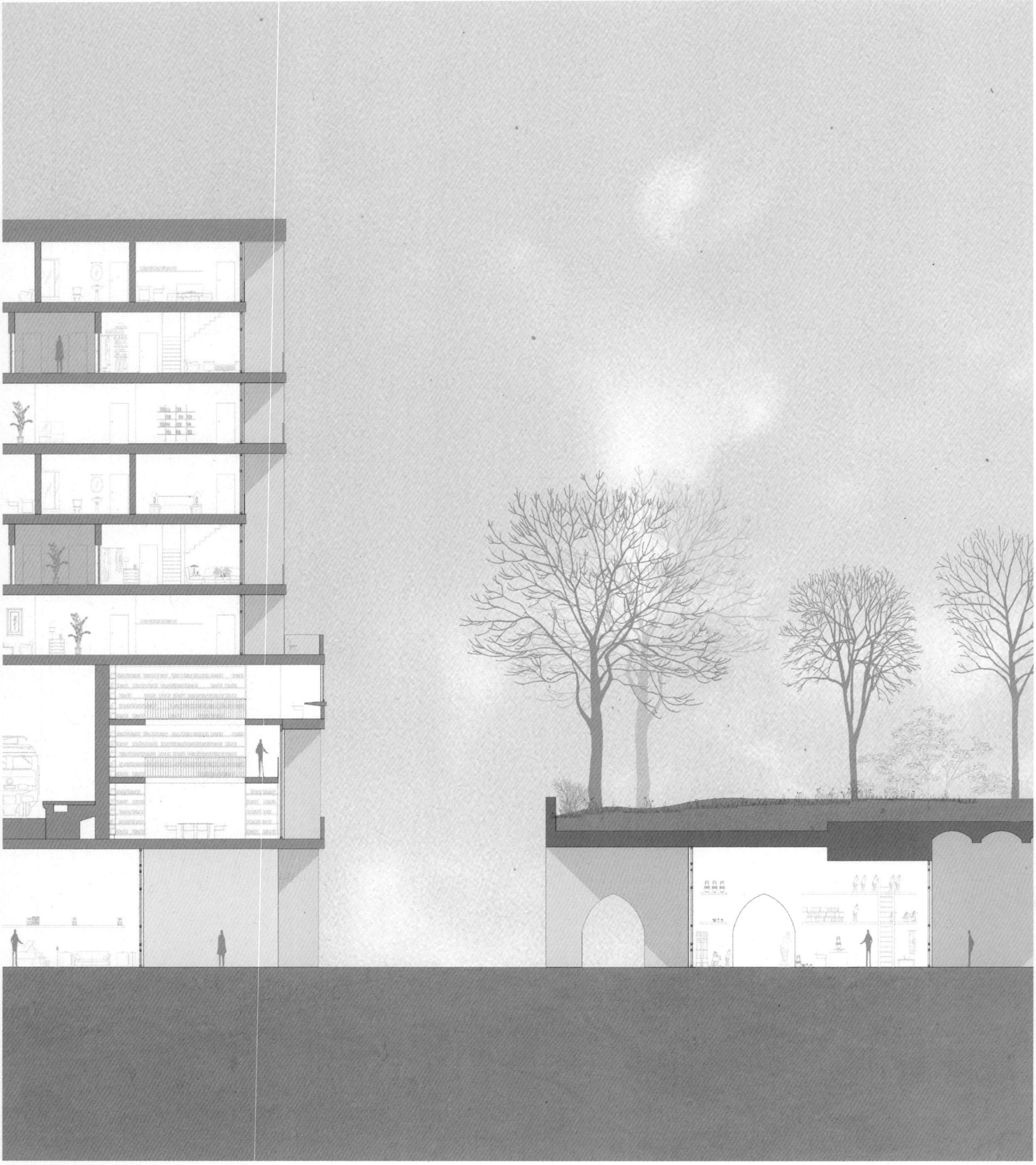

56 North-south section detail

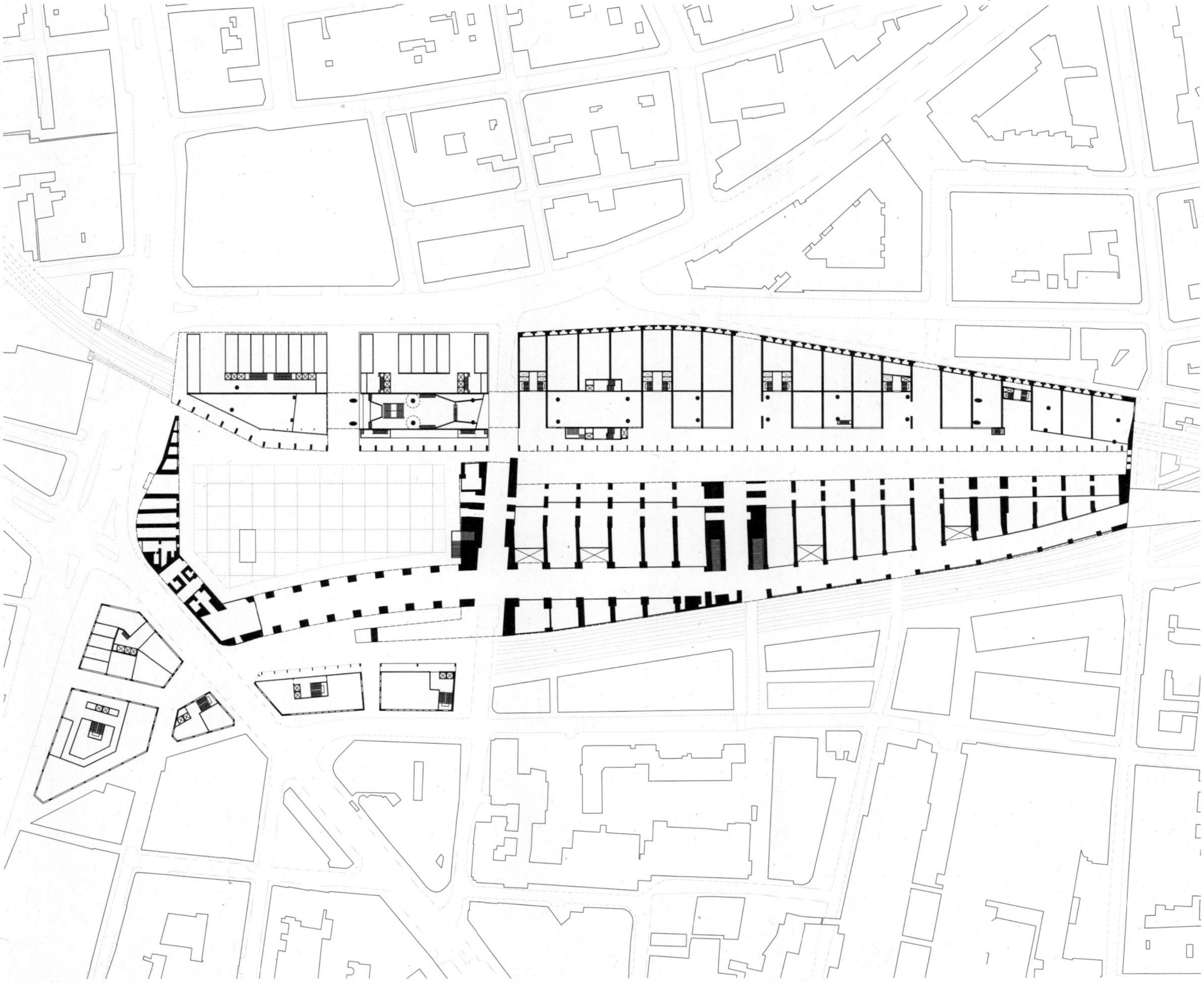

57 Ground level floor plan

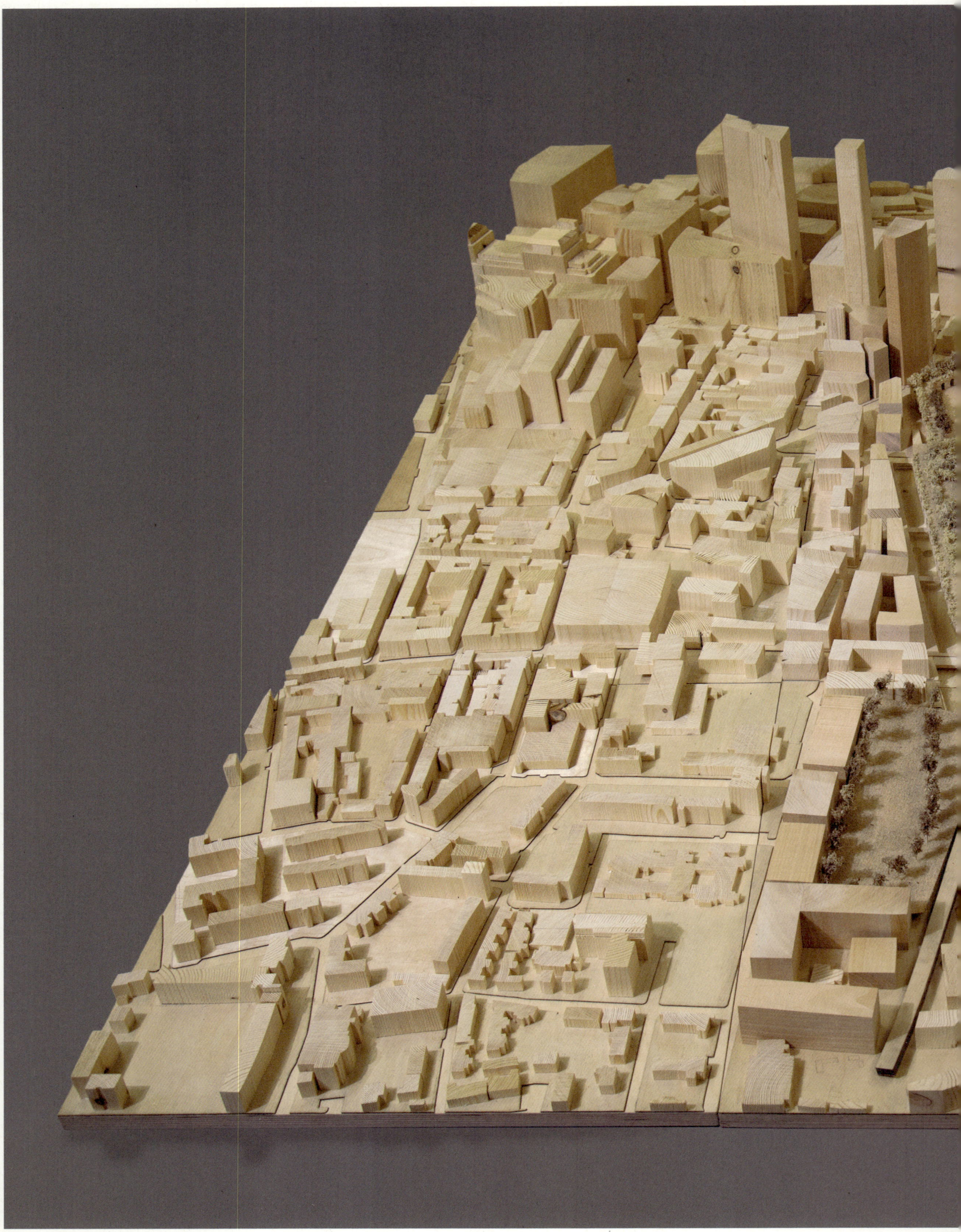

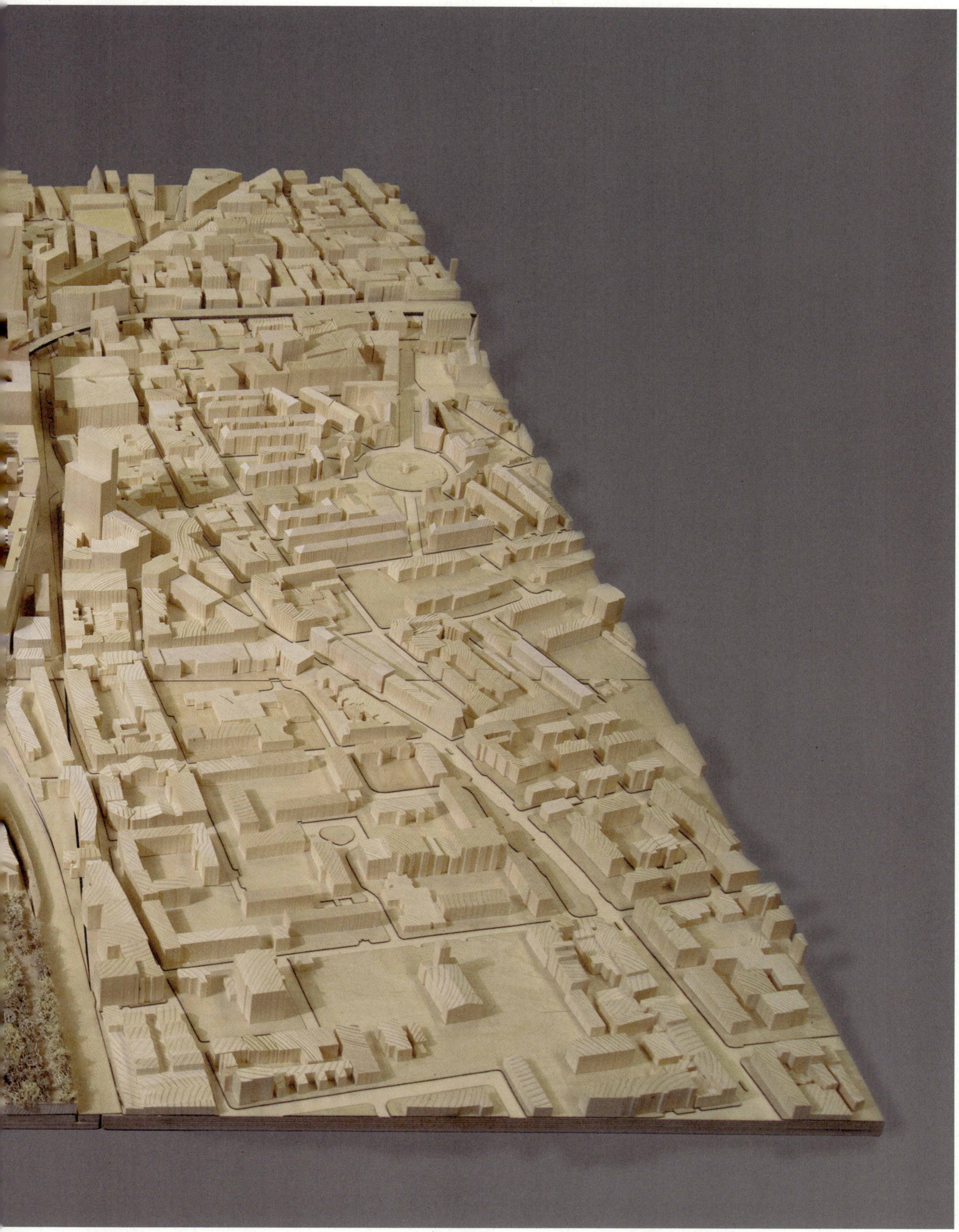

VII Walk in the Park

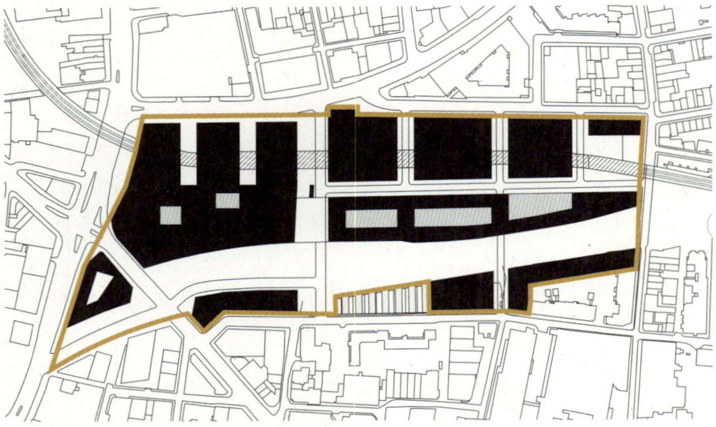

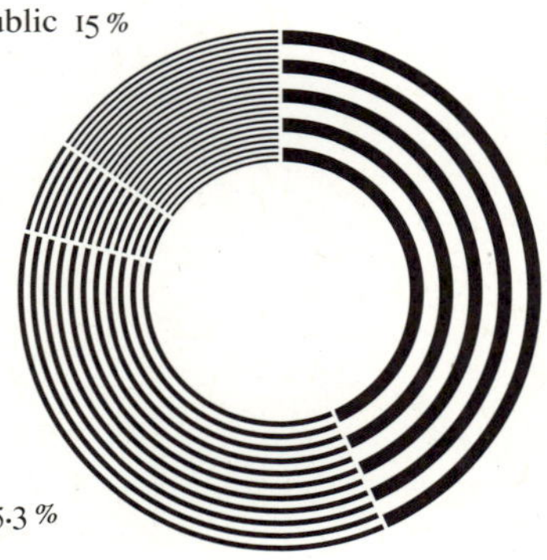

Site Area		58,497 m²	
Floor Area		195,270 m²	100 %
	Housing	85,139 m²	43.6 %
	Offices	69,012 m²	35.3 %
	Commerce	11,797 m²	6.0 %
	Public	29,322 m²	15.0 %
Density (FAR)		3.34	

What if, where presently the trains of the London Underground rattle through an urban ravine dividing the neighbourhoods, bicycles were to roll and pedestrians stroll? What if this space was not only used by the surrounding neighbourhoods, but was also an essential part of a longer sequence of public spaces connecting Liverpool Street Station to Allens Gardens? (fig. 60)

This type of urban space is the basis and conceptual spine of this proposal. It emerges along the ruins of the goods yard as a new connecting path, the curved design of which follows the structure of the old ruin, in turn based on the course of the rail tracks. The southern bend of this urban linear park connects to Liverpool Street Station (fig. 59).

This strategic intervention has a big impact, because it succeeds in bypassing many of the site's current constraints. Rather than an isolated island in the city's fabric, the site now becomes a logical extension of it. This concept is implemented by extending the existing street network and making it accessible for cars (fig. 61). Along both sides of the new path, the urban fabric is densified, with higher buildings lining the south-facing facade.

The concept works successfully because by simply covering the rail tracks and transforming them into an urban linear park, no additional representative public space has to be created. The rest of the site remains available for construction, with the ambition of densifying while still maintaining moderate building heights (fig. 64). Around the Shoreditch High Street station, integrated office and exhibition spaces for services and technology firms are settled around a small square, while the south and east parts of the site feature mostly residential units profiting from the large open space (figs. 62 and 63).

The proposal proves how one thoughtful intervention can cut the Gordian knot, which had been tied by the layering of the site's diverse and complex constraints. It uses the freed-up space to sensitively densify the area, and merges with the surrounding neighbourhoods by extending them rather than creating a 'lighthouse' project (fig. 65).

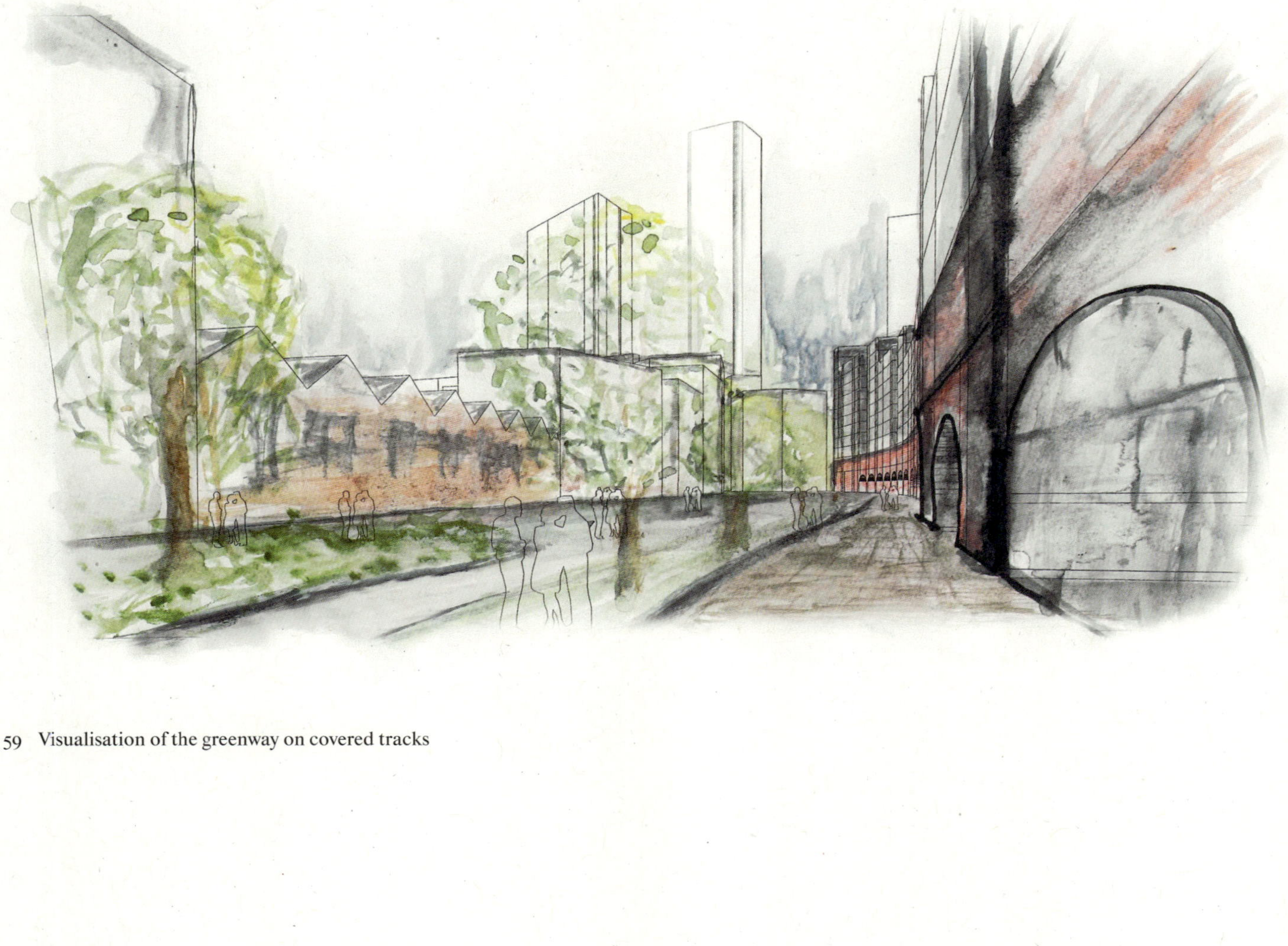

59 Visualisation of the greenway on covered tracks

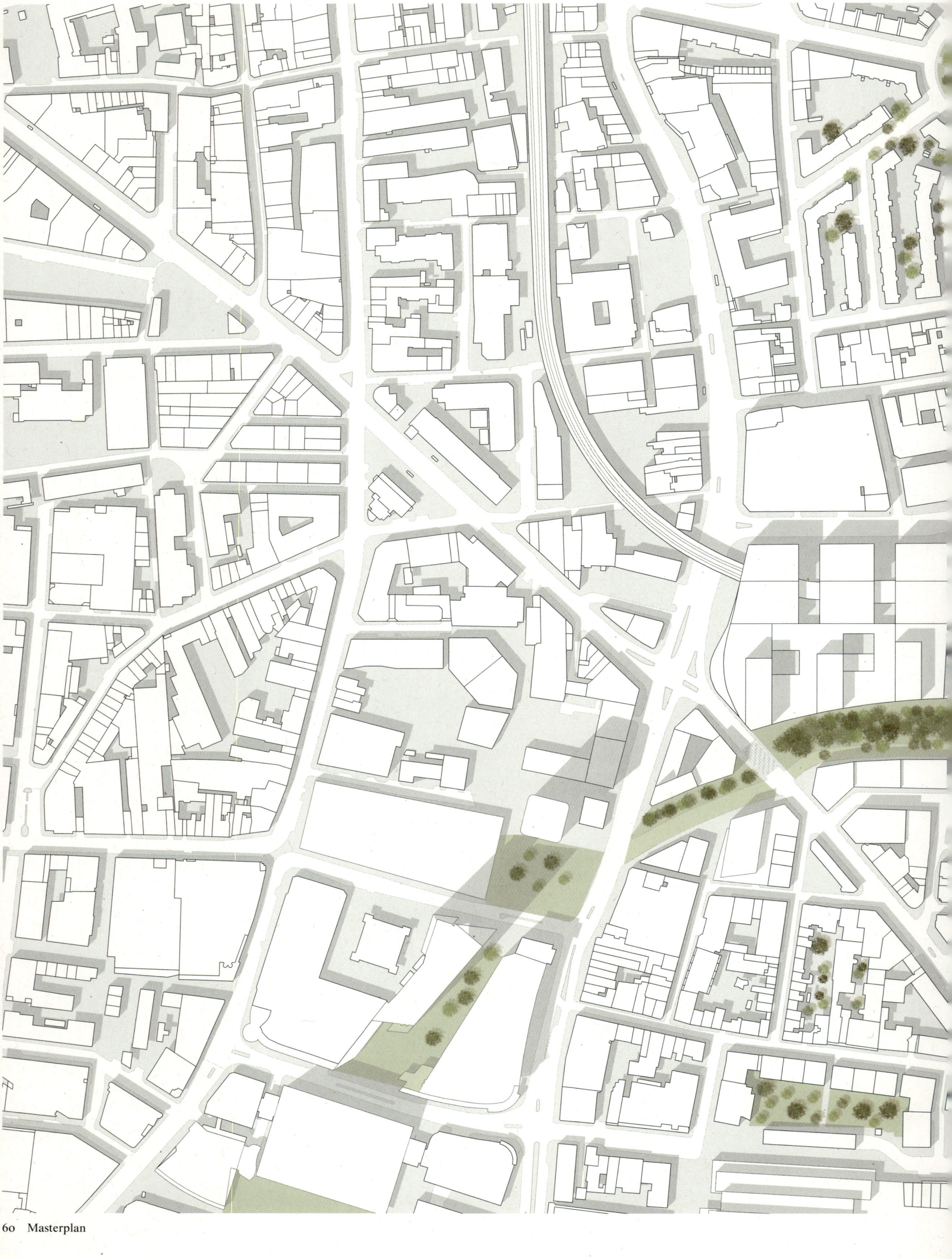

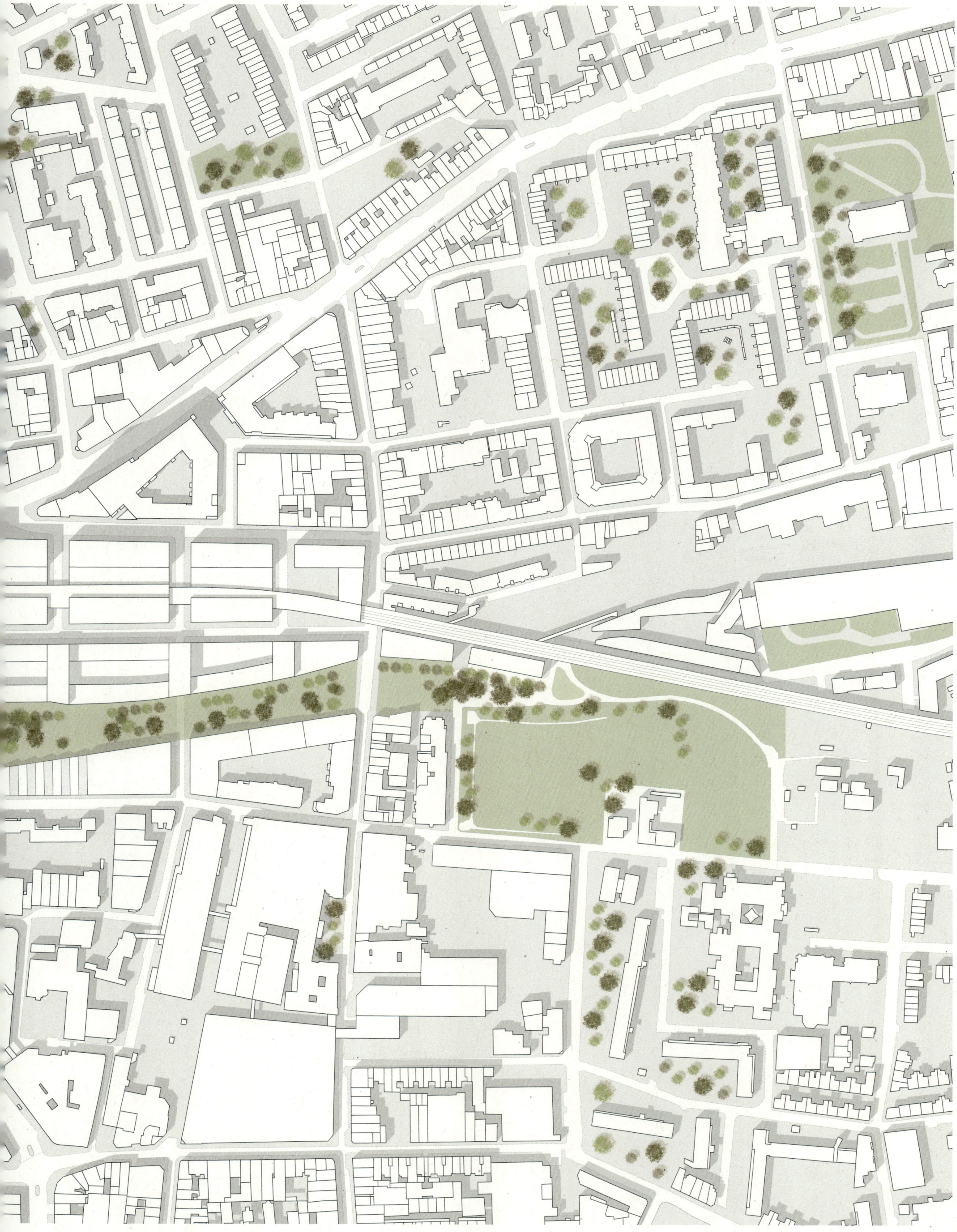

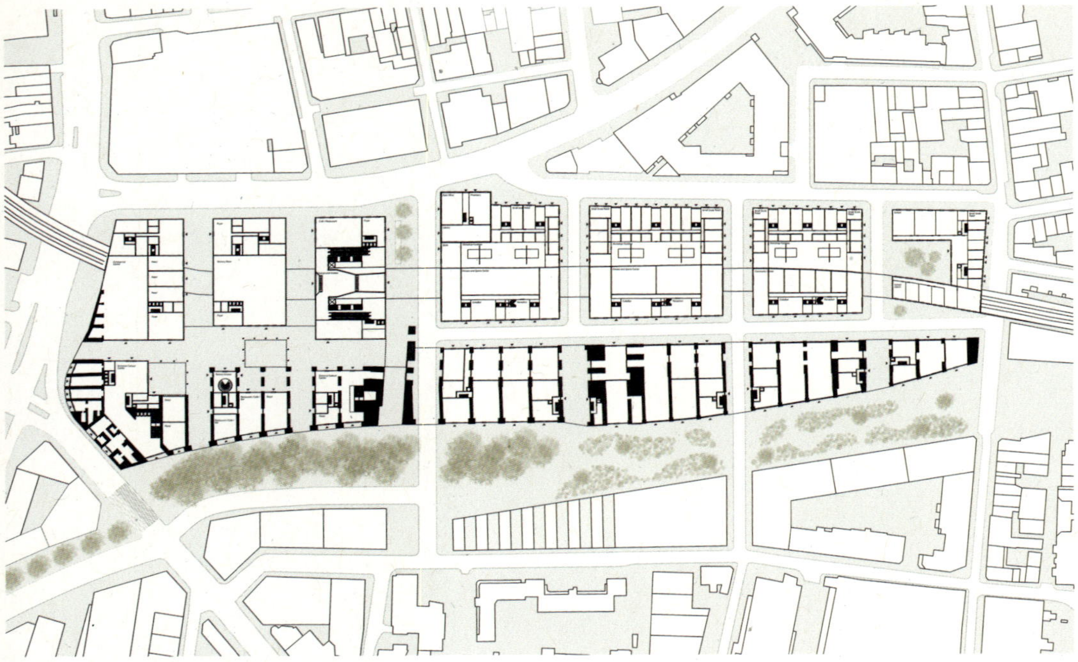

61 Ground level floor plan

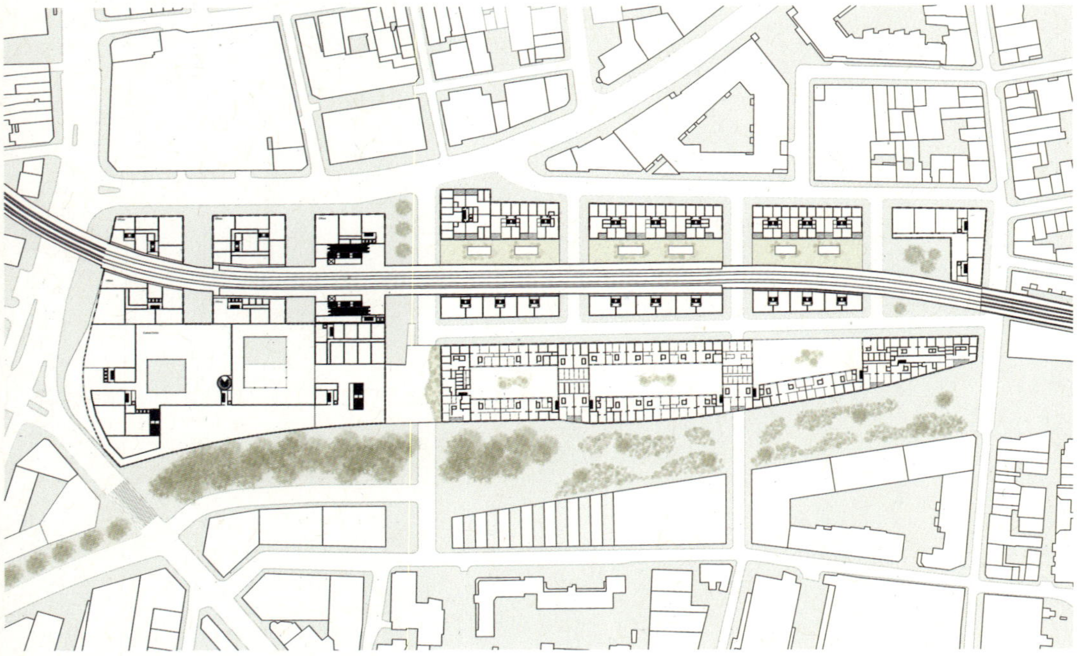

62 Third level floor plan

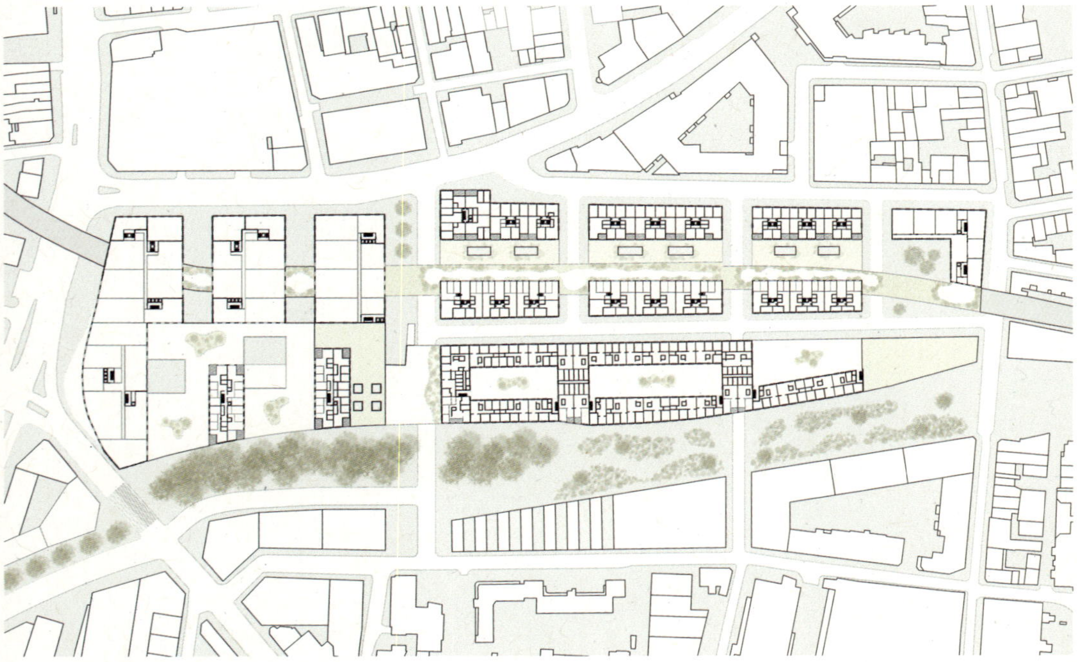

63 Fifth level floor plan

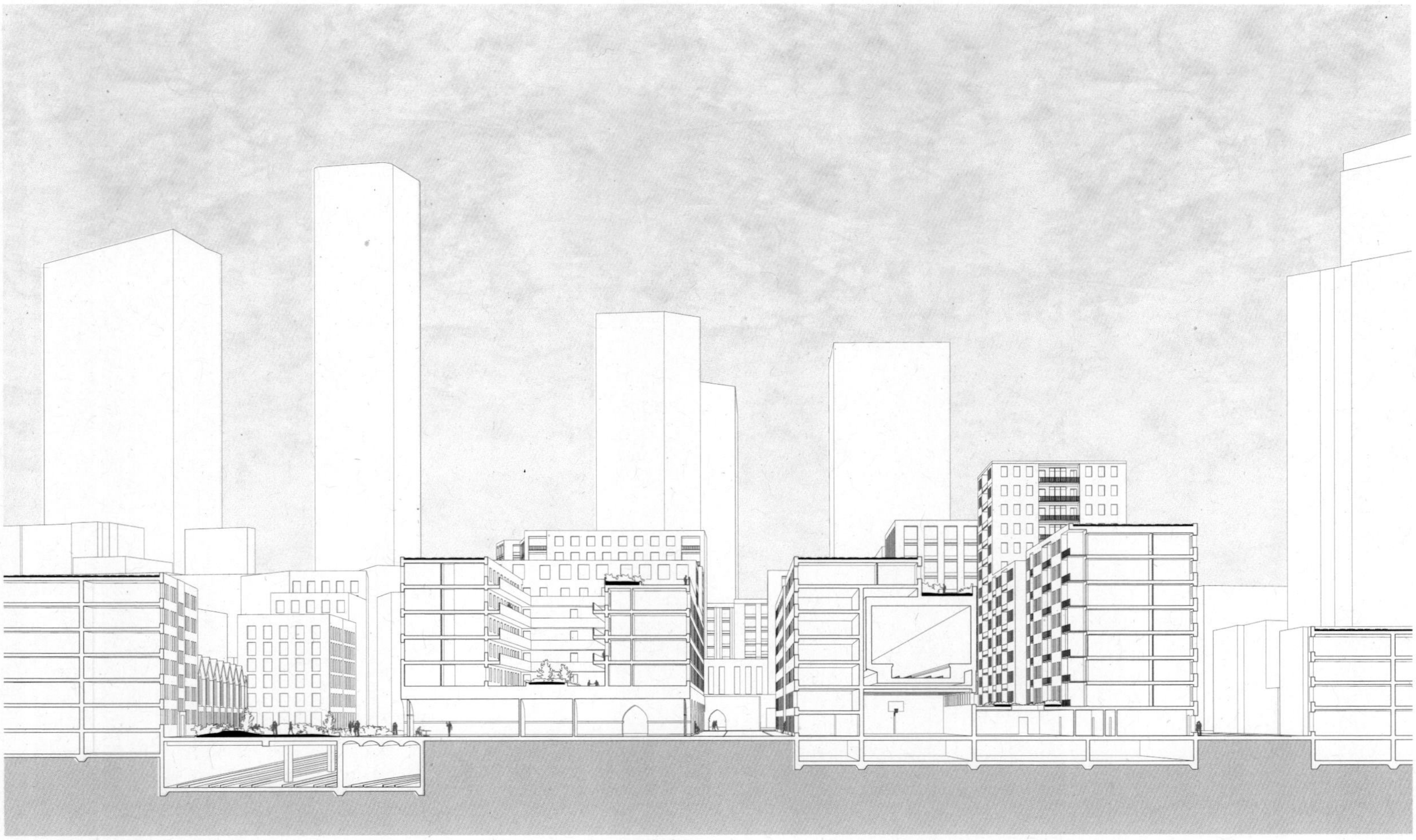

64 South-north section

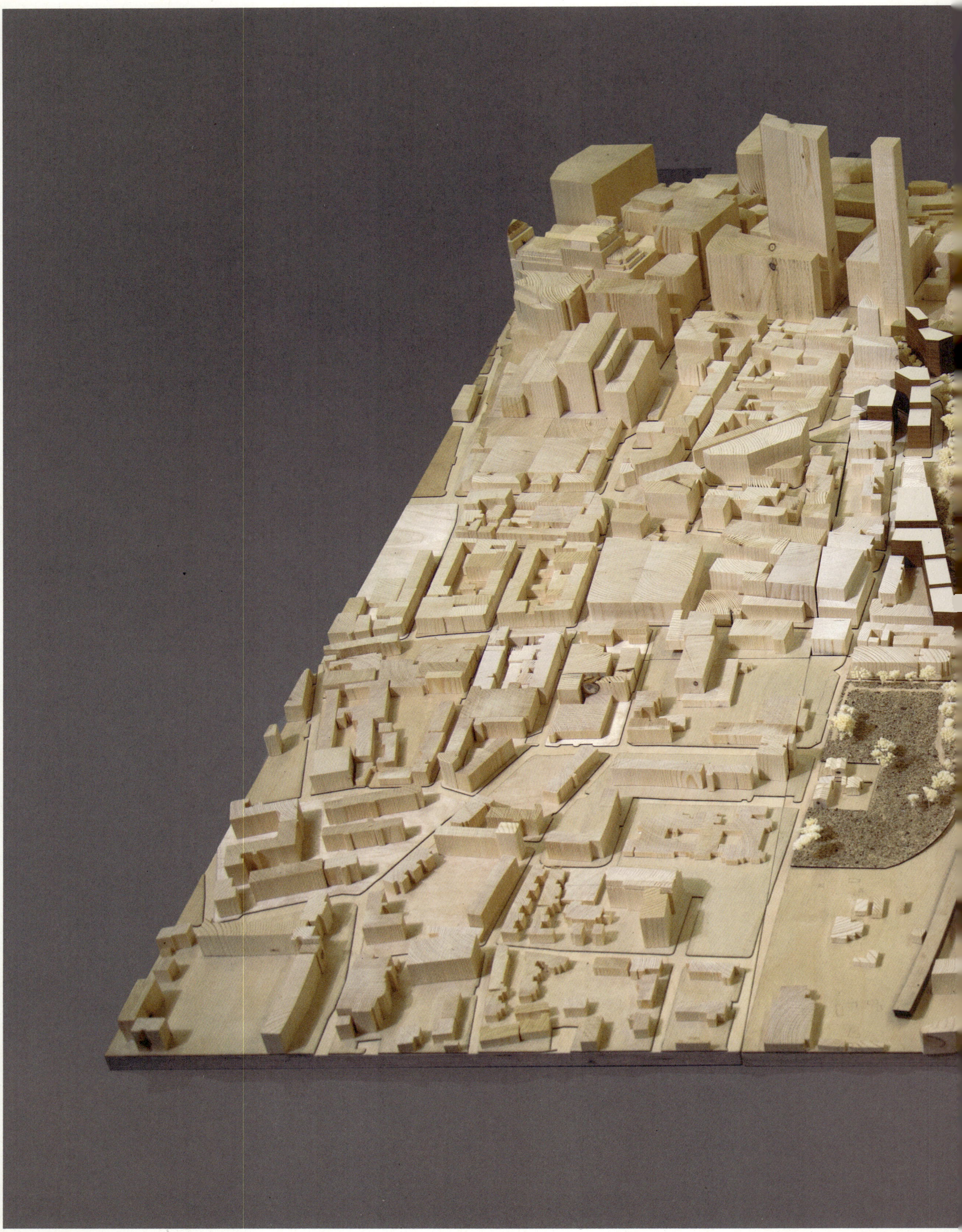

 Model 1:500

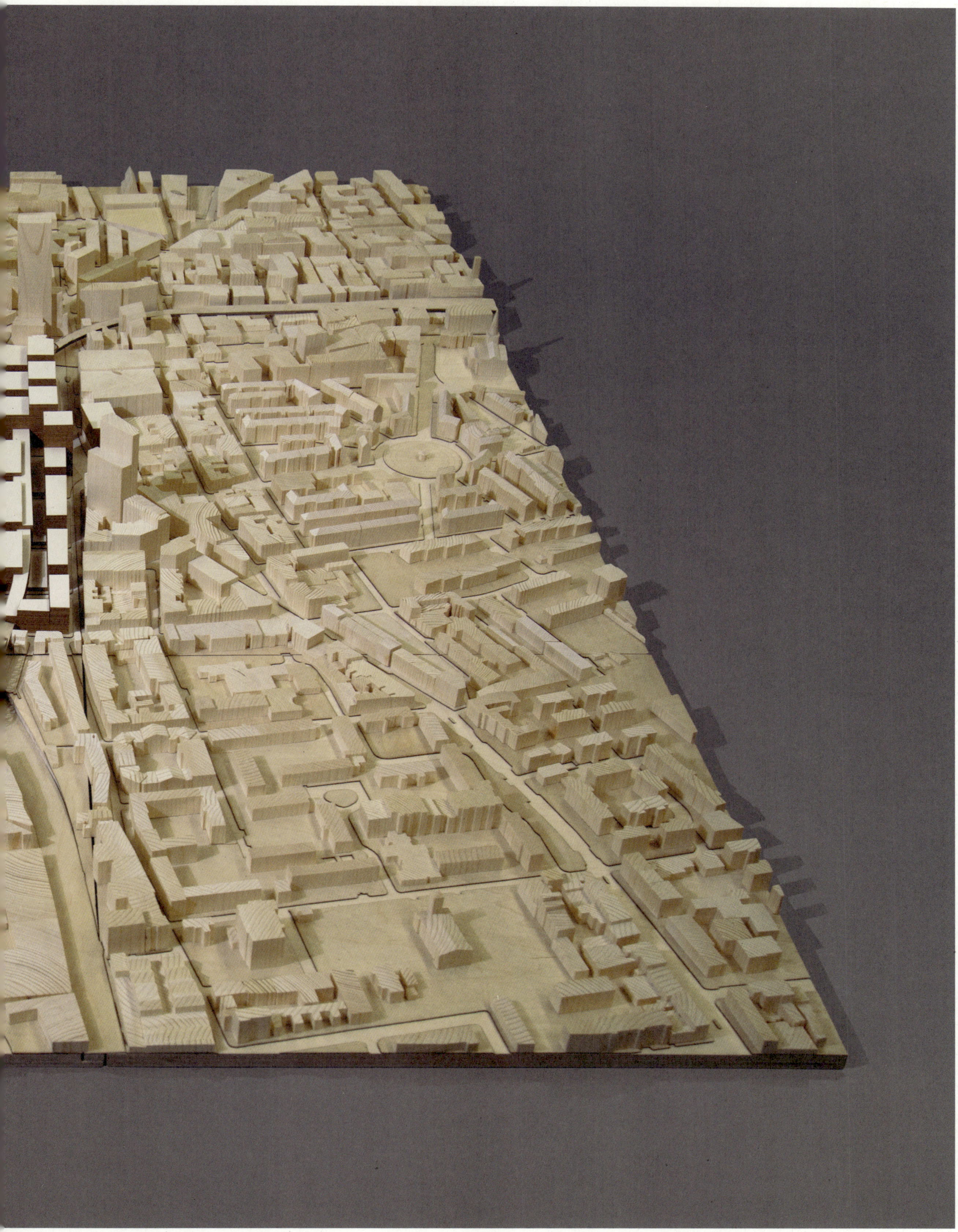

VIII Bishopsgate Courtyards

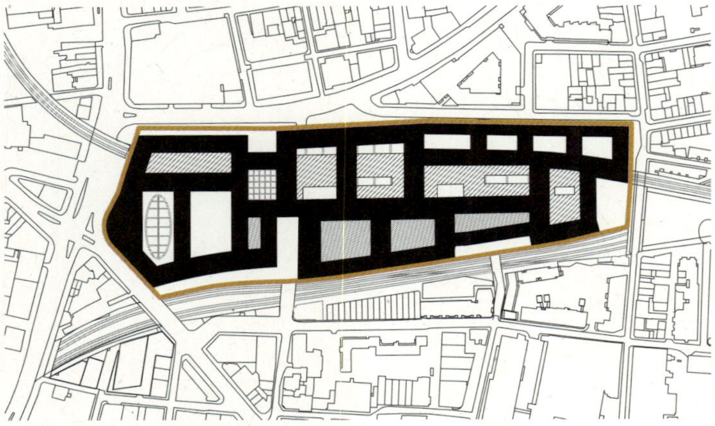

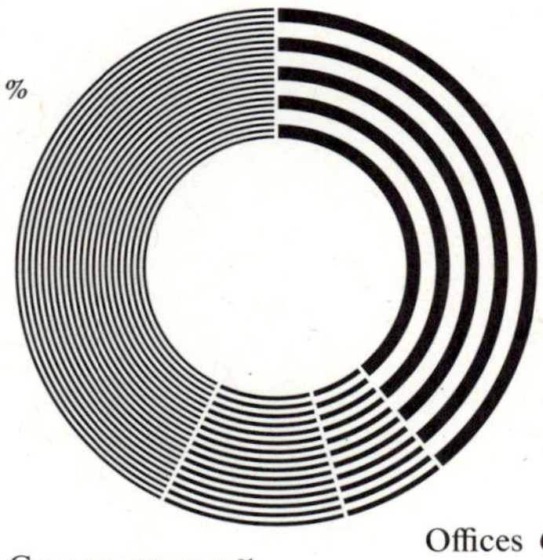

Site Area		41,886 m²	
Floor Area		165,130 m²	100 %
	Housing	64,730 m²	39.2 %
	Offices	11,095 m²	6.7 %
	Commerce	18,943 m²	11.5 %
	Public	70,362 m²	42.6 %
Density (FAR)		3.94	

Similar to Test Project II, this proposal explores the potential of a horizontally oriented large-scale project. The starting point in this case is a structural experiment: the site is overlaid by a complex cluster of convoluted courtyards (fig. 68). Even though it replicates the volume of the former goods yard, the resulting composition appears less massive and manages to adapt to the urban patterns of its surroundings (fig. 72).

At its edges, the structural approach proves to be flexible; its entrances from and access points to the surroundings are carefully chosen and designed. The integration into the city is fostered by the porosity of the ground floor and its diverse public uses (figs. 66 and 67). The two most important access points in the east and west of the site are connected by an outdoor alleyway. Courtyards, retail and entrances to the residential units are arranged along this passage. The seemingly rigid 'corridor' is opened upwards and sideways at several points, opening the view to the upper storeys, and attempting to foster an experience of a sculptural, engaging interior, yet not indoor, space.

While the corner of the west end of Shoreditch High Street is accentuated by a prestigious building with cultural uses, the eastern end is connected to the residential neighbourhoods by the placement of a new school (fig. 70). Residential units of various sizes and characteristics span between these two anchor points (fig. 71). Diverse and sophisticated courtyards lend specific qualities to the apartments (fig. 69).

Locating the most important public uses in the centre of the building bears high risks. The intimacy of the central alley and its hybrid character of both indoor and outdoor space create a relative separation from the city. Thus, the project risks to either develop into an isolated enclave, whose privileged inhabitants are the only ones benefiting from the exquisite spatial qualities, or in the opposite direction, to become a ghetto of extreme contrasts. Further, its success or failure largely depends on the architectural realisation. If executed well, however, and if proper management of the public spaces were to be guaranteed, the proposal could provide novel qualities to London's East.

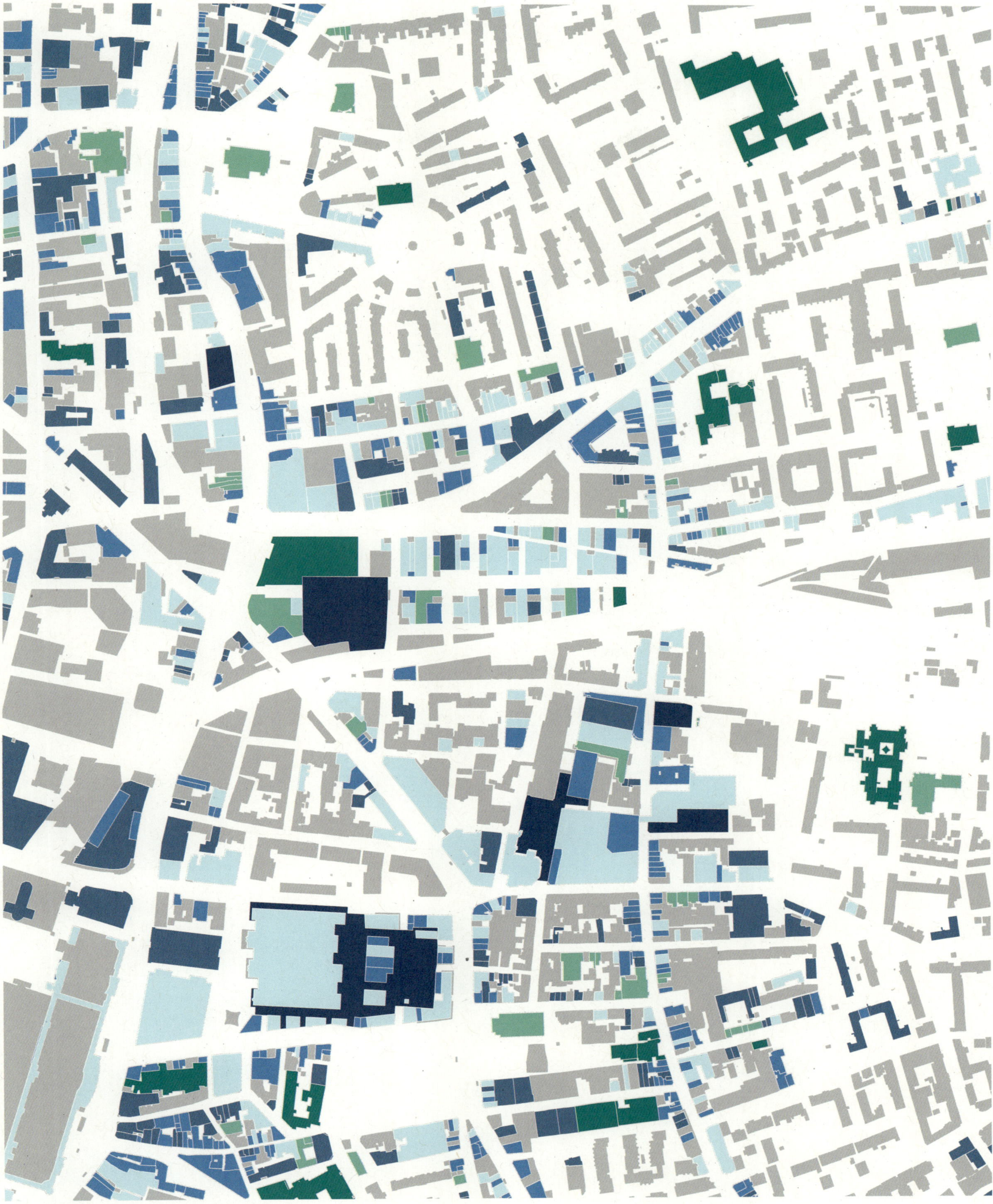

66 Ground level uses in the neighbourhood

- Education
- Culture
- Services
- Gastronomy
- Industry
- Market, festival, temporary functions

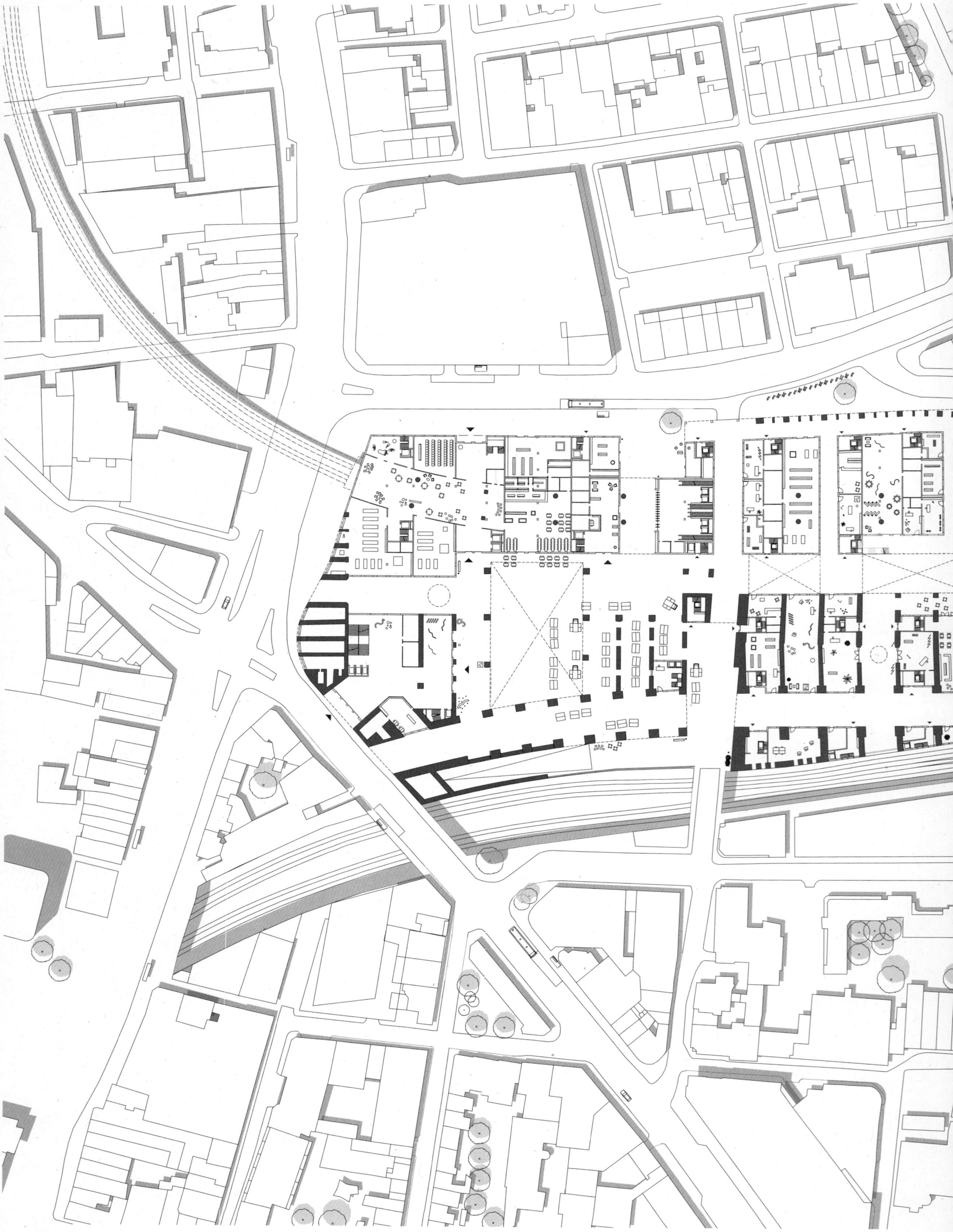

67 Ground level floor plan

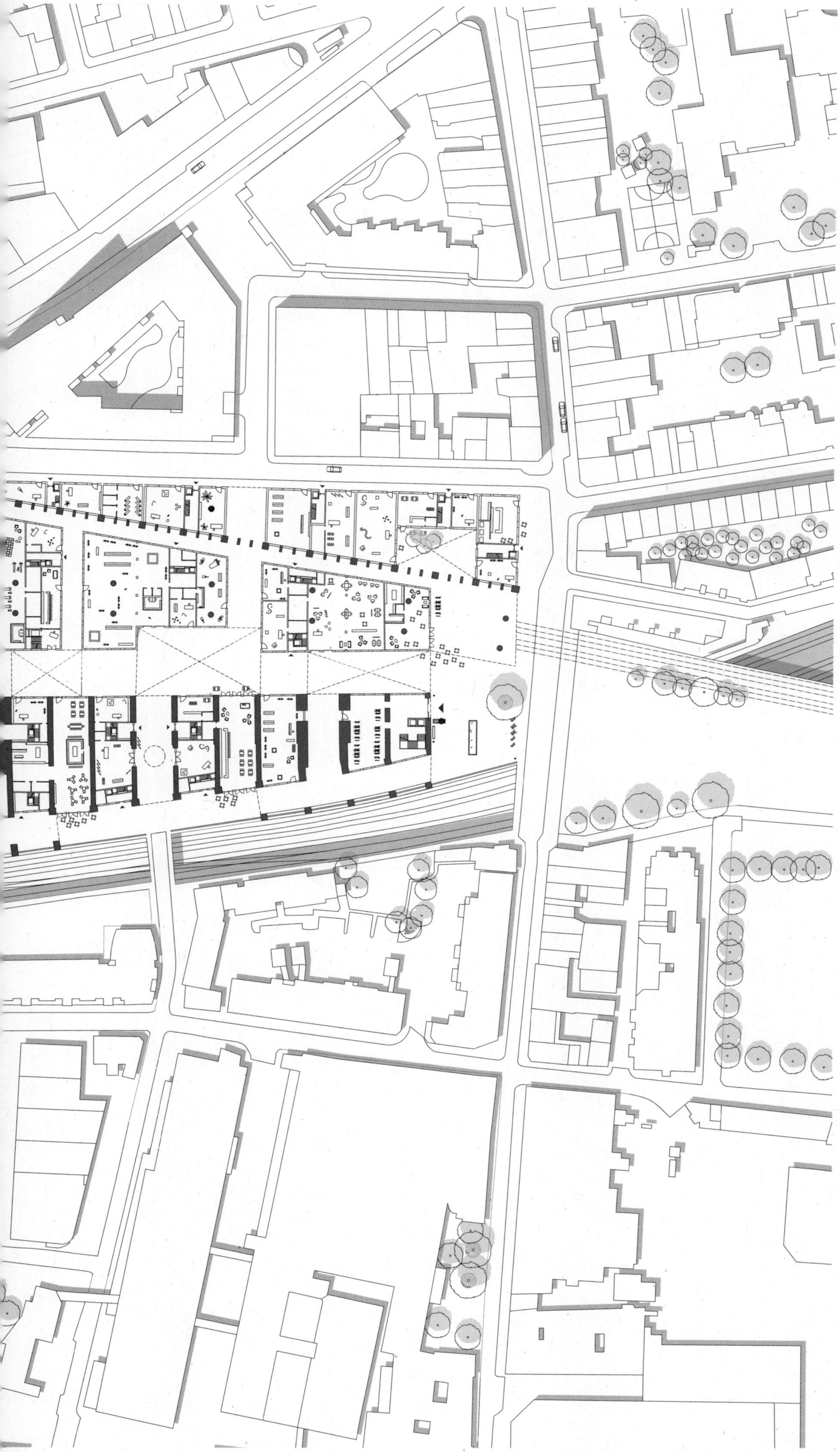

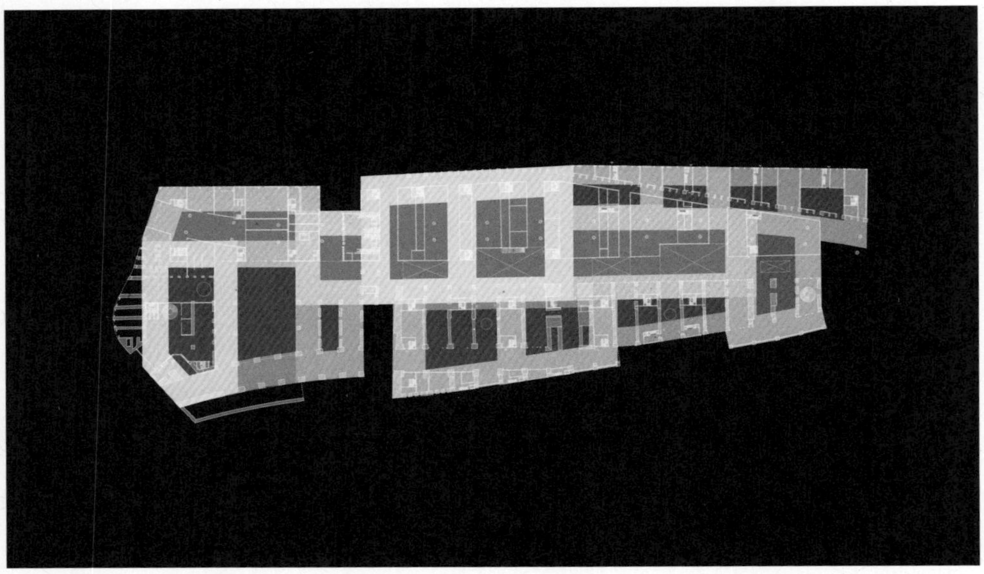

68 Visualisation of the spatial concept

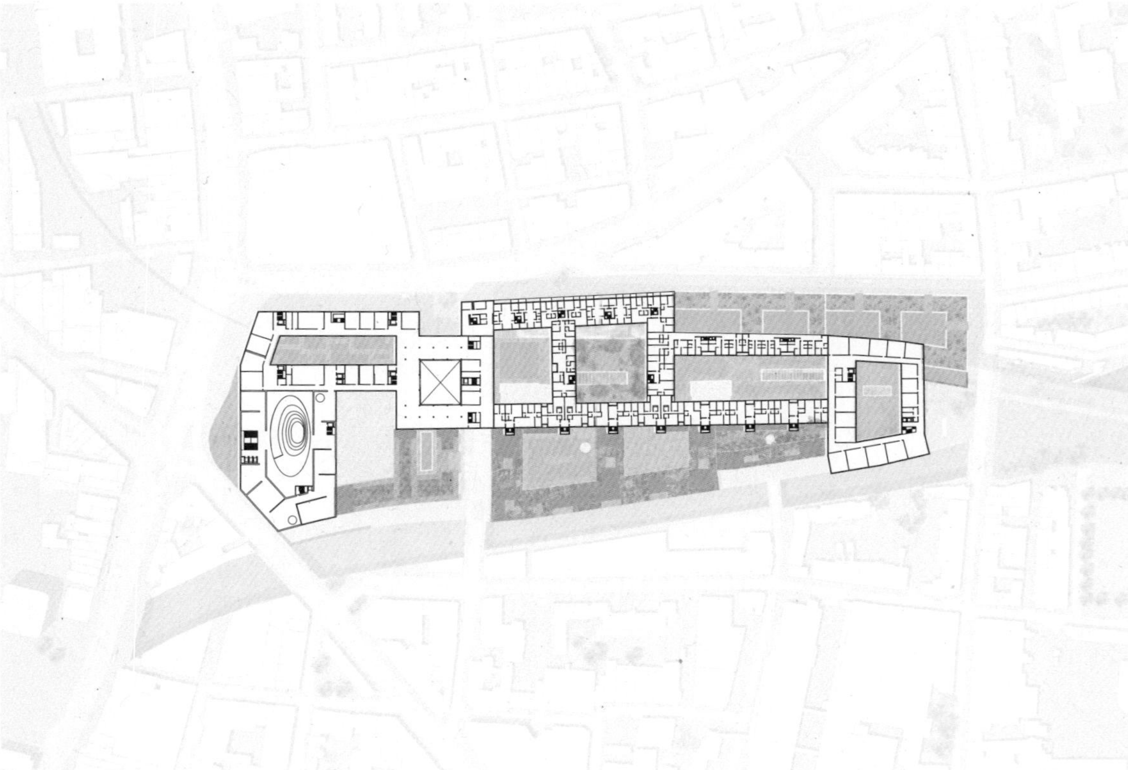

69 Fifth level floor plan

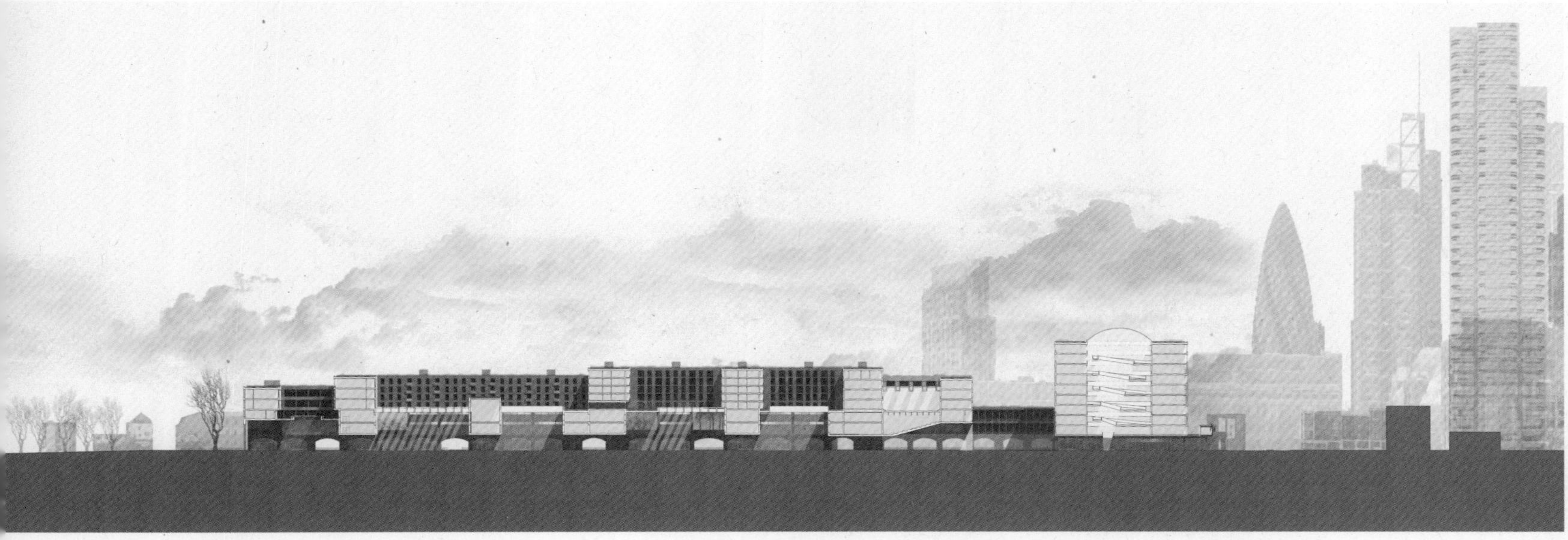

70 East-west section

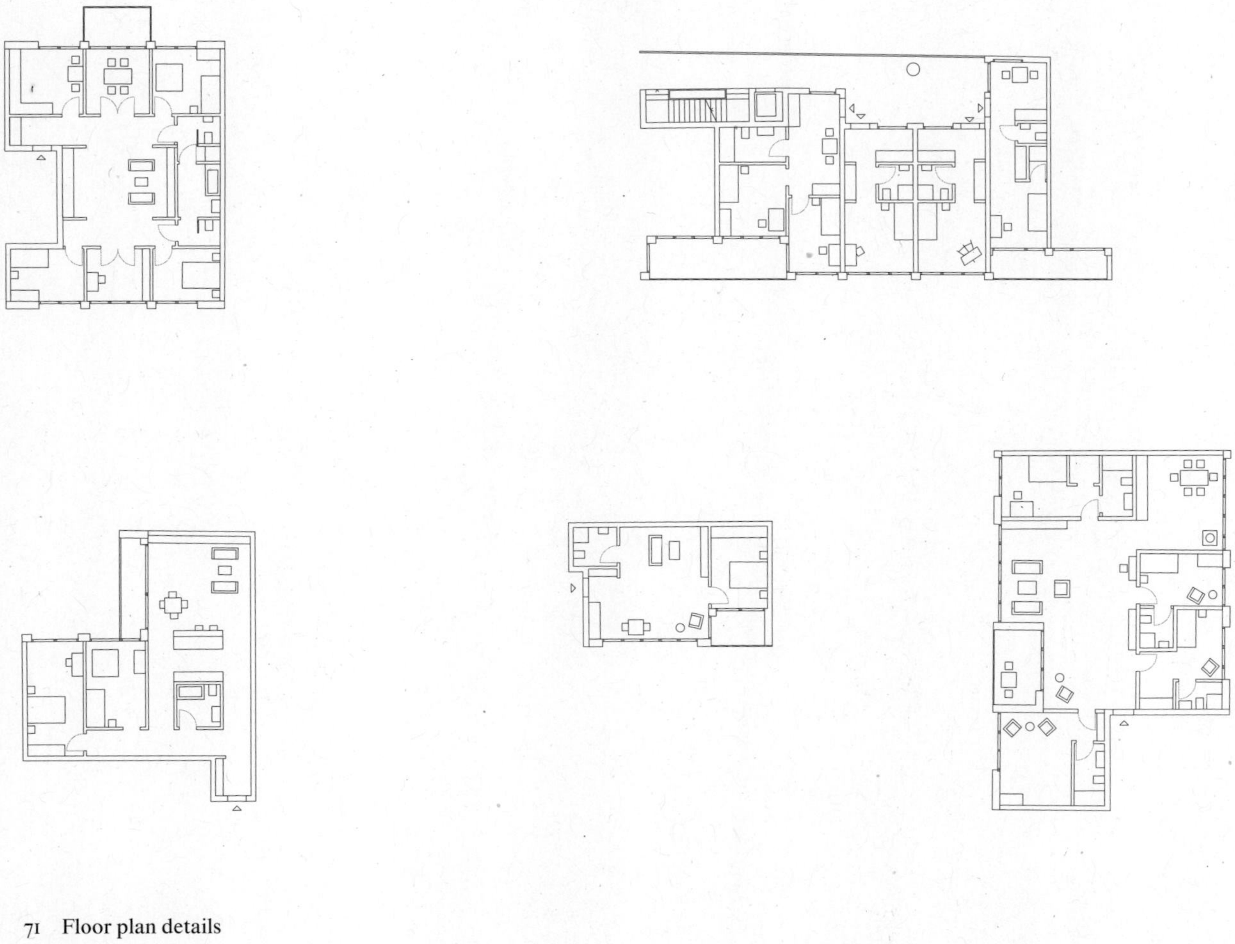

71 Floor plan details

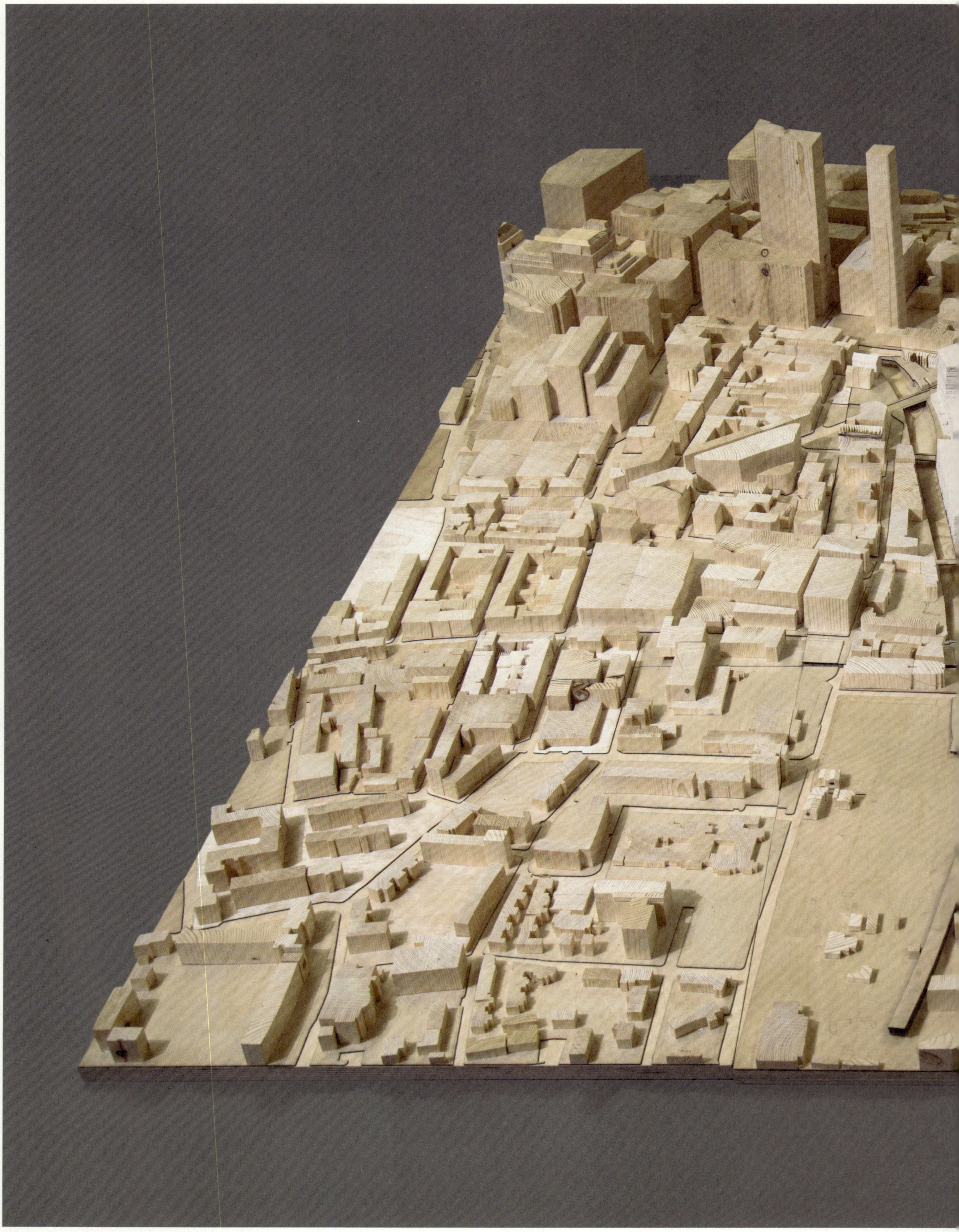

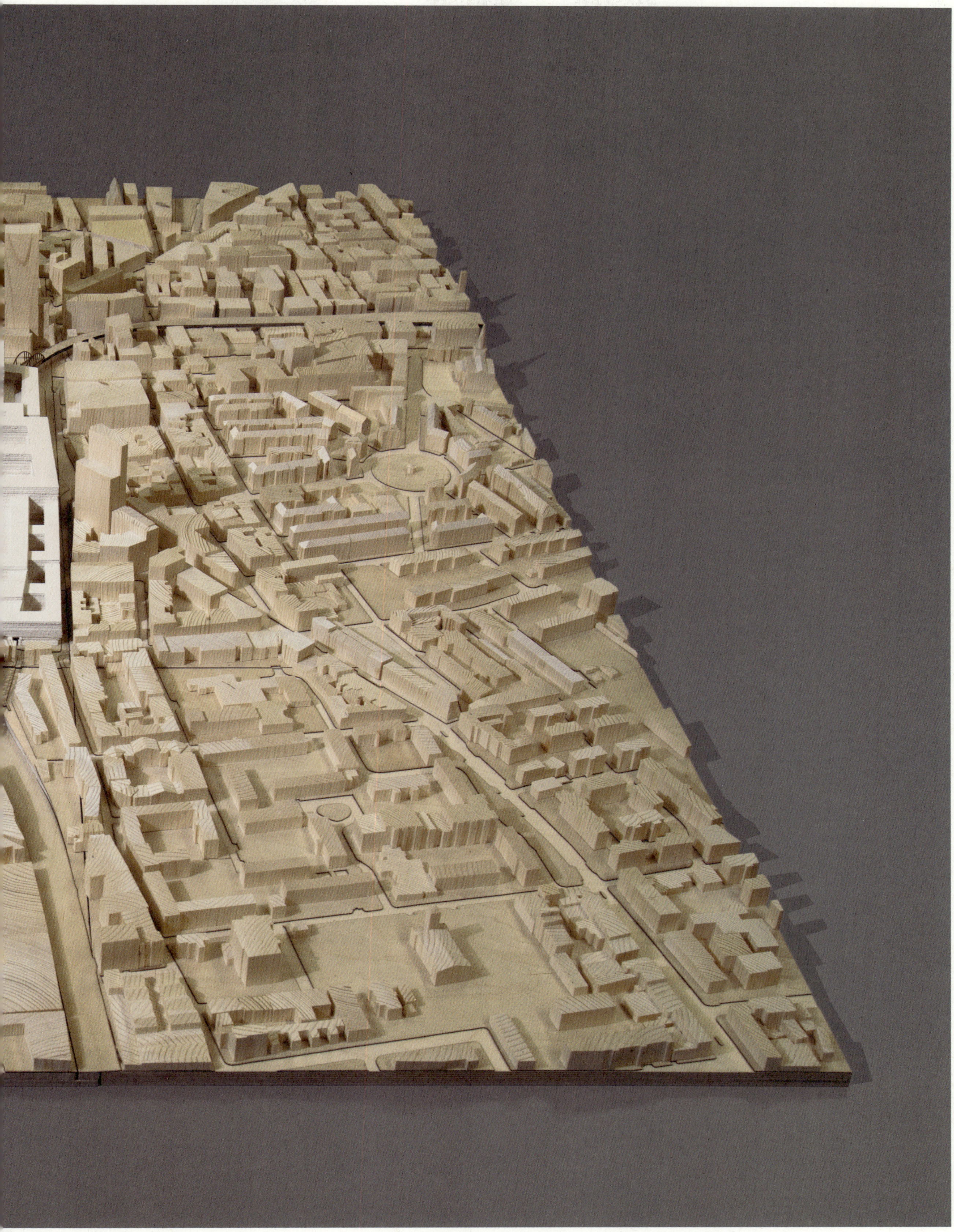

IX London Line

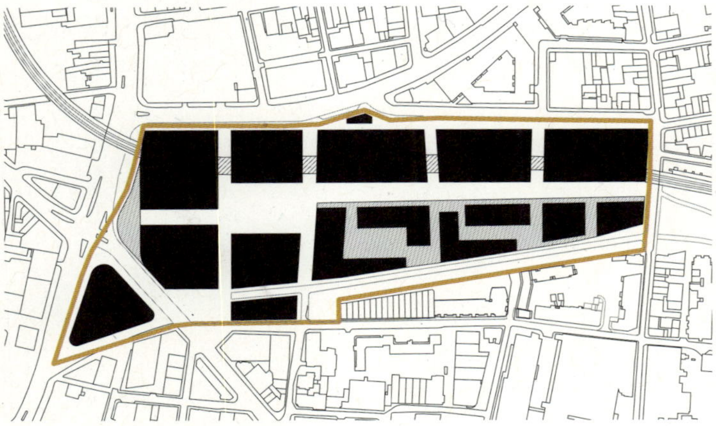

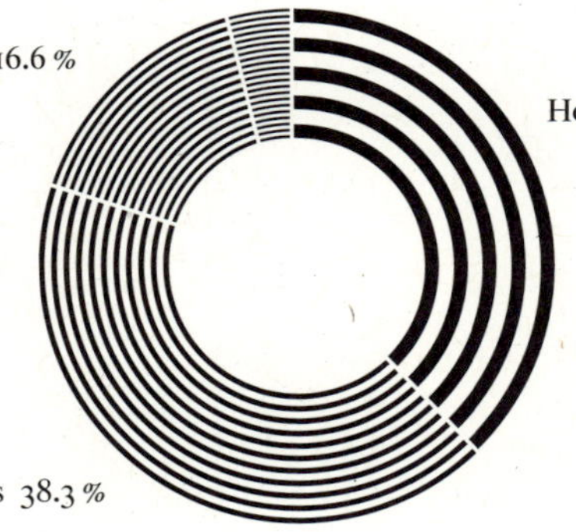

Site Area		43,700 m²	
Floor Area		199,510 m²	100 %
	Housing	80,502 m²	40.3 %
	Offices	76,495 m²	38.3 %
	Commerce	33,187 m²	16.6 %
	Public	9,326 m²	4.7 %
Density (FAR)		4.57	

The key concept of this project is its clear antithesis to the sprawling towers of the City. The proposed public spaces are not balanced by punctuated concentrations of extremely high density, but rather by a continuous and linear distribution along a wide pedestrian axis. Because of the moderate and well-balanced building heights along this axis, the project integrates well into the surrounding neighbourhoods. The historical and heterogeneous city grid is extended and adapted (fig. 78). The buildings can be grouped into three distinct parts: west, north and south.

The project also unites the appeal of the small scale with the strength of a clear spatial concept covering several scales. The central pedestrian promenade is extended towards the east by a conceptual corridor. It connects the City with Mile End Park through both the goods yard and Allens Gardens and then continues along the rail tracks. At the metropolitan scale, the corridor is part of a green grid of concentric and radial green spaces (fig. 75). The particular location of the goods yard at the intersection highlights the site's importance within the green grid of London. The proposal identifies this potential of the urban development area to alter the topology of the city and create a new node of metropolitan importance.

This metropolitan connection is realised on the site as a central open space running from east to west. Lined with public and commercial uses, this space mediates between the metropolitan and the local scale (fig. 74). Its structural integration into the city grid is facilitated by continuing the existing streets north and south of the site (figs. 76 and 77).

The second main urbanistic element of the proposal is the square located at the train station in the western part of the site. This public space defines the *western area* of the project, and is accentuated by the project's only high-rise, smoothening the transition to the City's high-rises and creating a visual link between the inner space of the goods yard and the Central Business District (fig. 73).

In the east, the basic layout of the project is organised in two distinct areas. In the northern part of the site where the elevated section of the London Overground runs through, new buildings encompass and integrate the trainline. In the southern part of the site, the ruin of the goods yard is used as a foundation. The elevated location enables a quiet residential situation with distinctive outdoor space, despite its centrality. The location is perfectly suited, however, for the shops, markets and trade set within the attractive vaults of the goods yard and in between two vibrant city districts, the Central Business District and the Brick Lane area.

The simple division into three sectors (west, north, south) guarantees flexible realisation of the project and facilitates the implementation of the development in urbanistic phases. Additionally, the project anticipates possible extension towards the East. The merging of two existing schools in a new spot defines a new edge of the Allens Gardens. It also exemplifies the future densification of the relatively sparsely built-up East (fig. 76). Generally, the proposal is convincing because of its simplicity and precision, operating at several scales.

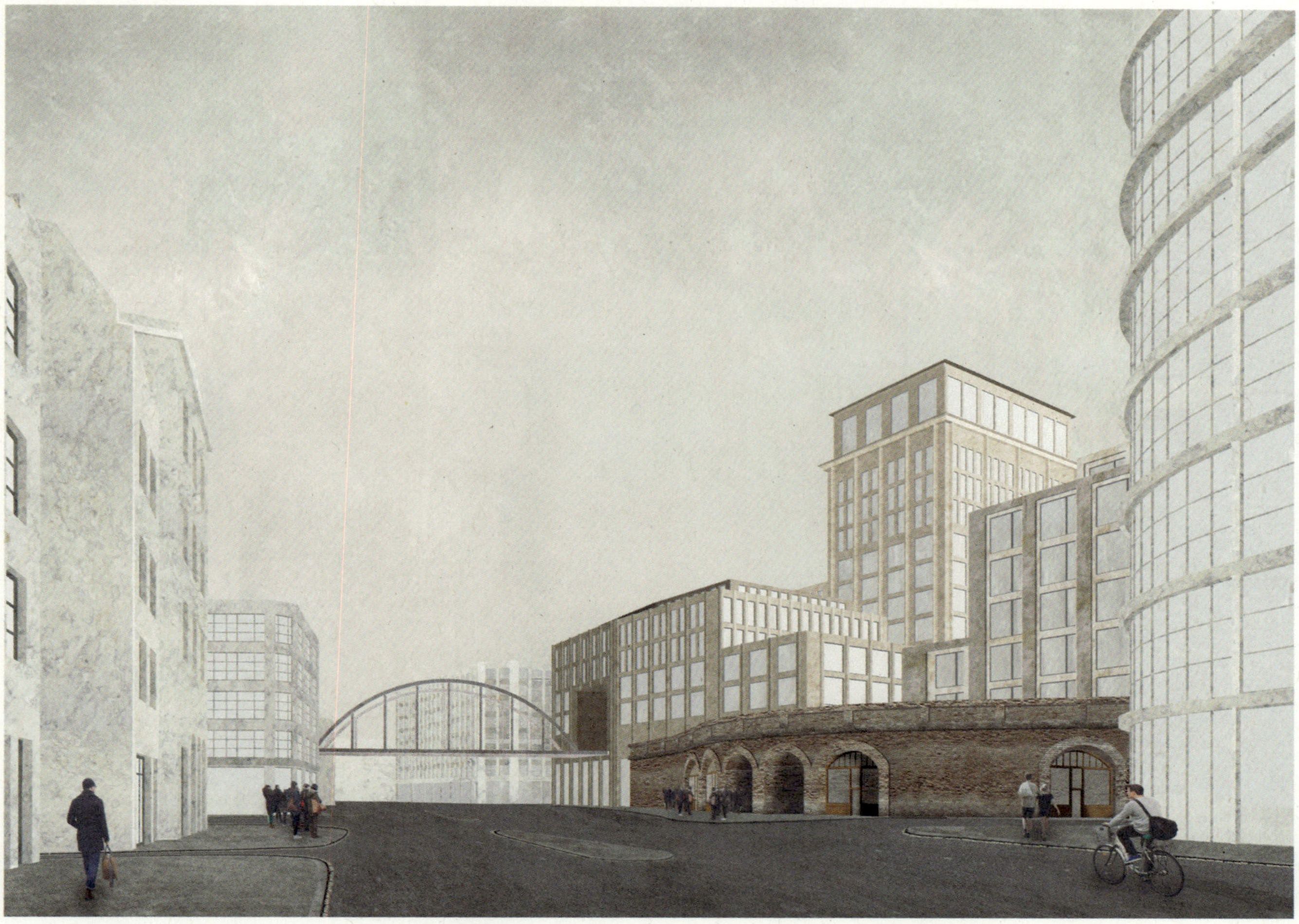

73 Visualisation of the south-western tip of the goods yard

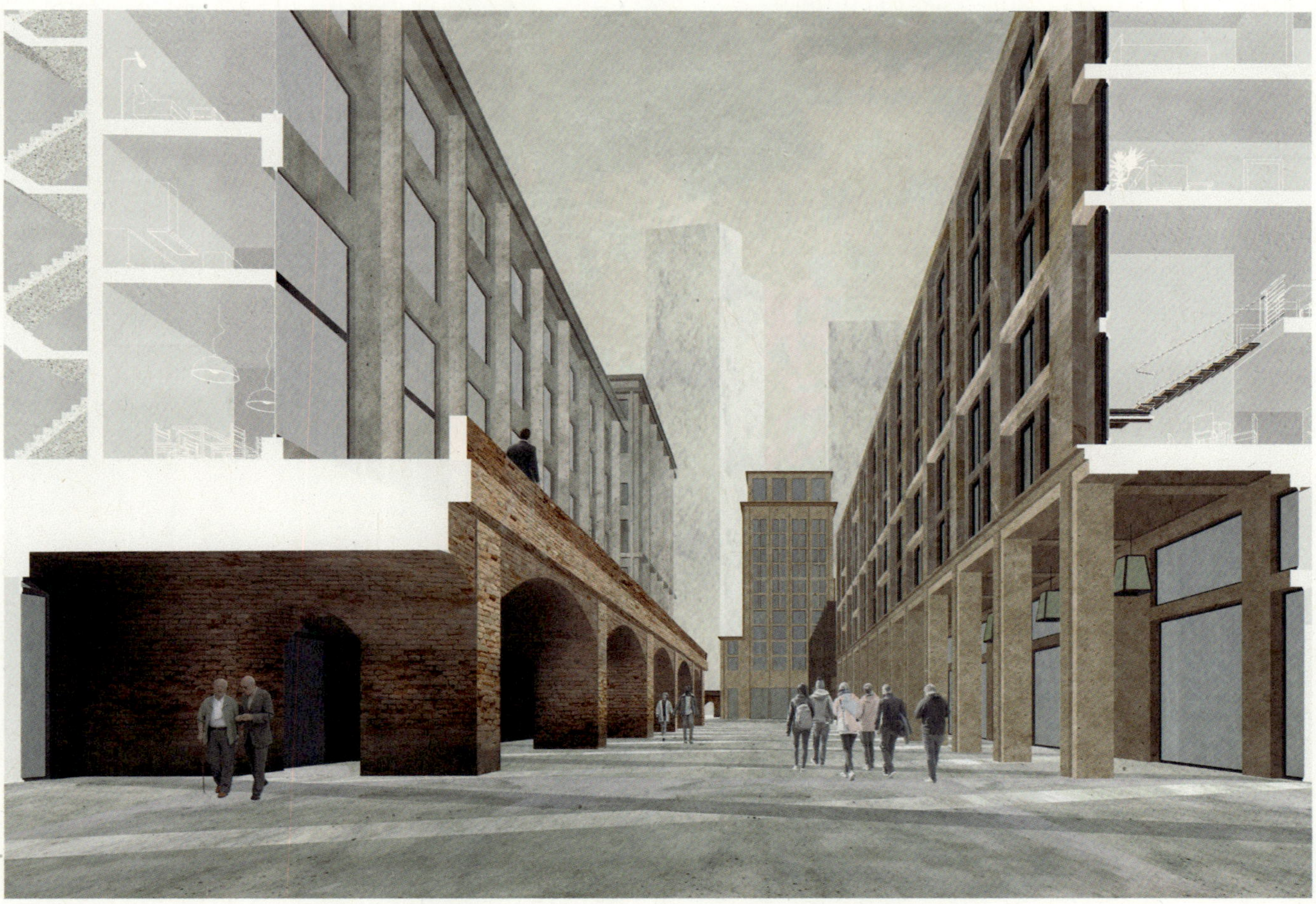

74 Visualisation of the internal east-west connection

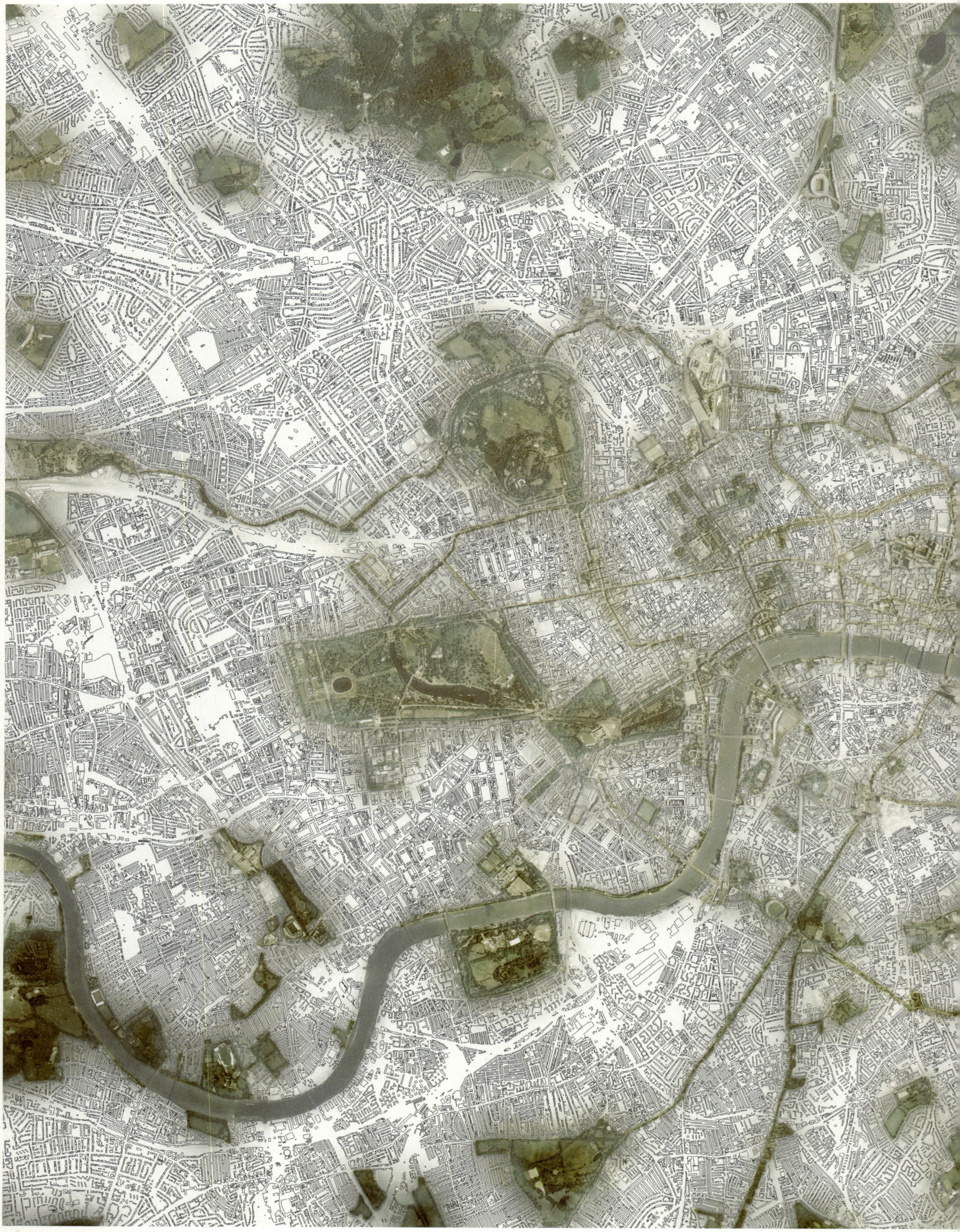

75 Visualisation of the regional integration

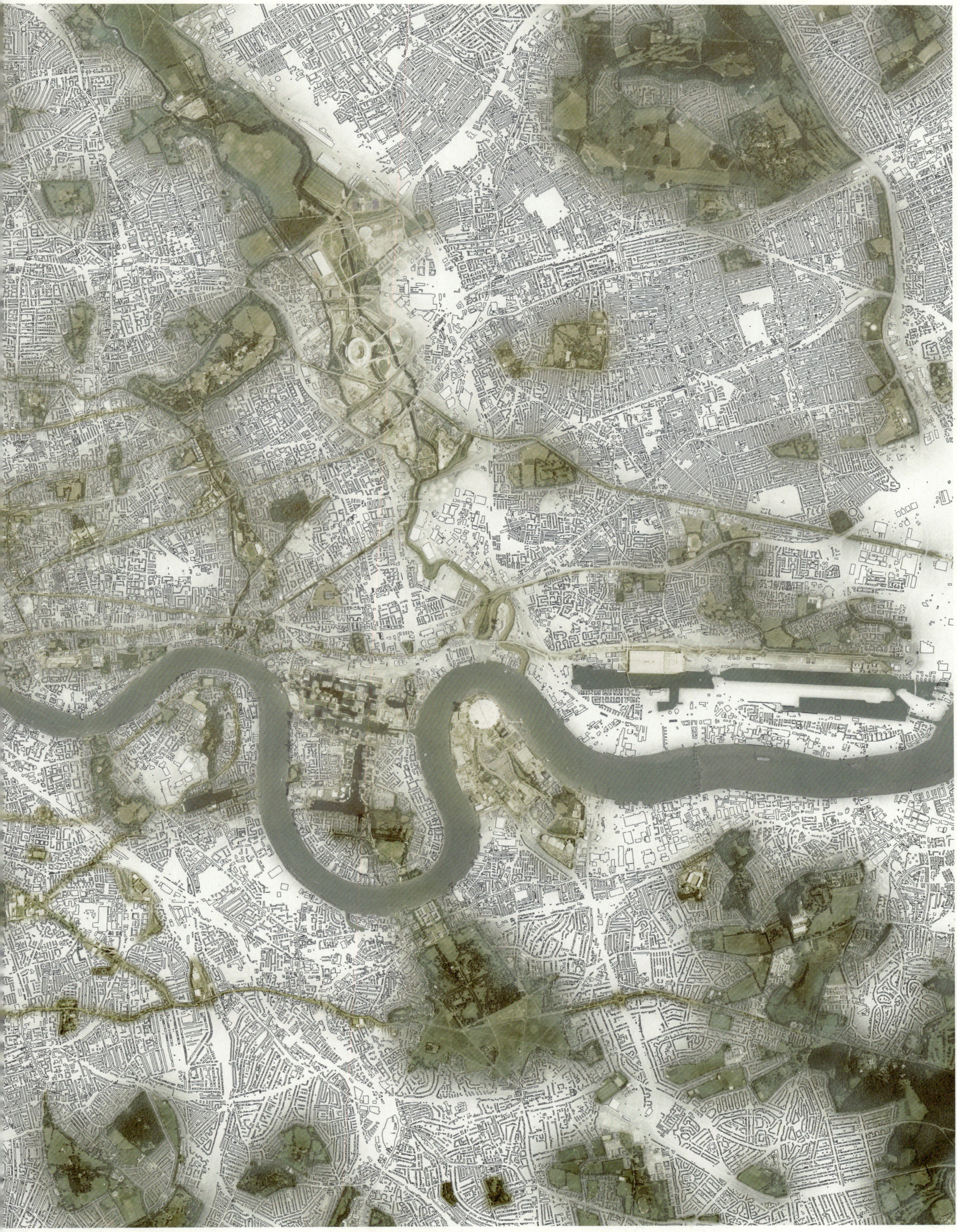

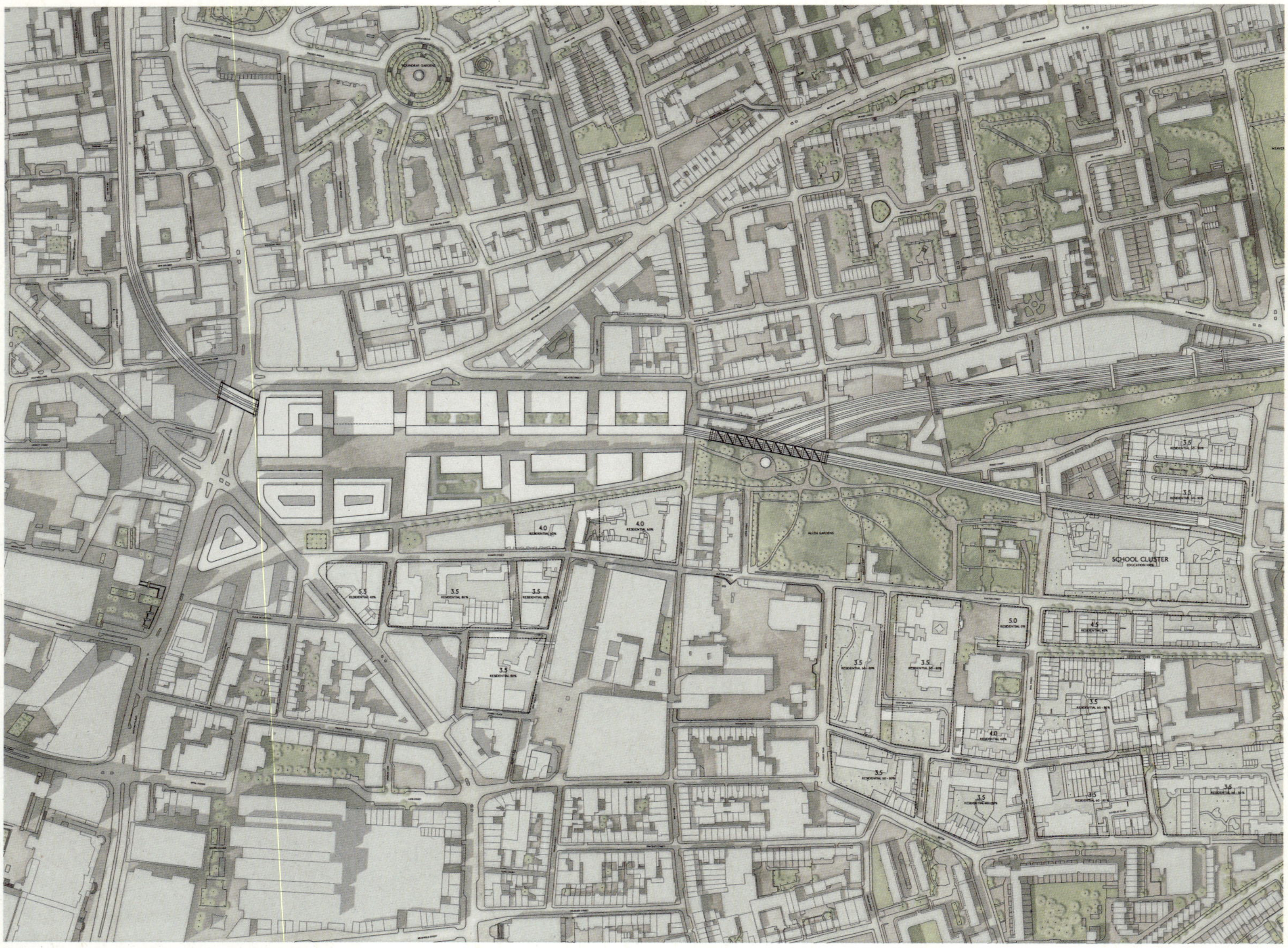

76 Masterplan

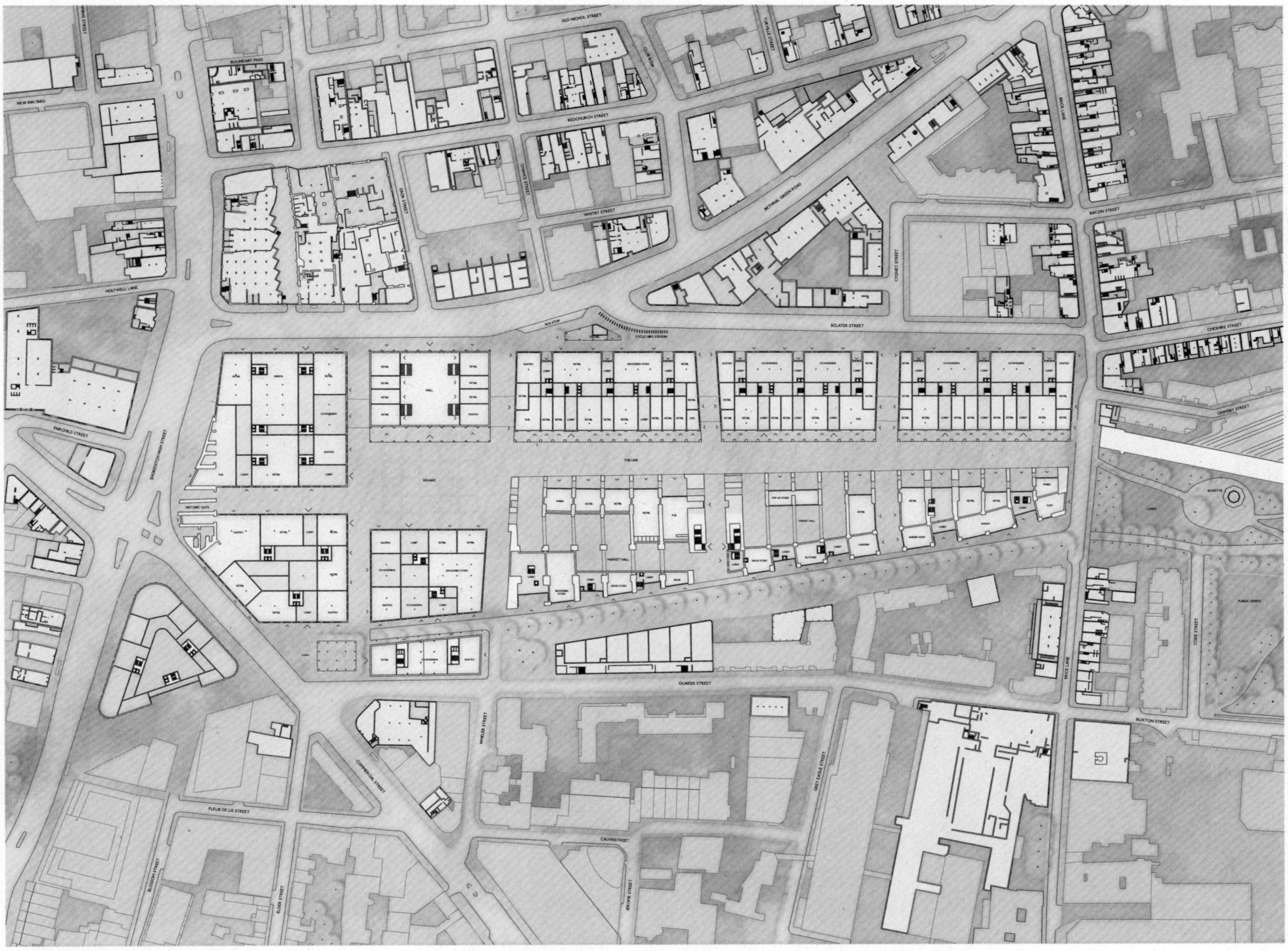

77 Ground level floor plan

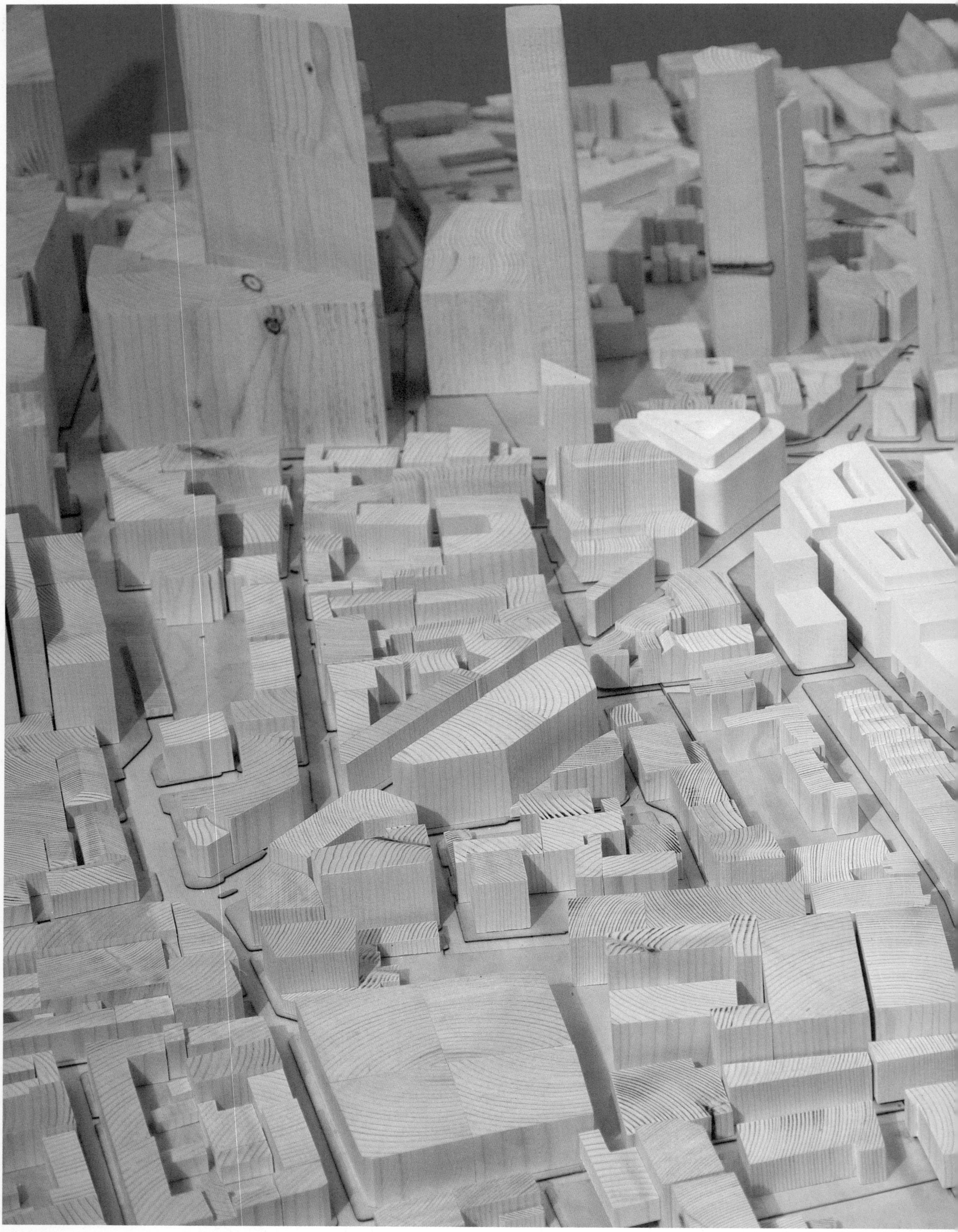

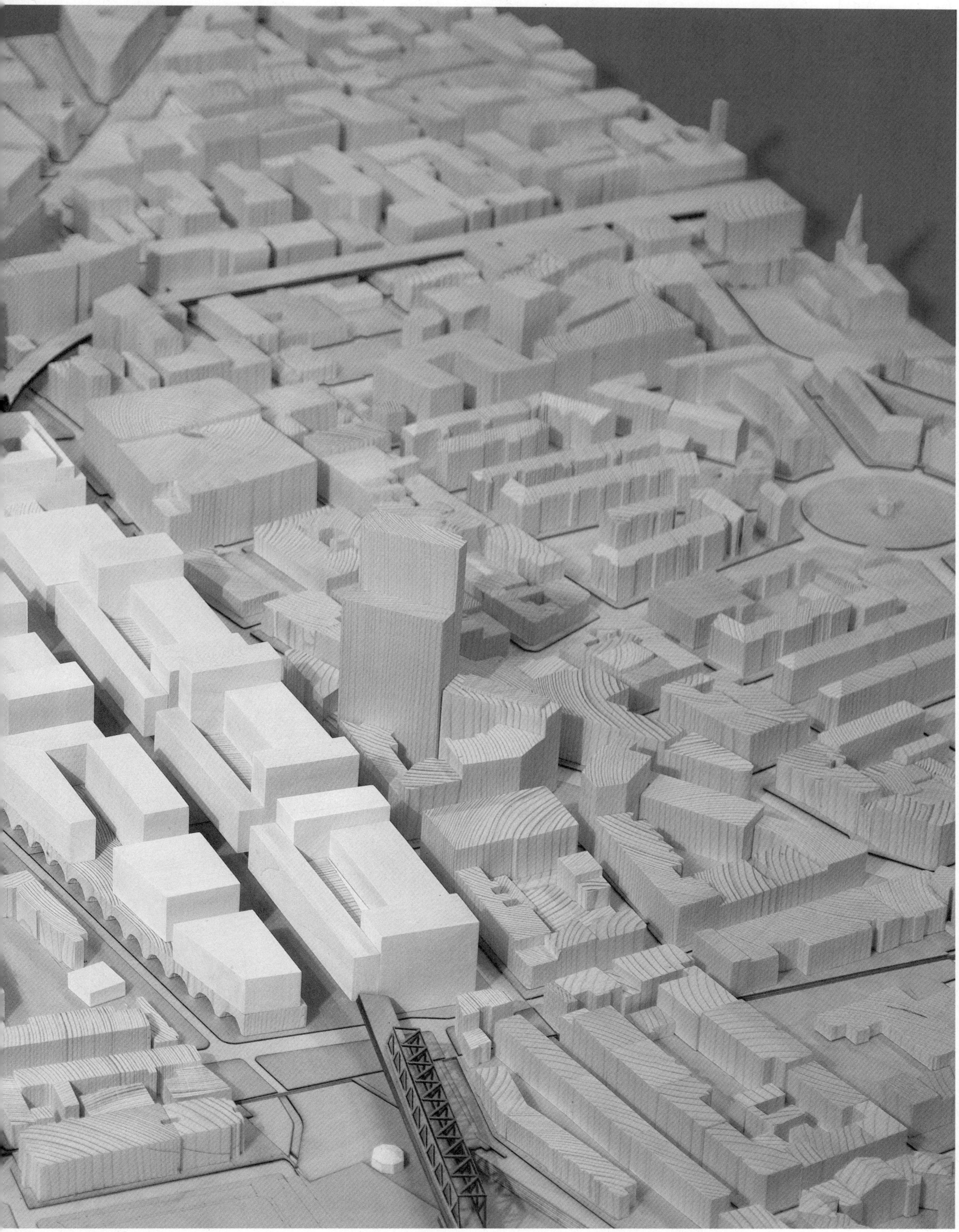

3.3 Synthesis

After evaluating and comparing the different project proposals in the last chapter, this chapter takes a step further and synthesises the most important findings. First of all, it is a product of the problem-finding process. Therefore, it should not be mistaken for a finished project. It is rather a design brief and a strategic vision for sound future development. Nevertheless, the synthesis also shows diagrammatically a viable solution for the former Bishopsgate goods yard and its surroundings, taking into consideration the basic developers' needs, Hackney Council's critique and the most important lessons from the project tests. Bridging the gap from problem finding to problem solving, it consists both of the most important goals and of strategic elements with which to achieve it. The synthesis sees the transformation of the goods yard foremost as an opportunity for London. Thus, it covers an area much larger than the developers' site, and not all strategic elements can be established by the developers. Some are simply not their responsibility. In order to integrate the goods yard in a larger strategy, the boroughs need to play a proactive role in this planning scheme. In order to channel positive effects for the good of the city, their role is to link-up the development of the goods yard with the development of the whole neighbourhood.

The strategic vision presented in this chapter can also be read as a result of an alternative planning model: one that extends the planning perimeter to the site's contexts, assigns the boroughs a more proactive role and believes in design as a tool for a discursive planning culture (fig. 79).

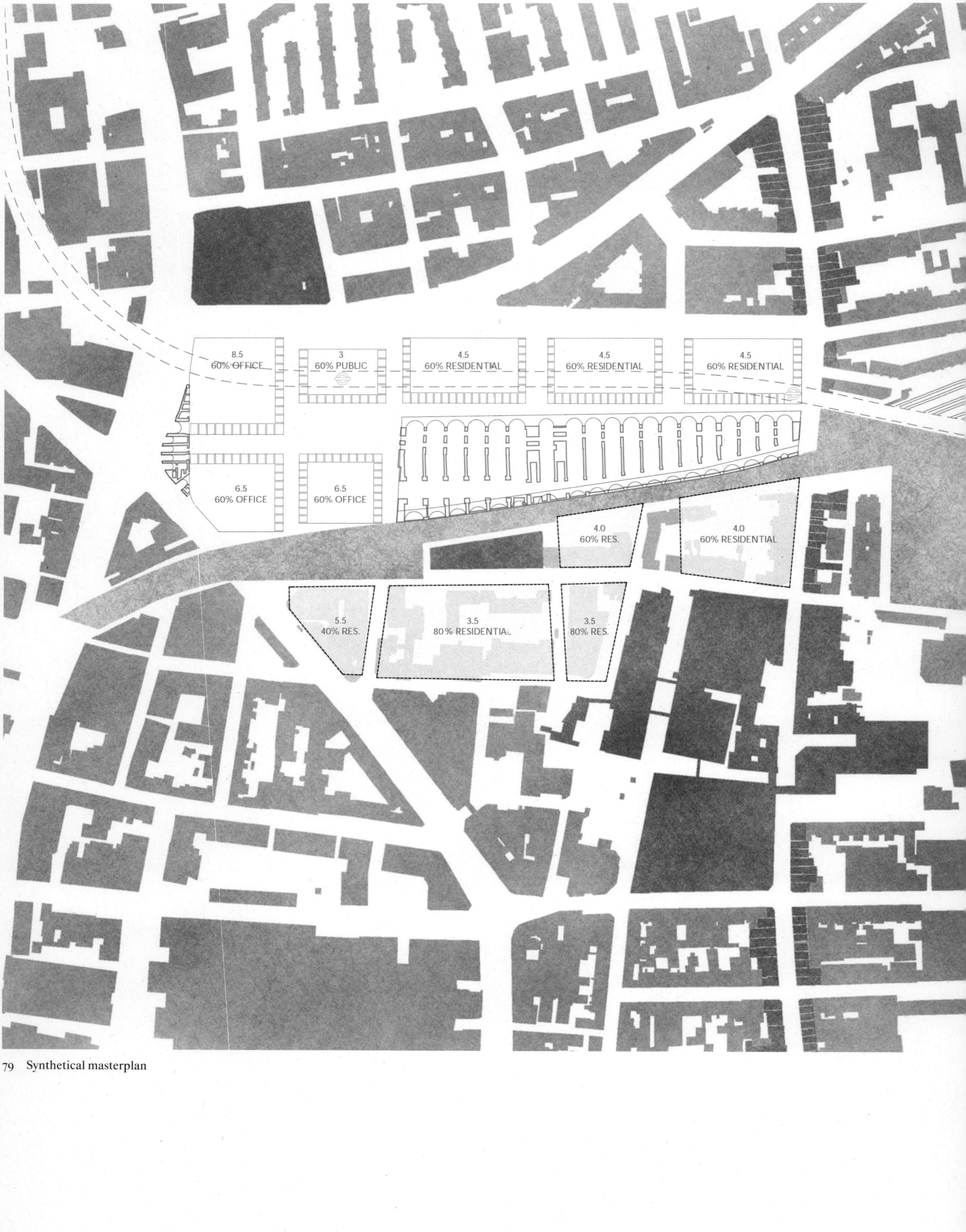

79 Synthetical masterplan

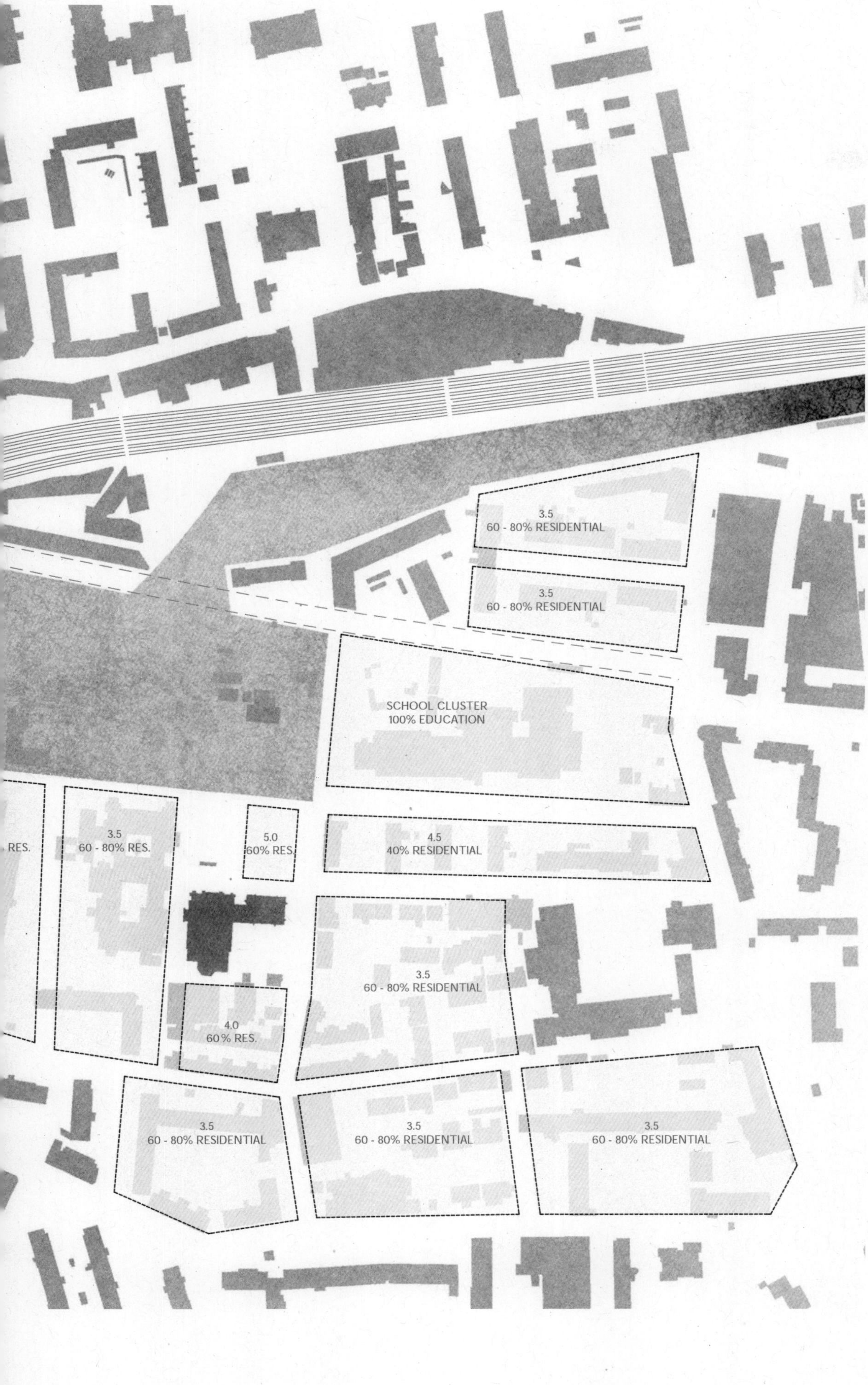

Special Buildings
Existing Urban Fabric
Greenway to the East
Brick Lane
Existing Viaduct
Double-height Spaces
Overground Line
Tube Station Entrance
Potential Densification Area
Density / Programme

Main goal:
create a centrality for multiple scales

For London:
a large public programme, e.g. market. This will create a city-scale centrality in combination with Brick Lane, Liverpool Street Station, Shoreditch High Street, Bethnal Green Road, Spitalfields Market and the Truman Brewery

For London's East:
a greenway to the Lee Valley, flanked by a development strategy for its fringes

For Shoreditch:
neighbourhood community services, spatial connections to the surrounding quarters, and public spaces at the edges of the goods yard

For new residents:
domestic and vernacular urban qualities for everyday life

Strategic elements, subdivided into three scales:

London scale (fig. 80)

1. Greenway to the East, most probably best on covered train tracks (fig. 86)
2. Large-scale densification strategy for the corridor between Bethnal Green Road and Whitechapel Road from the City of London to the Lee Valley
3. Large public programme, e.g. market in the existing viaduct as an addition to the Brick Lane Street Market

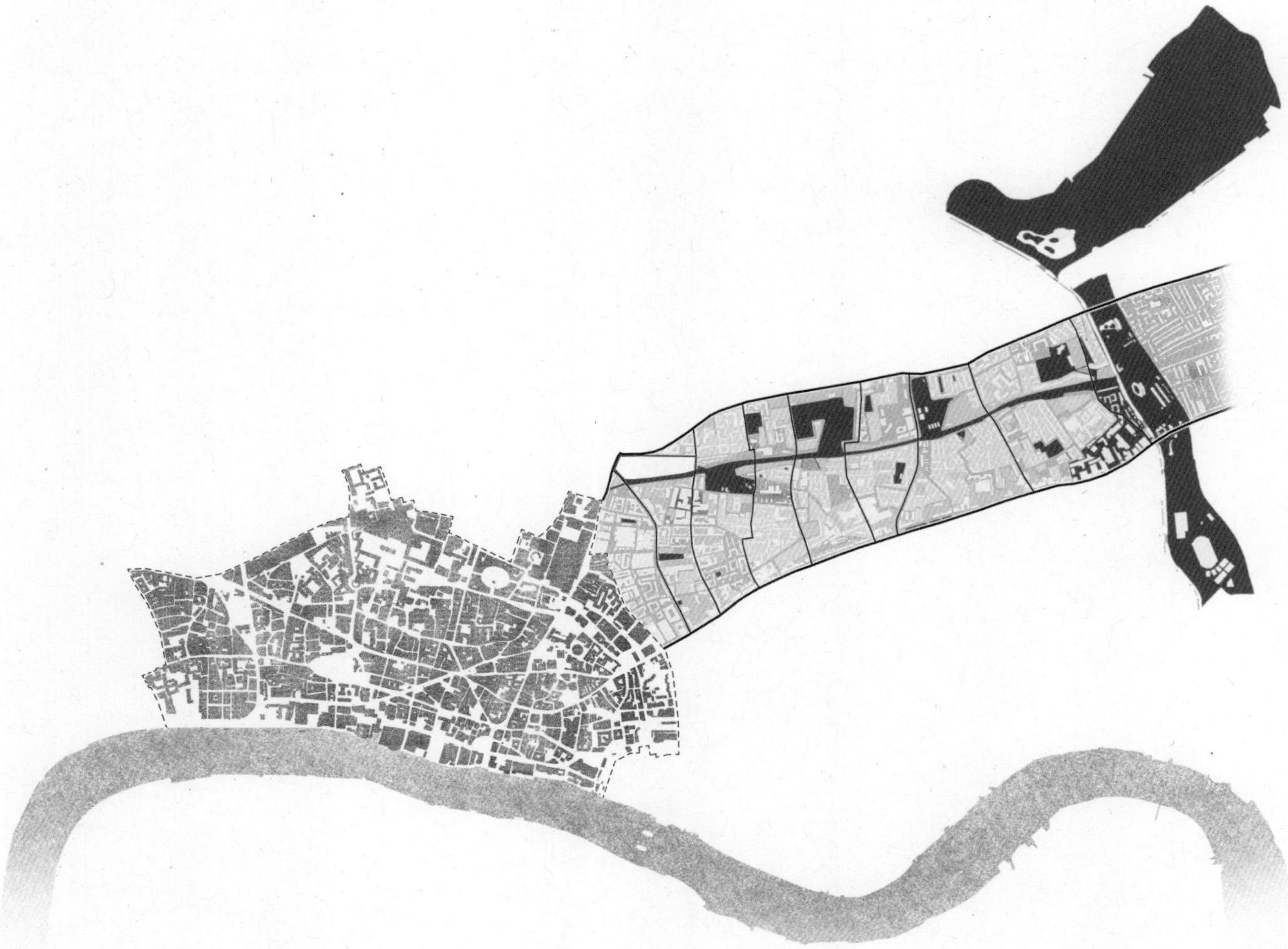

80 Regional scale spatial concept

- Bishopsgate Goods Yard
- Main Streets
- Greenway to the East
- City of London
- Key Public Facilities
- Existing Urban Fabric
- Services
- River Thames
- Densification Potential

Neighbourhood scale (fig. 81)

4. Reconfiguration and integration of Allens Gardens
   - 4.1 Spatial reorganisation of Allens Gardens (fig. 85)
   - 4.2 Densification strategy at the fringes of Allens Gardens
   - 4.3 Reorganisation of the uses of Allens Gardens
   - 4.4 Public space as a spatial link between the goods yard and Allens Gardens

5. Connecting and urban integration of Spitalfields
   - 5.1 Connect street grid
   - 5.2 Cover train tracks to create a public space (fig. 86, see points 1 and 6.4)
   - 5.3 Densification strategy for the area south of the goods yard

6. Creating public spaces as meeting points between the site and its surroundings
   - 6.1 Square in the east as a link between the goods yard, Brick Lane and Allens Gardens
   - 6.2 Junction in the west at Shoreditch High Street
   - 6.3 Public square at Shoreditch High Street station and a link between the station and Bethnal Green Road
   - 6.4 Greenway in the south by covering train tracks (see points 1 and 5.2)

7. Integrating neighbourhood services (e.g. a library, sports fields, educational programmes, religious programmes. The viaduct could also be used for temporary uses serving the neigbourhood)

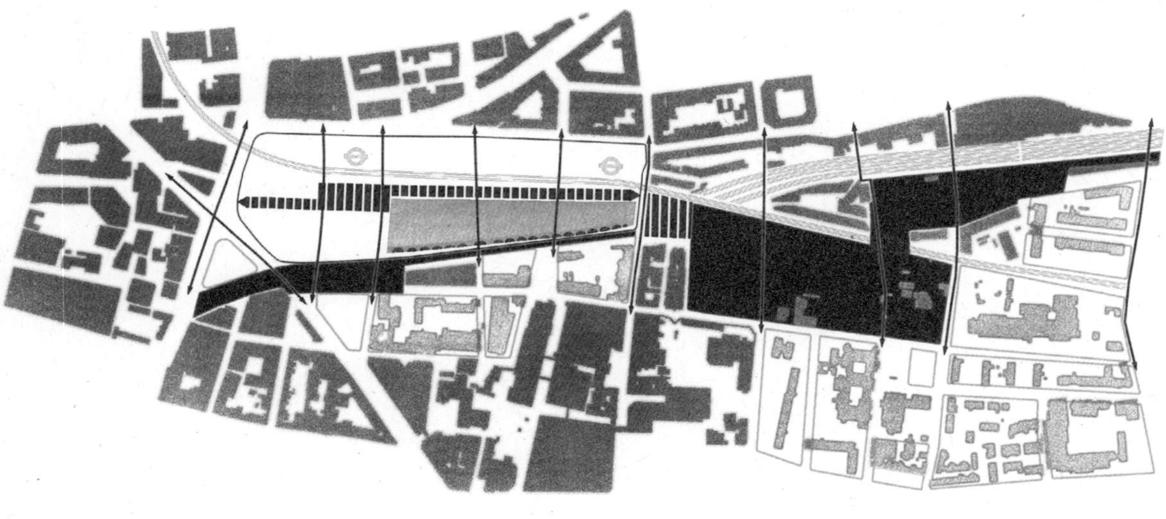

81 Neighbourhood scale spatial concept

- Site Perimeter
- Greenway to the East
- Key Connections
- Existing Urban Fabric
- Potential Densification Area
- Overground Line
- Existing Viaduct
- Tube Station Entrances

Quarter scale (fig. 82)

8. Internal east-west connection, preferably north of the listed viaduct
9. Shoreditch High Street station square, preferably part of the internal east-west connection
10. Achieving a relatively high density (FAR between 3.7 and 4.6) without resorting to high-rise as the primary means in order to create domestic and vernacular urban qualities on the public street level (figs. 83 and 84)

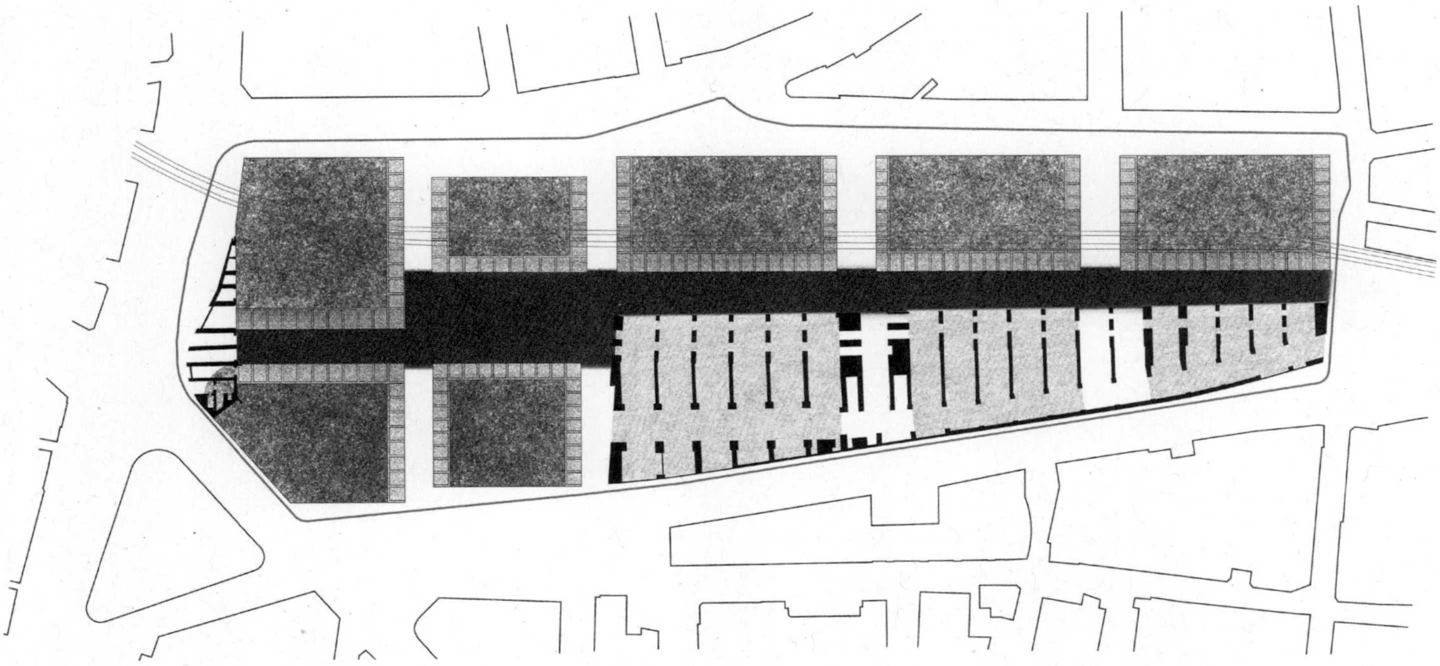

82 Local scale spatial concept

Site Perimeter
Existing Viaduct
Overground Line
East-West Connection
Existing Urban Fabric
Building Plots
Double-height Spaces
Goods Yard Extensions

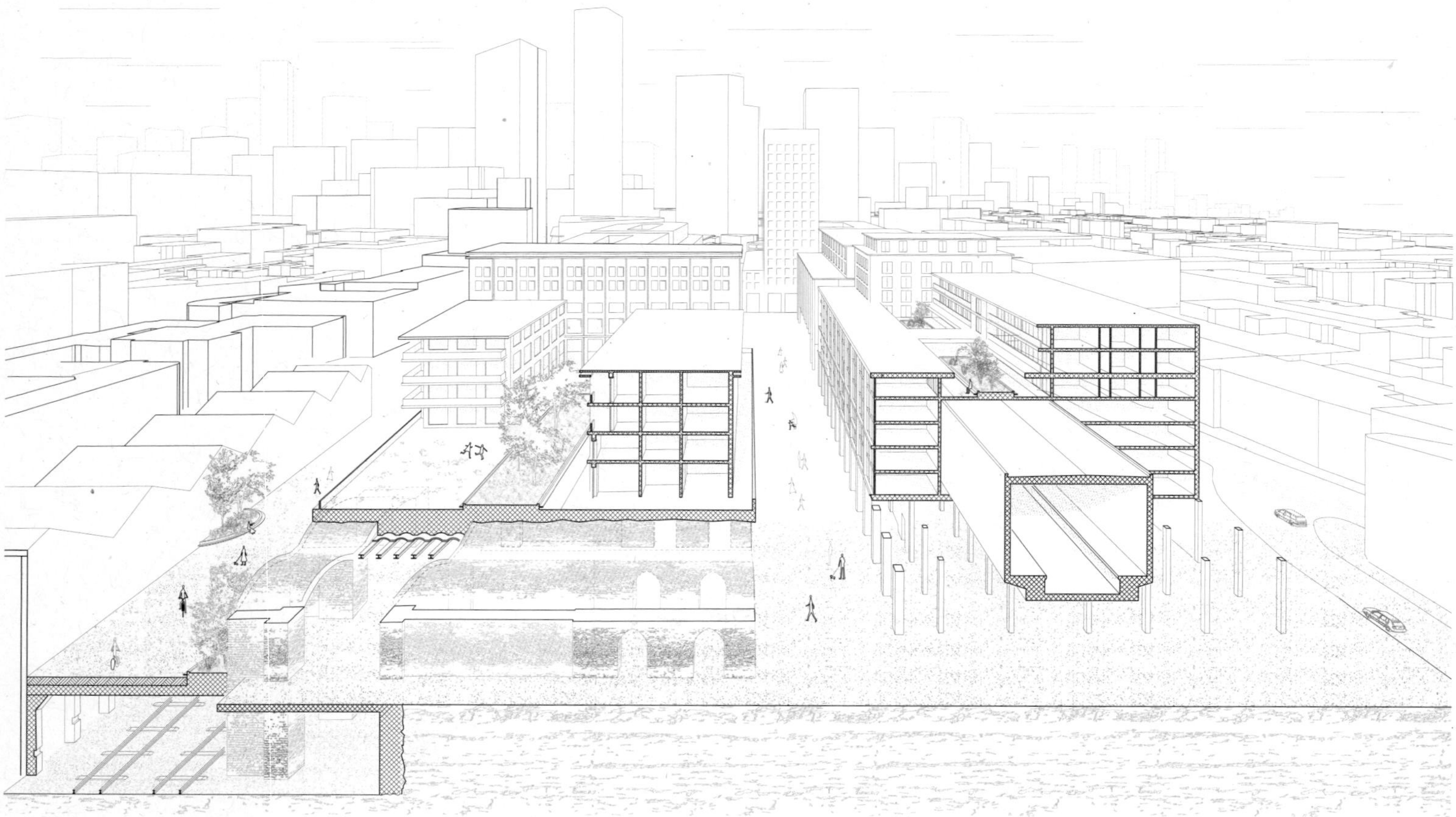

83 South-north section

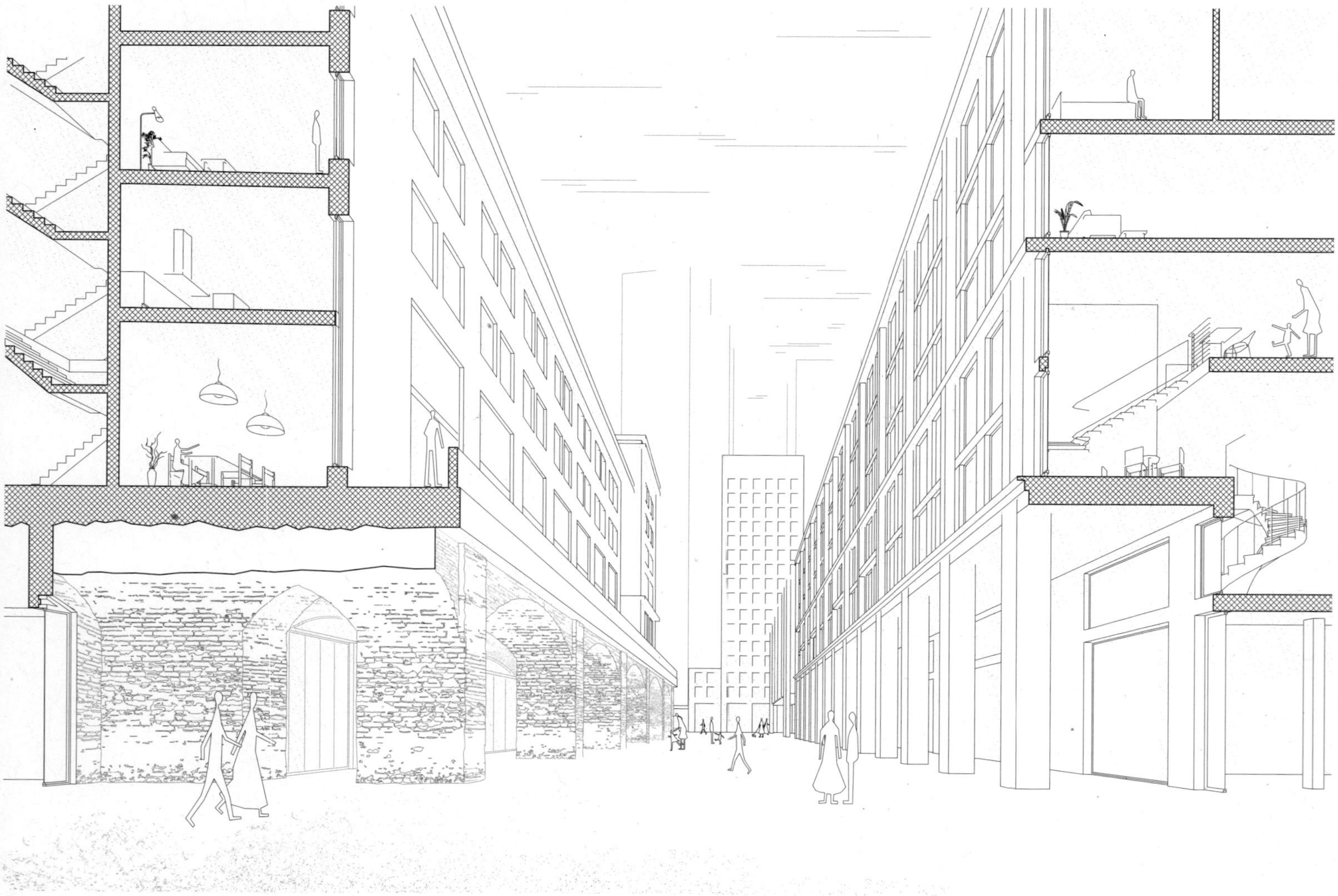

84 South-north section detail

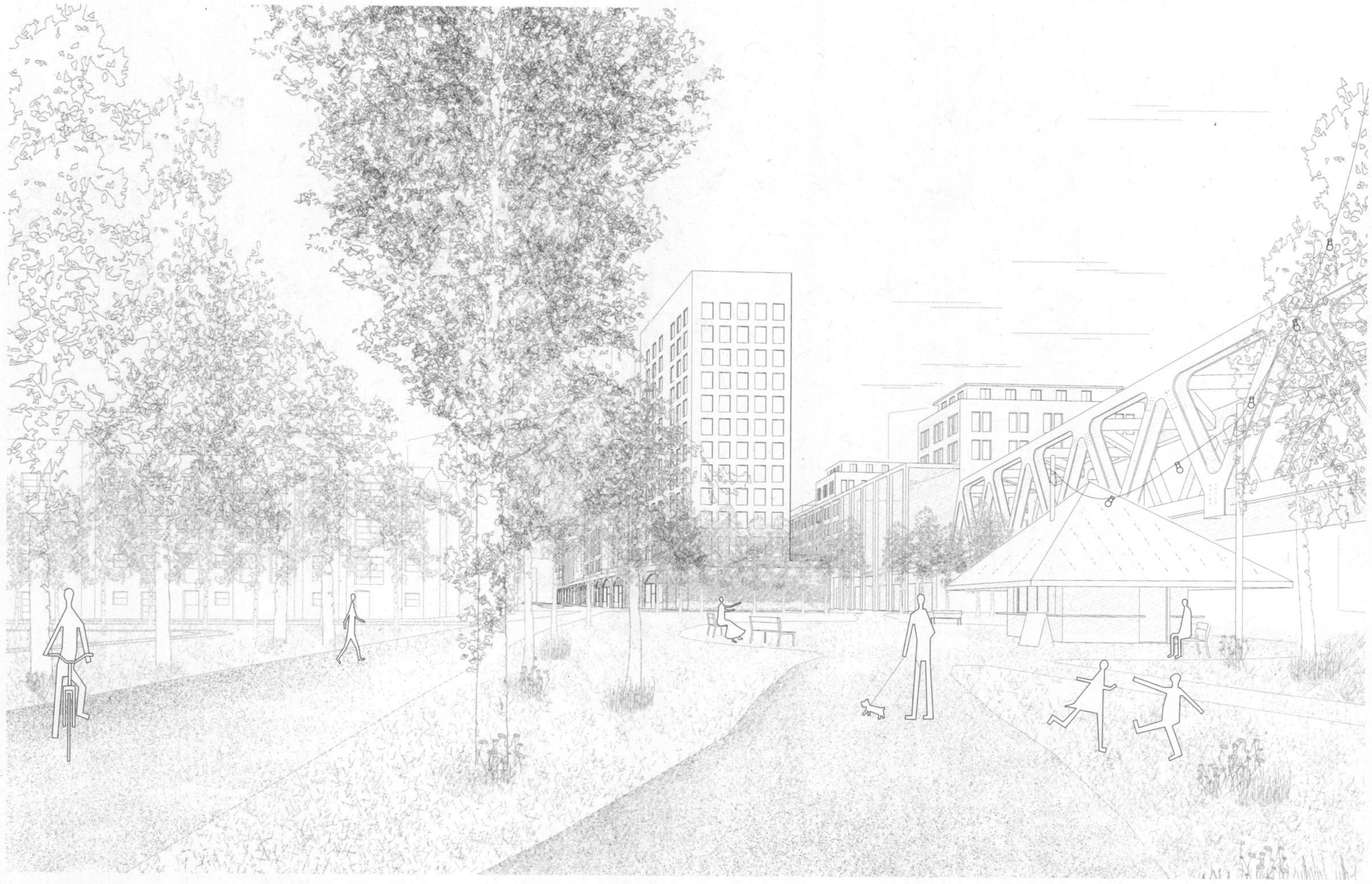

85 Visualisation of the view from Allens Gardens

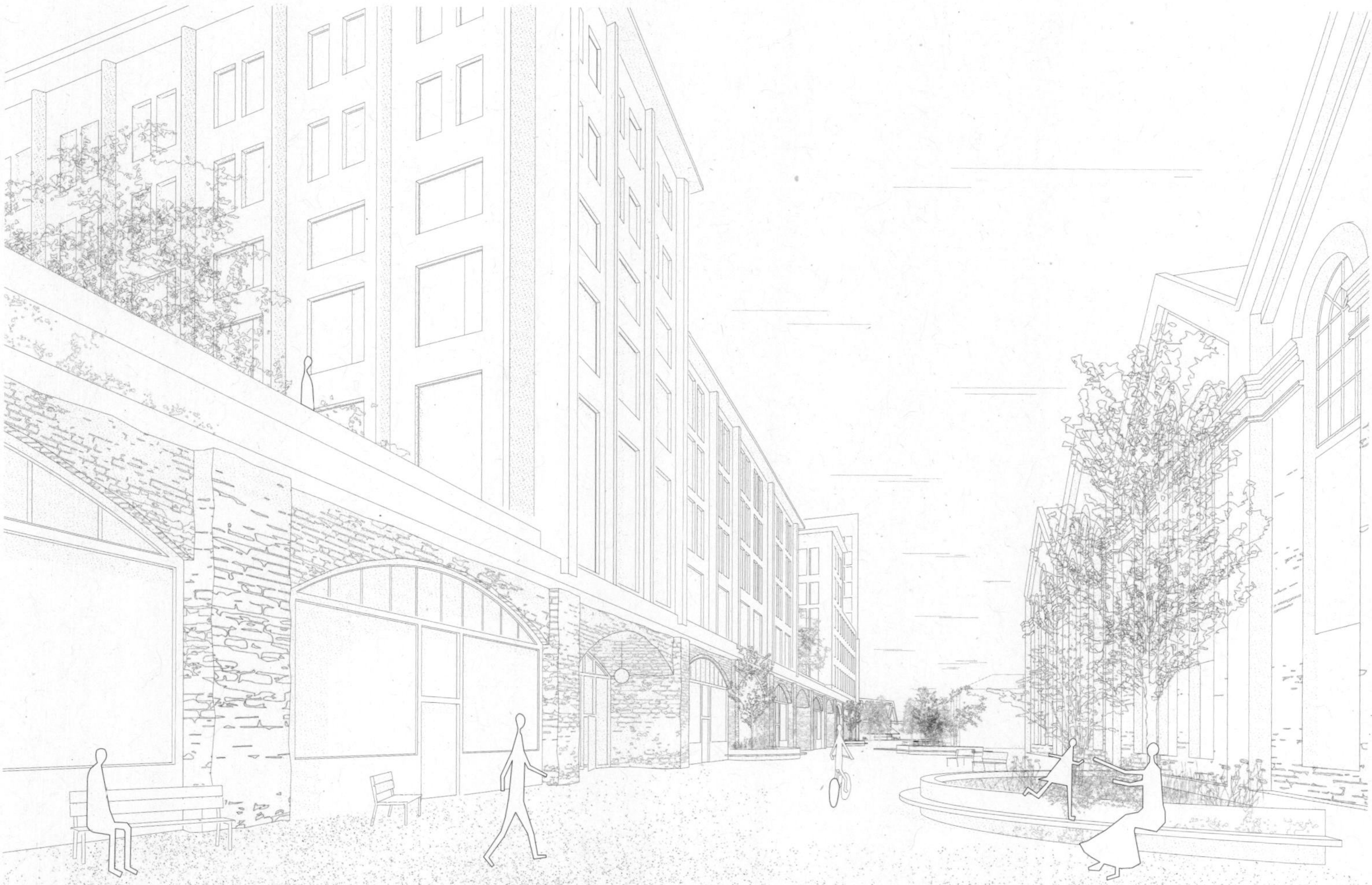

86 Visualisation of the greenway on covered tracks

4 Reflections

This chapter aims at summarising the most important findings of the case study in the form of listed statements. Its goal is to contribute to a paradigm change in planning processes, to shift these towards mouldable discourses and away from merely technocratic necessities or commercial deals. The following statements are split into two headings. The first deals with the culture of planning, the second with its methodological aspects. Together, they can be seen as an apparatus for guiding involved communities, stakeholders, developers and experts, as well as for a general discourse on urban development.

4.1 Towards a Culture of Planning

Focus on Urbanity Instead of Urbanisation

Given that urbanisation is the process of producing our built environment, the term urbanity can be described as the specific spatial and temporal conditions of how societies arrange, organise and live under the overarching process of urbanisation. Processes of urbanisation do not necessarily lead to symbiotic forms of coexistence. On the contrary: while urbanisation seems inevitable, urbanity is a very fragile quality that needs to be cultivated. Therefore, urban development projects should not be seen purely as constructions of buildings and marketable places. Instead, a positive urban impact has to play a part in their realisation. At best, they contribute to achieving social and spatial goals, and facilitate the realisation of a collective idea and form of a city. In this context, urbanity is the goal and urbanisation its vehicle. By creating synergies between the process of urbanisation and the targets of urbanity, urban resources are not only used more efficiently, but can also be steered towards meaningful common goals. The creation of such synergies is a challenging task and is certainly not costless. However, taking into account the urban impact, the financial investment can be seen as modest. If the development of a city is understood as a process of long-term urban valorisation, planning should be interpreted as one of its investments.

Create a Discourse through Design

Design is not only the product of an engaged discourse, it also has the potential to initiate discourse. The depiction of potential realities, an act inherent in design, enables the spectrum of possible and impossible futures to be explored. By dissolving the thin line between reality and fiction, design alters perspectives, regarding both the future and the present. Design experiments not only reveal and demonstrate possible solutions but also highlight unresolved problems. Their analytical and political dimensions, while often hardly visible, perform highly effectively. Through them, design manipulates and steers discourses – wanted or not. However, designs are not inherently suited to stimulate debate. If a project employs interpretation and manipulation as an end to legitimise its own purpose, it does not contribute to a collective discourse. In the worst case, design oppresses an ongoing discourse through its glossy renderings and assertive diagrams. Only designs that genuinely attempt to gain knowledge through experimentation are of high discursive value. Their enquiring dimension is the core. In the best cases, this sets up a discourse, especially by highlighting potentials, questions, conflicts, aspirations and imagery that is open for debate. In any case, design has to be understood as an active and effective force in the creation of public discourses.

Pointing out Problems rather than Blurring Them

In urban planning, conflicts, problems and disagreements do not need to be considered as disruptive and, therefore, as features to be hidden. They should rather be used as resources for the genesis of a project. If explicitly formulated and integrated in an open debate, they can stimulate both mutual understanding and unconventional and creative solutions. Although images seemingly unite and issues divide, the blurring of problems is a very short-sighted strategy that should be seen as a missed opportunity. Firstly, suppressed problems have a tendency to erupt in the worst moments and create frustration, opposition and animosity. Secondly, disagreements are one of the most potent design resources at an early conceptual stage, leading towards a clear problem statement. Thirdly, the multi-perspective view, created by the productive convergence of different agencies and their interests, is a core societal resource of urban democracies for the solving of complex problems, amongst them urban design and planning issues. This is made possible by the holistic ideal and the inherent complexity of such a multi-perspective approach, both bearing the ability to cope with the intricate issues of contemporary urban societies.

Establish an Independent Space for Experts

The role of experts, such as city planners, architects, traffic engineers and heritage protection specialists, has dramatically changed in the wake of neo-liberalism. Their role has shifted from consulting cities to advising developers. What first seemed to be a smart way of saving costs for public budgets, resulted later in the rather confusing situation of specialists no longer performing according to their expertise but helping to furnish a development narrative instead. Since their commission relies on their willingness to conform, developer-friendly experts have the best chances of becoming consultants. After a couple of generations, such a modus of working leads to the disestablishment of sovereign competences. This auto-propelled process results in shifting dominance over the narrative from public towards private agencies. If a city is without resources, therefore lacking the help of experts, and faces a private real estate developer armed with a team of consultants, the result can easily be imagined. The focus will lie clearly on local land valorisation, which is a worthwhile goal but most definitively not the only one of an urban development project. It is time to create spaces for independent experts, especially because of their potential to bridge the gap between public and private. The balancing role of independent expert bodies is currently underestimated and often blatantly missing. Given that a high-quality urban future based on a balanced development is one of our core societal goals, such independent expert bodies are essential.

Design Planning Processes

The way planning processes are structured has substantial influence on the resulting design schemes. For example, a linear process structure leads to a very different urban layout than an iterative one. Additionally, the way different agencies are empowered in the process is a key aspect of planning, and the orchestration of the information flow is also critical. Who defines the problem statement and the design brief, and at what point in the process? All these aspects have to be considered when procedures are to be set up. Yet planning processes do not only pre-arrange design solutions, they also have to be designed themselves. Most professionals would agree that good architectures and public spaces can hardly make up for badly conceived planning processes. Many would also acknowledge the importance of urban planning and the inherent processes leading to urban spaces and architecture. However, hardly any of them has the will and courage to tackle one of the most underrated, yet fundamental tasks of the production of space: the design of skilful planning processes.

Embrace Stockholder and Stakeholder Complexity

Reducing ownership heterogeneity and political complexity may be a centrepiece of process efficiency and short-term investment. In contrast, cities are long-term projects. Diversification is a core ingredient for long-term stabilisation, not only in economic terms. Following this line, ownership heterogeneity is important. It leads to different investment models, some riskier than others, and to different scales of investment. This mix results in different socio-economic patterns with different time horizons and tenancy concepts, indirectly leading to different social groups and milieus inhabiting an urban quarter. This multitude of particular interests generates an urban space with a high degree of political complexity, but also with a lower risk of collapsing from shocks and other imponderables. This multitude is also potentially able to adapt to new phenomena and challenges, step by step. Integrating a multitude of stakeholders in a very early phase of planning is crucial when designing an urban project. It is not only a political duty to include different perspectives, but it is also important to activate local and specific knowledge, to address conflicts and potential forms of consensus as generating parts of the project, and to use the multi-perspective potential of stakeholder heterogeneity as a tool for robust developments. Fixating on a single – and therefore highly vulnerable – perspective is not helpful.
The shaping of the urban realm as a collective and transparent endeavour further helps to avoid frustration, inefficiencies, unnecessary follow-up costs and political mistrust. In contrast to this diversity-driven concept of urban space, many contemporary urban developments aspire to large-scale undercomplexity and create spaces for rather homogenous social milieus, camouflaged by urban tropes of diversity such as colourful buildings in diverse shapes. What really counts when it comes to the diversity of a city is its DNA, consisting of different land ownership patterns and different user groups using and sharing the same physical space.

Enforce Ownership Transparency

When ownership is opaque, responsibilities become (at least ethically) unclear. Developers assemble experts and investors and then convince the authorities with a compelling narrative. Since most authorities are politically in a relatively weak position, it is more likely that they will follow the developer's narrative. Only public protests can put the authorities under pressure and raise counterarguments to the proposed imperatives. After a couple of tiresome redesigns, public protest is usually worn down. As ownership conditions become more and more opaque, fewer people are either able or willing to take long-term responsibility. Who feels morally accountable for the quality of an urban development? The city is too weak to take responsibility, while the developers develop their urban product only until the construction is finished.
At which point, they can finally hand it over to the owner, which is potentially an investment fund financed by thousands of people all over the globe, most of them not even aware of their ownership. The main deficiency of such a combination of both local and global irresponsibility is its political fogginess, resulting in both haphazard urban processes and unwanted urban impacts. That is why nowadays many cities seem to happen to their residents instead of being projected by them. Obviously, this condition leads to a high degree of frustration. Ownership transparency and ownership accountability could be a first step towards a responsive and responsible urban future.

Avoid Antagonising Developer and Public

The simplistic dualism of 'developer' and 'public' has gradually come to an end, its practice as a confrontational set-up having proven to be unproductive. Increasingly, it is being replaced by a more complex actor network and power geometry. This shift is mirrored in a wide variety of local groups with political agendas, potentially leading to a multilayered and engaged urbanistic discourse and to new concepts of development, financing and tenancy. If new projects are directed towards a positive urban impact, an engagement with the dendritic political topography, its dynamics, potentials and pitfalls is crucial, both on the local and the city scale. In this changing context, simple antagonisms are not helpful.

Use Informal Planning Instruments as Ice Breakers

The concerns of different stakeholders of the planning process matter: the boroughs, the city, investors and developers, local enterprises and residents as well as their public institutions and clubs. By integrating a wider public in the early stages of the planning process, the political acceptance of a project can be fostered. In this context, informal planning tools such as scenario workshops and test planning are very helpful. They can be seen as both a positive exercise and professional shortcut within the discourse between stakeholders, since political processes are simulated to a certain extent. Applied in the early stages of planning processes, informal planning instruments are effective in creating a shared mental space for unusual thinking, open debate, surprising synergies, satisfactory solutions, mutual understanding and trust.

Support Civic Forces Deliberating about the City

Orchestrating individual development potentials with a collectively shared urban vision is not currently taking place because of the underlying trend to de-cultivate and de-politicise planning. In order to find a new balance and to re-cultivate and re-politicise planning, a weak state needs strong civic forces to compensate. A public debate on the future of our cities and the way planning processes are crafted is of the utmost importance, as it brings with it the potential of leading to majoritarian visions and shared political intentions. Shifting the momentum of civic action from frustrating and impactless protests against fully planned projects to the embryonic stage of urban planning processes is crucial, where vision is needed and impact still possible. Such a forum is still to be created.

4.2 Methods

Think in Multiple Scales

Cities are composed of houses, streets, squares, parks, subway networks, social milieus, economic systems and many more elements – all linked up in a complex network of relations. This link-up of different aspects and scales is the basis for the concept of transscalarity. It encompasses the knowledge that contemporary urbanisation processes do not only affect specific development sites, but reach out to the wider metropolitan area and are highly connected to national and international regulations, capital flows, technological innovations and employment markets. As stated in the first chapter, this line of thought leads to a comparison between urbanistic projects and other transscalar disciplines, such as environmental impact studies. Not unlike the analytical concept of the 'ecological footprint' for measuring negative human impact on the Earth's ecosystem, an 'urban footprint' could be established as a metaphorical concept for positive human impact on a city's socio- and ecosystem. An advantage of such a transscalar approach to urban space is that it encompasses effects on different scales and conceptualises the metabolism of cities. Thinking in different scales, and being able to purposefully relate actions with effects on different scales, are therefore core qualities of contemporary urban design.

Reconfigure the Planning Perimeter

The plot boundary of a single development project should not determine the planning perimeter. Important spaces to be transformed are often located outside the plot boundary. In the case of the former Bishopsgate goods yard, for example, derelict land, infrastructures, an underused public park and cut-off backyards fringe the actual goods yard. As highlighted in the design tests, they play a crucial role in the development of the neighbourhood. Therefore, the planning perimeter must include the surroundings and should be defined by the planning authority for three reasons: firstly, transscalar urban relations can be integrated in a better way; secondly, the urban impact of the development can be anticipated and steered; and thirdly, the social benefits and financial profits can be spread. Determining an adequate planning perimeter is one of the main strategic decisions of every planning process. If the planning perimeter is defined too narrowly and encompasses only one singular building site, many relevant questions regarding the urban integration of the site into the city remain invisible and consequently unanswered. If defined too loosely, challenges and potentials of the specific site get lost in the shuffle. Therefore, spatial designs must be integrated into urbanistic conceptions that both anticipate the transformation of the immediate surroundings and further extend into the metropolitan scale. Thus, the initial parameters at all relevant scales are to be set and put in relation. Sometimes it can be helpful to differentiate two perimeters: a larger one to contextualise the development and a smaller one to investigate the urban form in greater depth.

Allocate Public Spaces at Interfaces

It is noticeable that many contemporary development areas establish open spaces in their respective centres, surrounded by buildings. This is for a couple of reasons: firstly, open spaces can be better controlled when located in the middle of a site – in terms of style, access, use and safety. Secondly, such a spatial arrangement homogenises the social groups, especially when connectivity is low. In times of socio-economic differentiation or even isolation, this effect proves useful. Thirdly, it is said that high-quality open space yields the highest return of investment when placed in the centre of a plot. Finally, the sheer complexity of today's development projects is extremely high. Most developers have to concentrate on internal challenges. All energy is spent on site-internal intricacies. The sum of these four points leads developers to take on a purely inward-looking perspective, concentrating on the inner qualities of a site, suppressing the urban potential a site could activate when better related to its surroundings. An aggregation of such inward-looking projects leads to splintered developments, solely connected by infrastructural devices. This results in the extinction of a continuous network of public spaces that could interweave different locations and milieus and create urbanity. In contrast to the often weak spatial logic of the inward-looking perspective, allocating public spaces at the fringes, borders and interfaces is key. Placed in between different developments, neighbourhoods and at infrastructural nodes, these public spaces become linking devices connecting quarters, relating different neighbourhoods to each other and creating urban centrality. As such a spatial disposition is neither obvious nor results from the rather short-term logic of a single development, an overarching perspective is needed.

Unearth Context-Specific Qualities

For a design proposal in the existing urban fabric to be potentially realisable, context-specific solutions have to be found. The situative design process metaphorically resembles an archaeological task: unearthing the specific potentials and challenges of the site and its surroundings. Generic top-down solutions are bound to fail, and simple diagrammatic schemes, ready-made patterns or pseudo-contextual imitations of the vicinity can't cope with the transscalar complexities of the urban realm. Therefore, the biggest challenge in transforming cities is to harmonise specific local solutions with a main urbanistic strategy. In this context, quick design experiments can highlight certain qualities of the existing environment and test ideas and concepts. Latent potentials and constraints of a site can be visualised and also potential impacts on its surroundings and on a larger scale. These are helpful tools to understand both the specific character of a site and its precise role in the city.

Anticipate the Urban Impact

Urban projects not only have internal qualities such as the beauty of their spaces or the functionality of their layouts, but also external qualities. These external qualities reside in the effect they have on their contexts. Urban development projects are analogous to acupuncture in Chinese medicine: a precise, focused process having a substantial impact on elements that it is more widely connected with. Does a project trigger a construction boom in the area? Does it raise the land-value of the neighbourhood? Does it enhance social diversity? Does it create a successful public space and a new centrality for the borough? Does it open up a natural resource for recreational use? Does it link up two splintered neighbourhoods? Are significant shadows cast on neighbouring buildings? Does it provoke traffic jams at the nearest junction? Does it change the character of a city, and in what way? All these external qualities can be understood as urban impacts. For many citizens these might be the most important issues of concern when it comes to urban transformation schemes. Even though the future is never fully predictable, anticipating the impact of a project is crucial. Following this line, singular developments should be embedded in an urbanistic (social and spatial) strategic goal, led by the question: how can a project be connected to the urban fabric while having positive urban impact both on the neighbourhood and the metropolis?

Link up. Don't Splinter

Splintering spaces, processes and social groups reduces interdependencies and complexity. Sometimes, and especially from a short-term perspective, this can be a decisive factor in the failure of urban developments. Splintering prevents meaningful relations, potential synergies and public accessibilities – all urban qualities of the highest order. In an urban context many new opportunities for activity may arise if people and artifacts are able to enter into a productive relationship: gardeners and streets, chess players and squares, dog-owners and parks. Smart urban design can lay the strategic and spatial foundations for such connections. Urban design can be understood as a craft that links up things, people, animals and plants in a diverse and manifold context of meaning, thereby enabling urbanity.

Produce Alternatives

The danger of a singular design lies in the fact that its formal coherence and necessary simplification often suppresses the intricacies of reality. Creating multiple design tests is a way to react to this problem. Working with alternatives and options helps to explore the field of possibilities. Methodically, a wide variety of proposals leads to an urbanistic discourse. Applied early in the planning process, a set of variations can act in many ways: firstly, it raises public awareness of the specific challenges and complexity of the site. Secondly, it eliminates spatial, social or economic concepts that are unrealistic or one-dimensional. Thirdly, it identifies disagreements and conflicts as well as the consent and synergies of different stakeholder groups. And finally, it can 'break the ice', sparking a public debate on a positive note and finding surprising solutions, instead of triggering public anger by imposing a definite solution.

Use Projects as Thought Experiments

Design projects are not only synthetical tools that can bring order to a confusing reality, they can also investigate reality, just like thought experiments: what if...? Design can also deliberately unsettle, change and reassemble an existing order. The destabilisation effect is an appropriate artistic means for triggering changes in perception among different groups of protagonists, building new bridges between supposedly contrary positions, and provoking unexpected solutions. As with thought experiments, design has both a productive and an enquiring dimension. On the one hand, it helps to develop viable future conditions. Therefore, it projects contingent possibilities to illustrate differences to actual reality. In this context, it can also solve identified problems. On the other hand, designing can be seen as an enquiring thought experiment that investigates the qualities of actual reality. In this case, the goal is to gain knowledge through design. Along these lines, design can also be understood as a problem-finding tool. Through testing, relevant questions emerge and major problems can be detected before any final solution is proposed. The aim is not to uncritically follow a predefined brief and solve its problems, but rather to define the brief by finding the relevant problems. Understanding and defining the problem plays a major part in the problem-solving task. In other words, problem solving and problem finding are two sides of the same coin. By relating the productive with the enquiring dimensions of design, the design process can be extended beyond the mere creative act to a more extensive formation of thought: the investigation of reality and its transformation potentials.

fig. 1 Ordnance Survey, OS OpenMap – Local, 2016
fig. 2 Ordnance Survey, 1916
fig. 3 subbrit.org.uk/sb-sites/sites/b/bishopsgate_goods_station/index.shtml, accessed 24.11.2017
fig. 4 Daniel Zielinski, 2017
fig. 5 Graziella Gini, 2017
figs. 6–11 Simon Kretz, 2017
fig. 12 Joris Jehle, Simon Kretz, ETH Zurich 2017
fig. 13 Simon Kretz, 2017
fig. 14 Yannick Dvorak, 2017
fig. 15 en.wikipedia.org/wiki/The_Goodsyard, accessed 21.12.2017
fig. 16 2.bp.blogspot.com/-K5kZG9DqofQ/U8tc5WBw07I/AAAAAAAAAwE/PNLRmk58bts/s1600/A3-Bishopsgate-2014_Page_5.jpg, accessed 27.10.2017
figs. 17–19 PLP Architecture, Tower Hamlets Planning Application PA/14/02011/A1, 2011, development.towerhamlets.gov.uk/online-applications/applicationDetails.do?activeTab=documents&keyVal=DCAPR_110776, accessed 30.10.2017
fig. 20 Graziella Gini, Jil Kugler, ETH Zurich 2017
figs. 21–25 Benjamin Artero, Jil Kugler, Noah Richner, Mark Zahran, ETH Zurich 2017
fig. 26 Model: Benjamin Artero, Jil Kugler, Noah Richner, Mark Zahran, ETH Zurich 2017; photography: Joris Jehle, ETH Zurich 2017
fig. 27 Model: Mathieu Bulliard, Graziella Gini, Adrian Kröpfli, Nicolas Wild, ETH Zurich 2017; photography: Joris Jehle, ETH Zurich 2017
figs. 28–32 Mathieu Bulliard, Graziella Gini, Adrian Kröpfli, Nicolas Wild, ETH Zurich 2017
fig. 33 i.pinimg.com/originals/a0/07/00/a00700d8dac0dd-34097874b28249ec35.jpg, accessed 27.10.2017
fig. 34 Model: Mathieu Bulliard, Graziella Gini, Adrian Kröpfli, Nicolas Wild, ETH Zurich 2017; photography: Joris Jehle, ETH Zurich 2017
figs. 35–38 Christopher Aebi, Nicole Bucher, Franziska Matt, Delia Wymann, ETH Zurich 2017
fig. 39 Model: Christopher Aebi, Nicole Bucher, Franziska Matt, Delia Wymann, ETH Zurich 2017; photography: Joris Jehle, ETH Zurich 2017
figs. 40–46 Laura Bernard, Leandra Krummenacher, Androniki Prokopidou, Sarah Stähle, ETH Zurich 2017
fig. 47 Model: Laura Bernard, Leandra Krummenacher, Androniki Prokopidou, Sarah Stähle, ETH Zurich 2017; photography: Joris Jehle, ETH Zurich 2017
figs. 48–52 Nik Bieri, Ileana Dan, Tobias Germann, Samuel Meier, ETH Zurich 2017
fig. 53 Model: Nik Bieri, Ileana Dan, Tobias Germann, Samuel Meier, ETH Zurich 2017; photography: Joris Jehle, ETH Zurich 2017
figs. 54–57 Demian Derron, Niti Malik, Alina Wyder, ETH Zurich 2017
fig. 58 Model: Demian Derron, Niti Malik, Alina Wyder, ETH Zurich 2017; photography: Joris Jehle, ETH Zurich 2017
figs. 59–64 David Brückmann, Yannick Dvorak, Tim Kappeler, Samuel Thomas, ETH Zurich 2017
fig. 65 Model: David Brückmann, Yannick Dvorak, Tim Kappeler, Samuel Thomas, ETH Zurich 2017; photography: Joris Jehle, ETH Zurich 2017
figs. 66–71 David Gössler, Alexandra Grieder, Jan Helmchen, Alisa Labrenz, ETH Zurich 2017
fig. 72 Model: David Gössler, Alexandra Grieder, Jan Helmchen, Alisa Labrenz, ETH Zurich 2017; photography: Joris Jehle, ETH Zurich 2017
figs. 73–77 Martin Achermann, Charly Jolliet, Gabriel Souto, Daniel Zielinski, ETH Zurich 2017
fig. 78 Model: Martin Achermann, Charly Jolliet, Gabriel Souto, Daniel Zielinski, ETH Zurich 2017; photography: Joris Jehle, ETH Zurich 2017
figs. 79–86 Martin Achermann, Charly Jolliet, Gabriel Souto, Daniel Zielinski, ETH Zurich 2017
Project Title Diagrams Graziella Gini, Jil Kugler, Thorben Westerhuys, ETH Zurich 2017

Editors
Simon Kretz, David Chipperfield

Authors
Benno Agreiter, David Chipperfield, Simon Kretz,
Christian Weyell

Urban Design Projects
Institute for Urban Design, Prof. Kees Christiaanse,
ETH Zurich: Benno Agreiter, Kees Christiaanse, Joris Jehle,
Eirini Kasioumi, Simon Kretz, Christian Weyell

Post-production
Martin Achermann, Graziella Gini, Charly Jolliet,
Simon Kretz, Jil Kugler, Gabriel Souto, Felix Tran,
Thorben Westerhuys, Daniel Zielinski

Coordination
Olivia Lawrence Bright

Photography
Benjamin McMahon, London

Proofreading
Brigitte Clements, Joris Jehle, Daniel Kiss,
Doris and Robert Kretz, William Lambie

Copy Editing
Matt Price, London

Graphic Concept and Design
John Morgan and David Vallance,
John Morgan studio, London

Lithography, Printing and Binding
Unicum, Tilburg

First published by Koenig Books, London
Koenig Books Ltd
At the Serpentine Gallery
Kensington Gardens
London W2 3XA
www.koenigbooks.co.uk

© 2018 editors, authors, ETH Zurich
and Koenig Books, London

ISBN 978-3-96098-300-2
1st Edition, 2018

Project Partners
Department of Architecture, ETH Zurich
David Chipperfield Architects, London
The Rolex Mentor and Protégé Arts Initiative, Geneva

ROLEX
Mentor & Protégé

Special thanks to
Sounding Board: Ricky Burdett, Yair Ginor
Guest Critics: Peter Bishop, Adam Caruso, Maren Harnack, Manuel Irsara, Günther Vogt
David Chipperfield Architects: Olivia Lawrence Bright, Evelyn Stern
Rolex Mentor & Protégé Arts Initiative: Rebecca Irvin, Martine Verguet
ETH Future Cities Laboratory: Anna Gasco, Naomi Hanakata
Proudfoot: Eddie Frost, Rory McGarrigle, Marc Rovira
Evelyne Gordon, Edwin Heathcote, Daniel Kiss, Doris and Robert Kretz, Christina Nater, Tina Ruisinger, Christian Salewski

All rights reserved. No part of this publication may be produced, stored in a retrieval system or transmitted in any form or by any means, electronic, mechanical, photocopying, recording or otherwise, without the prior permission of the publisher.

Although effort was made to find the copyright holders for the illustrations used, it has not been possible to trace them all. Interested parties are requested to contact Institute for Urban Design, ETH Zurich, ONA G41 Neunbrunnenstrasse 50, CH-8093 Zürich

Distribution

Germany, Austria, Switzerland / Europe
Buchhandlung Walther König
Ehrenstr. 4,
D – 50672 Köln
Tel: +49 (0) 221 / 20 59 6 53
verlag@buchhandlung-walther-koenig.de

UK & Ireland
Cornerhouse Publications Ltd. – HOME
2 Tony Wilson Place
UK – Manchester M15 4FN
Tel: +44 (0) 161 212 3466
publications@cornerhouse.org

Outside Europe
D.A.P. / Distributed Art Publishers, Inc.
75 Broad Street, Suite 630
USA – New York, NY 10004
Tel: +1 (0) 212 627 1999
enadel@dapinc.com

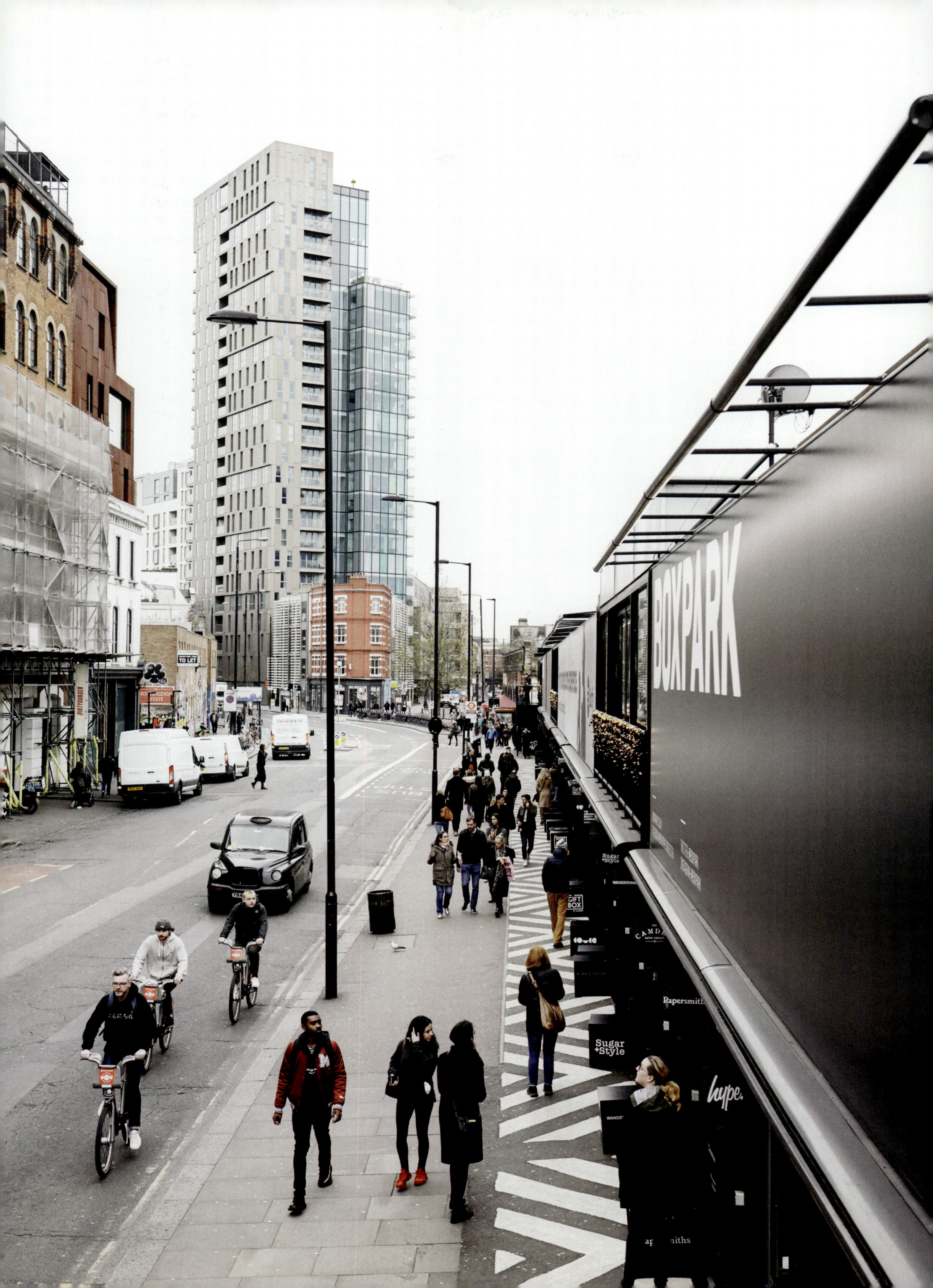
BOXPARK
TO LET
Sugar
+Style
hype.

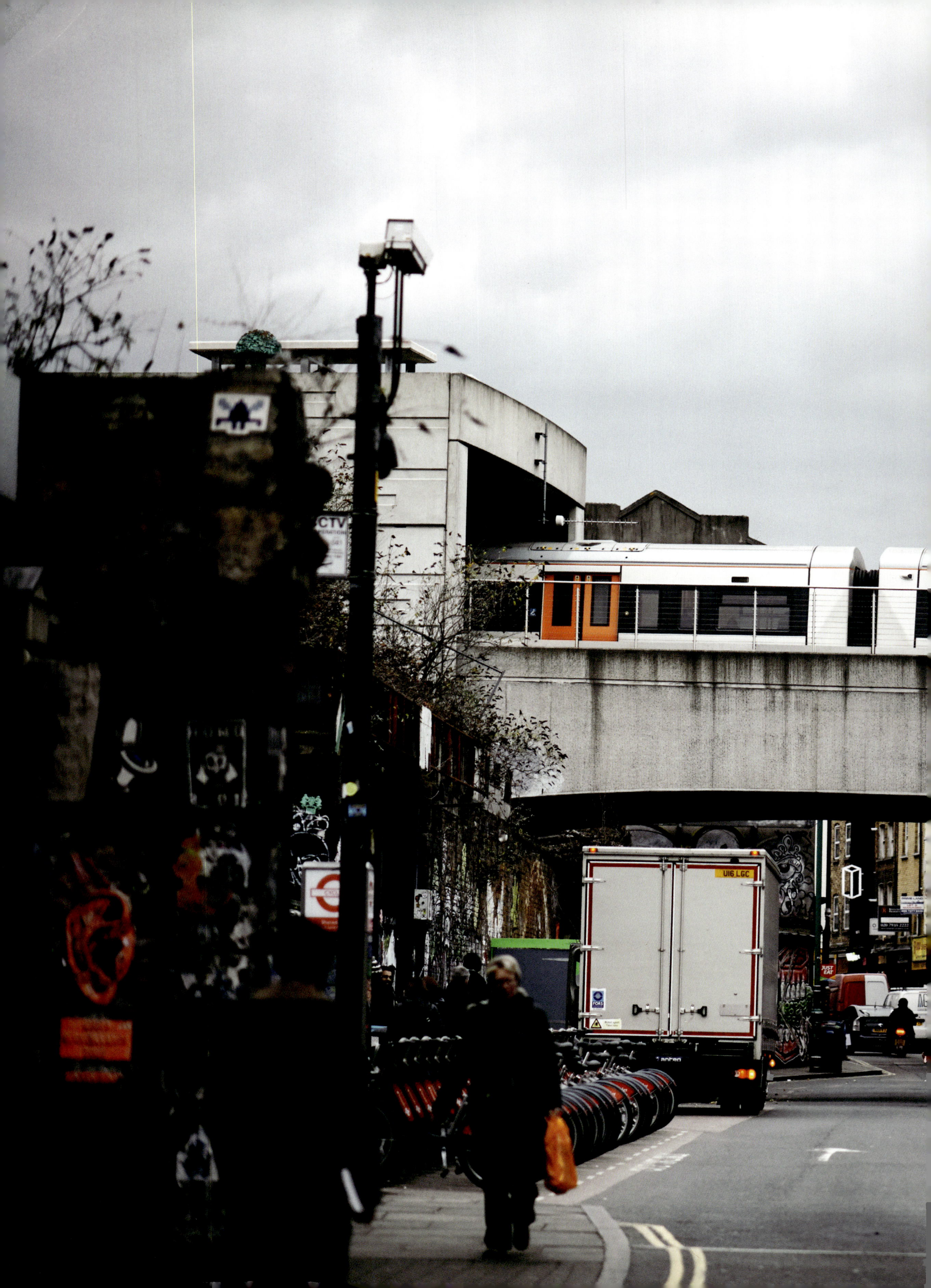
U16 LGC

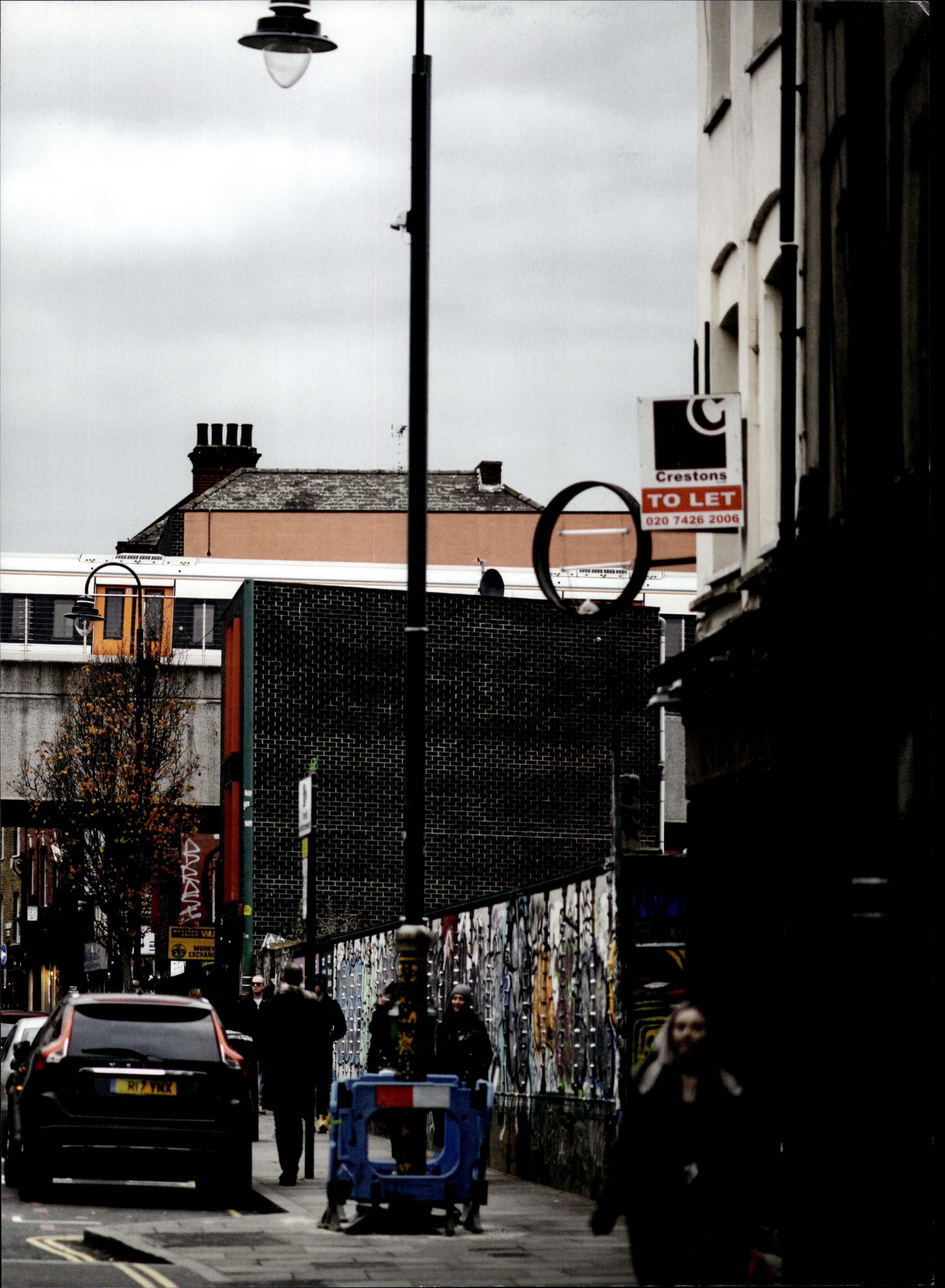
Crestons
TO LET
020 7426 2006
MONEY EXCHANGE
R17 YMX

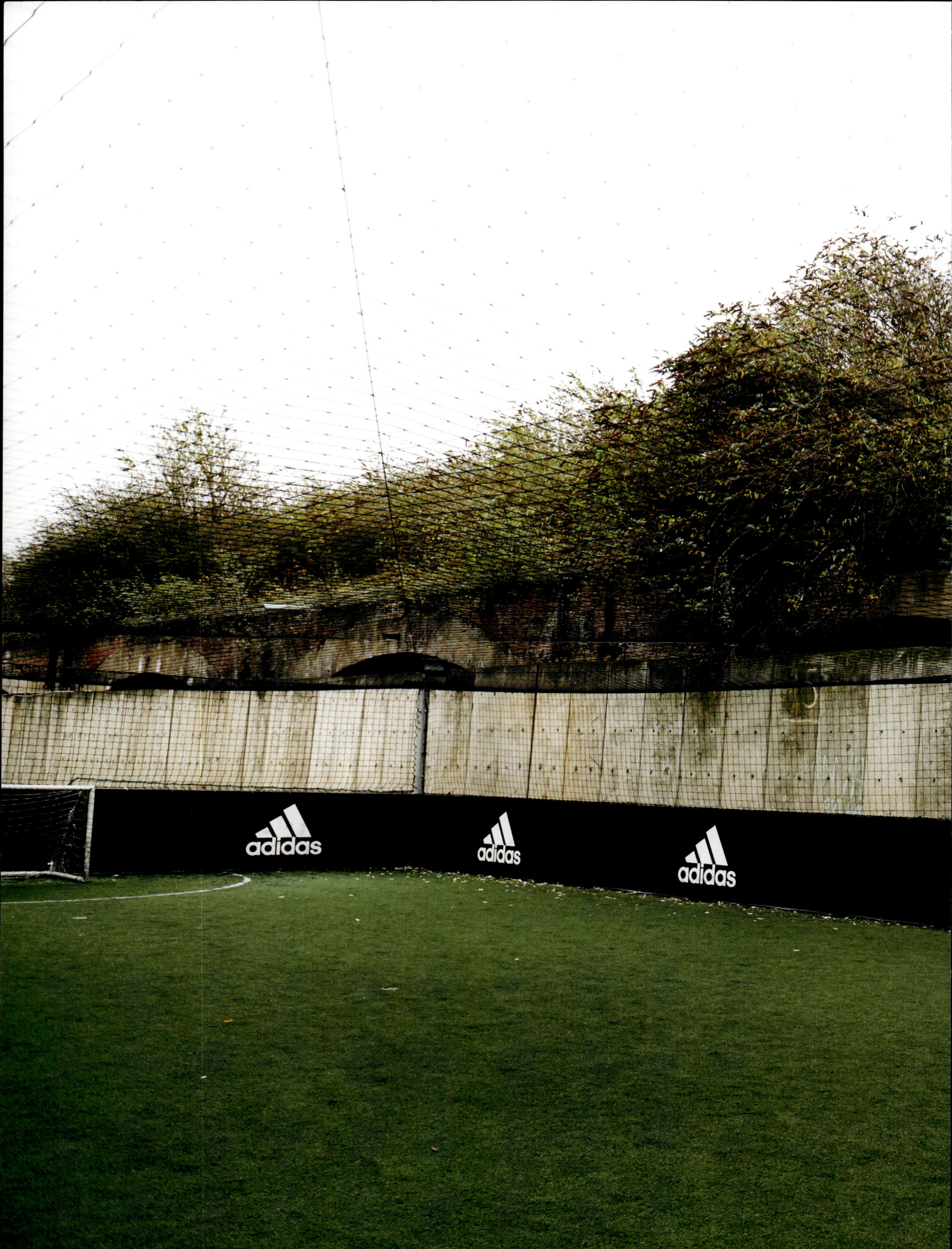
adidas
adidas
adidas

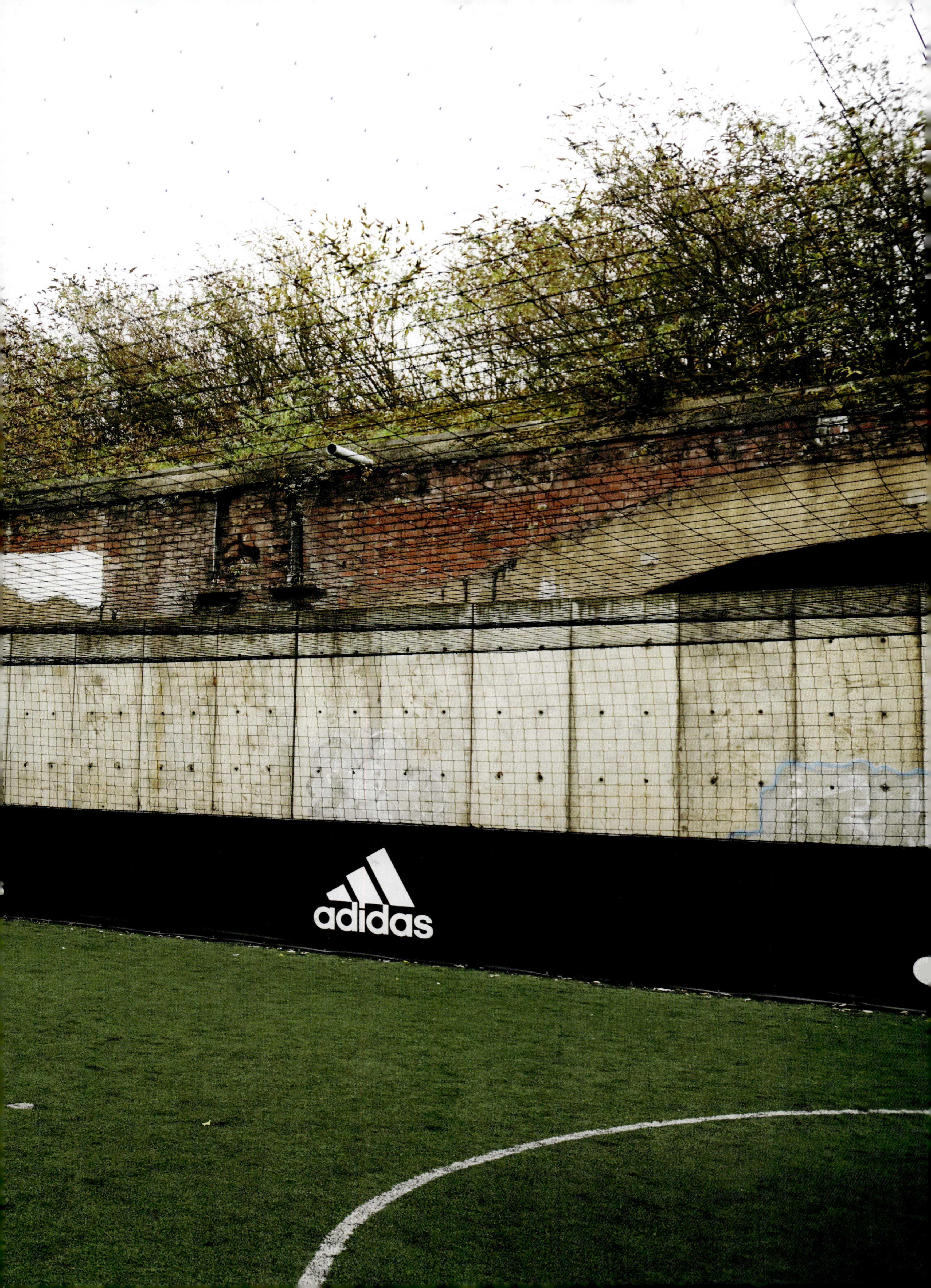
adidas

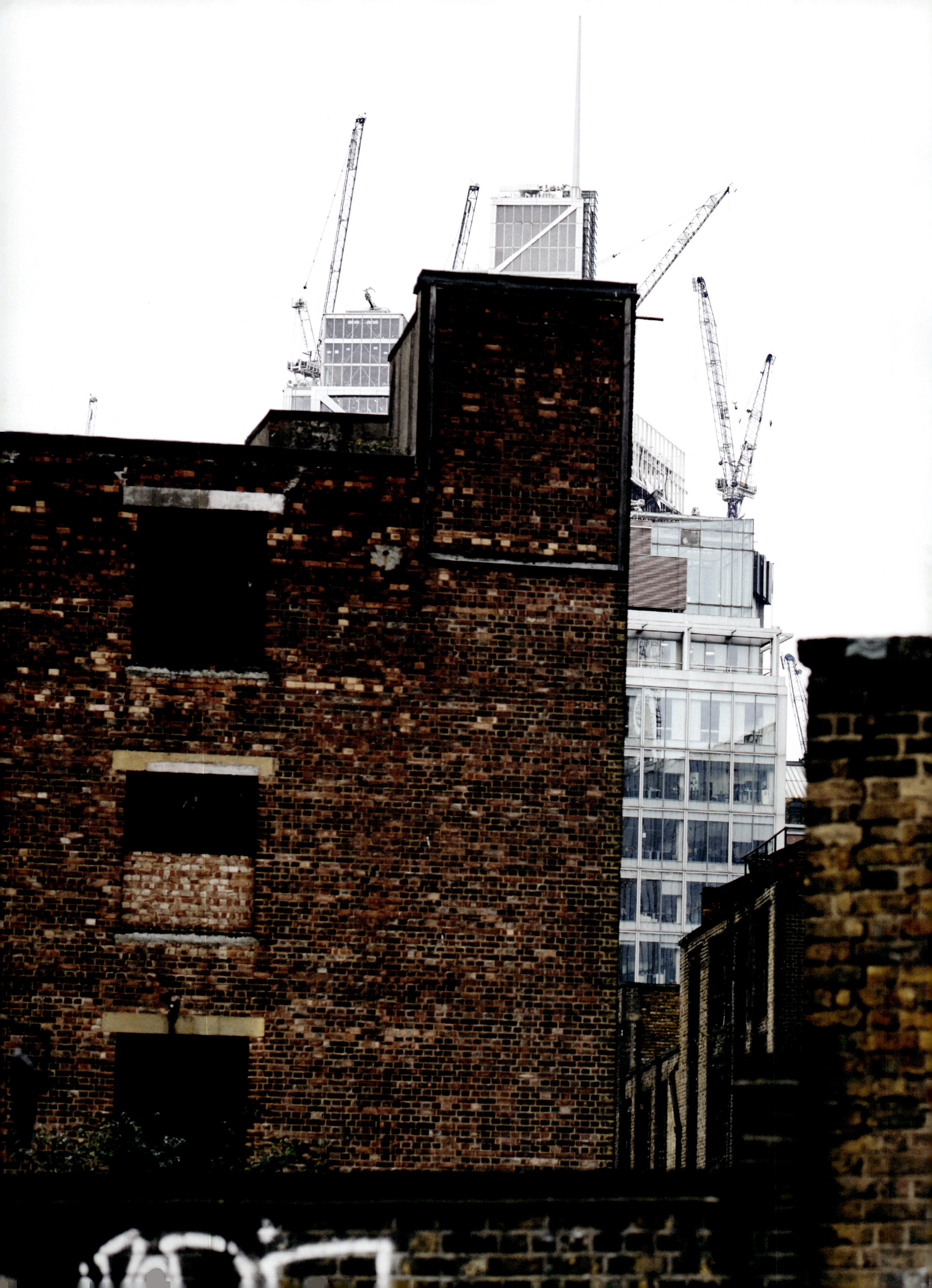

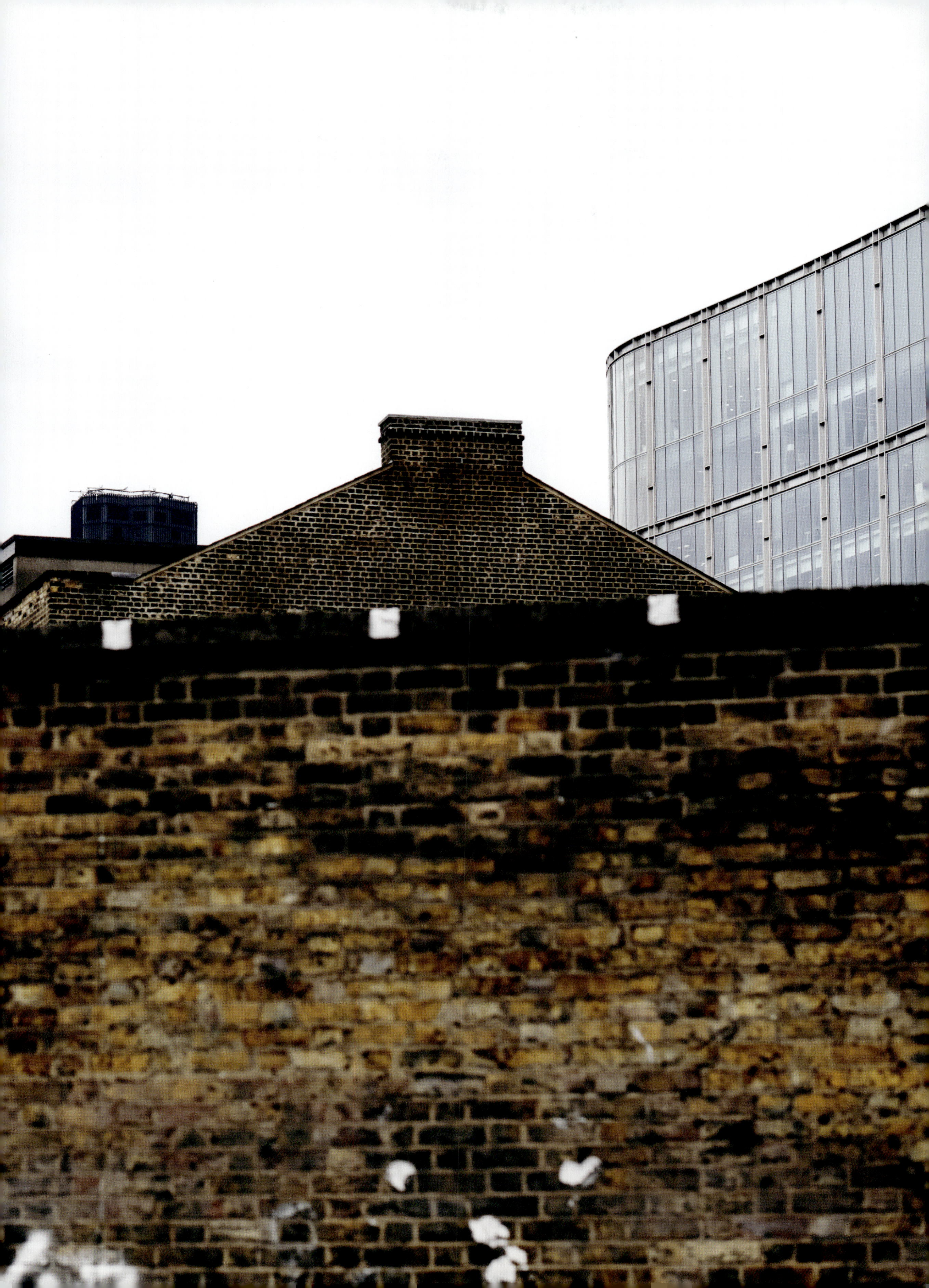

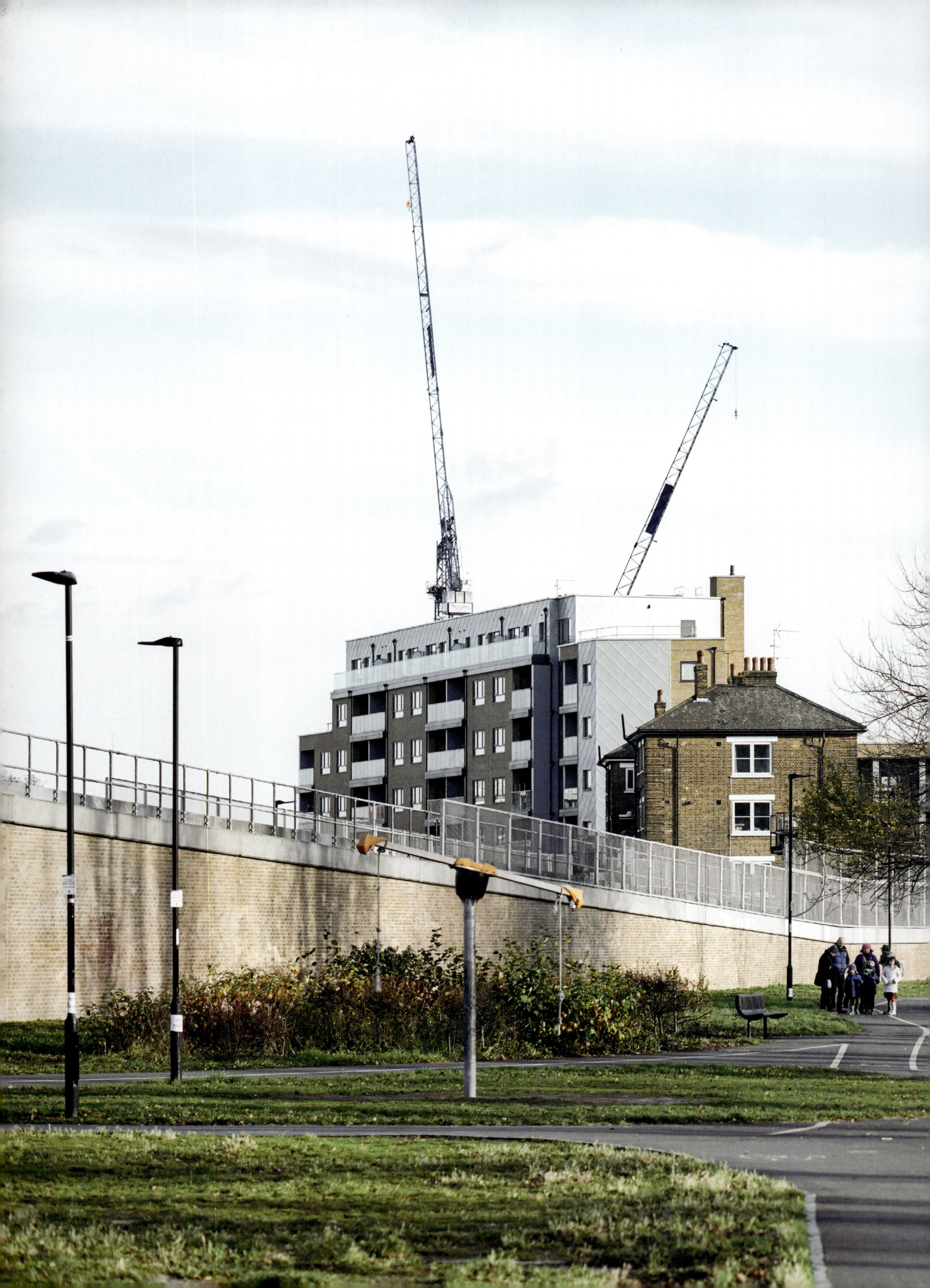
Higgins

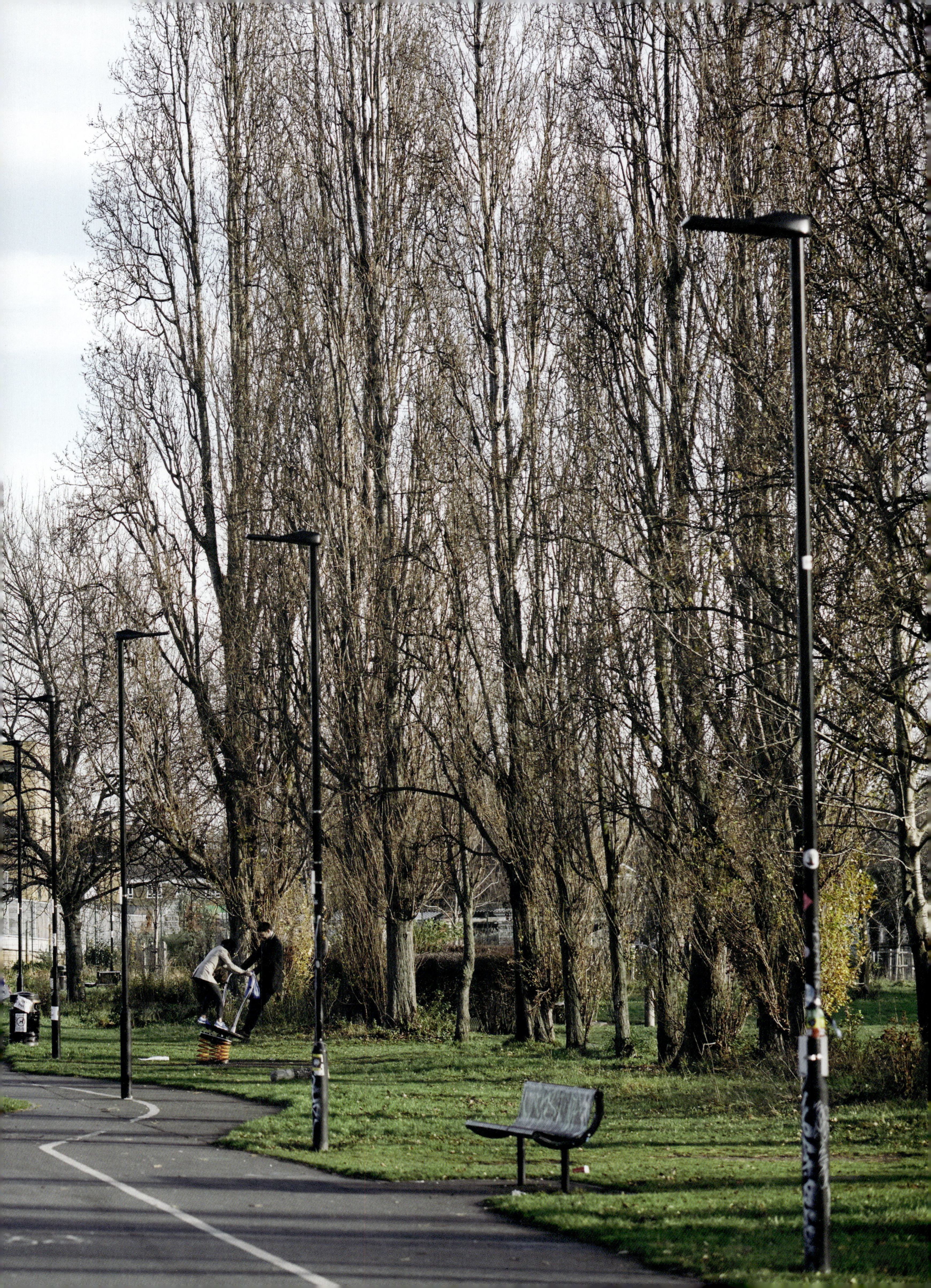

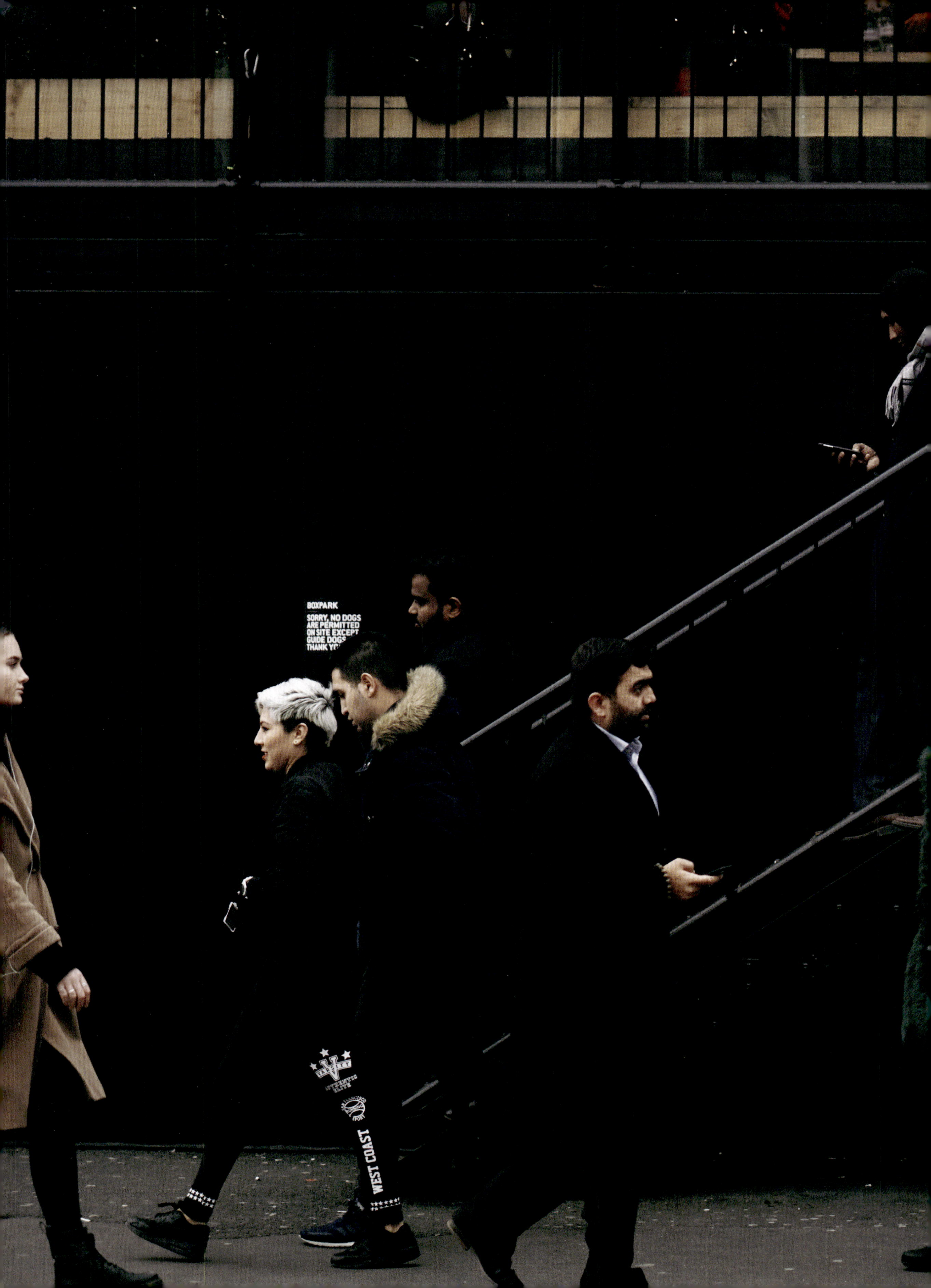
BOXPARK
SORRY, NO DOGS
ARE PERMITTED
ON SITE EXCEPT
GUIDE DOGS
WEST COAST

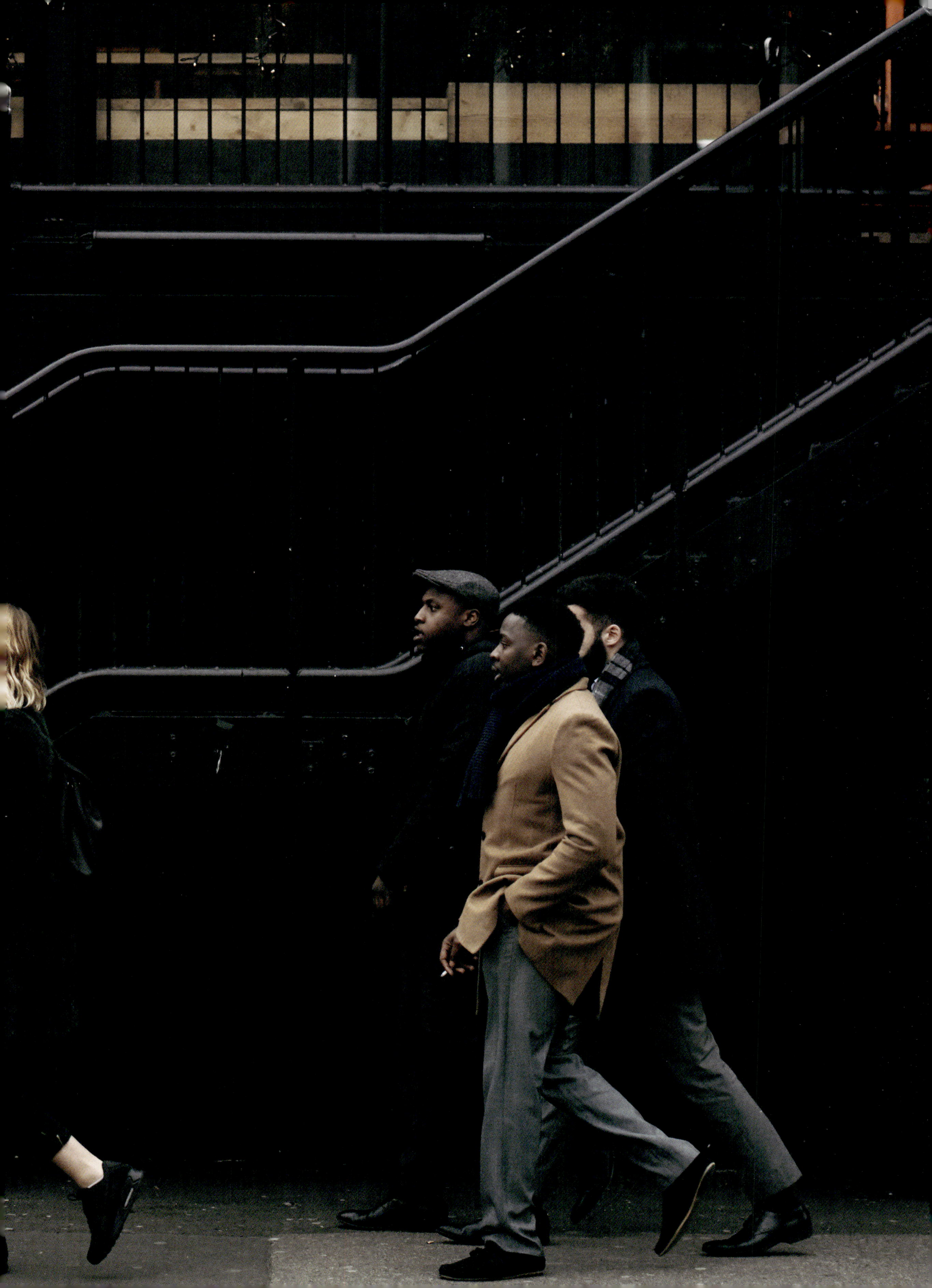

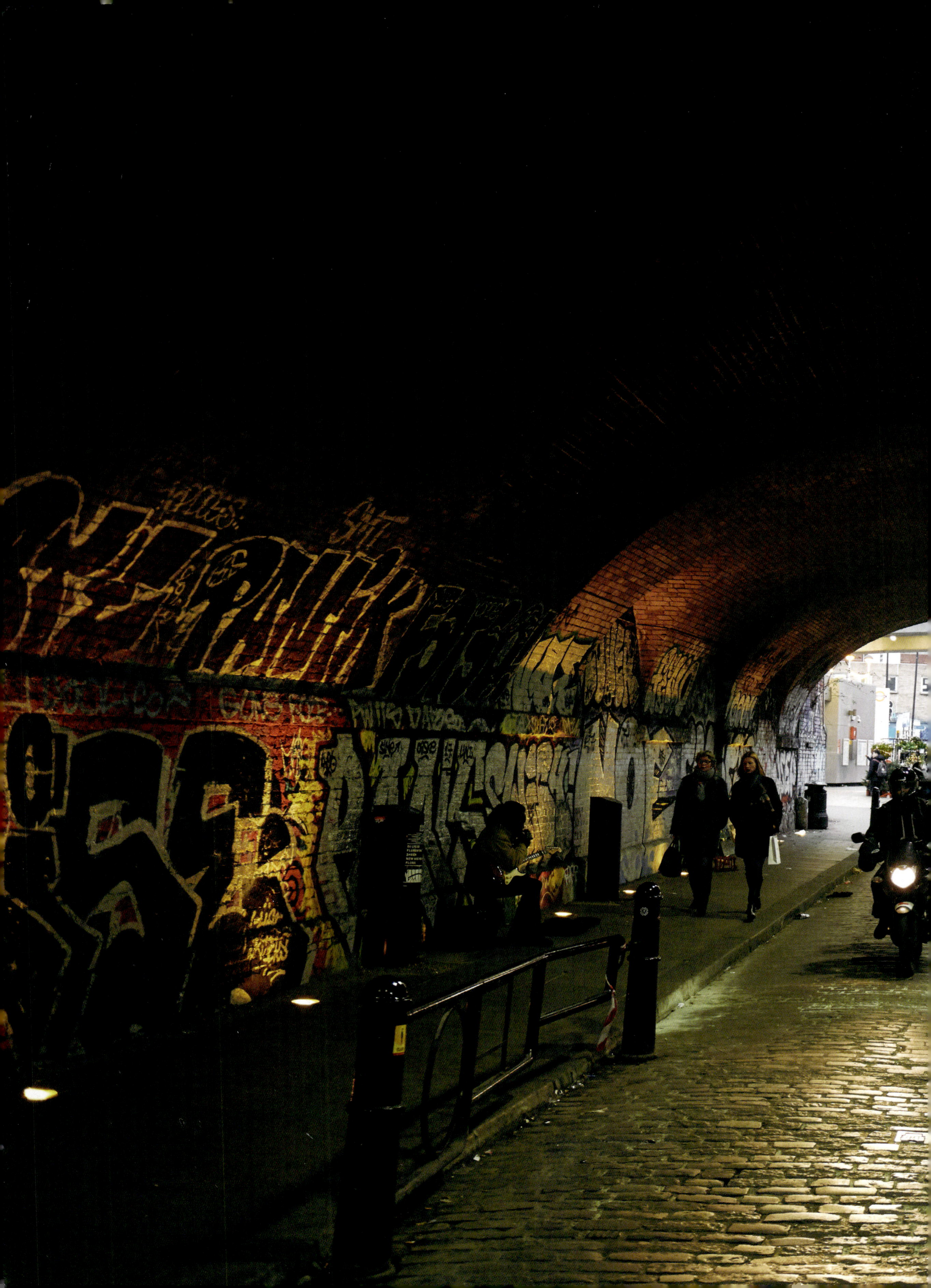

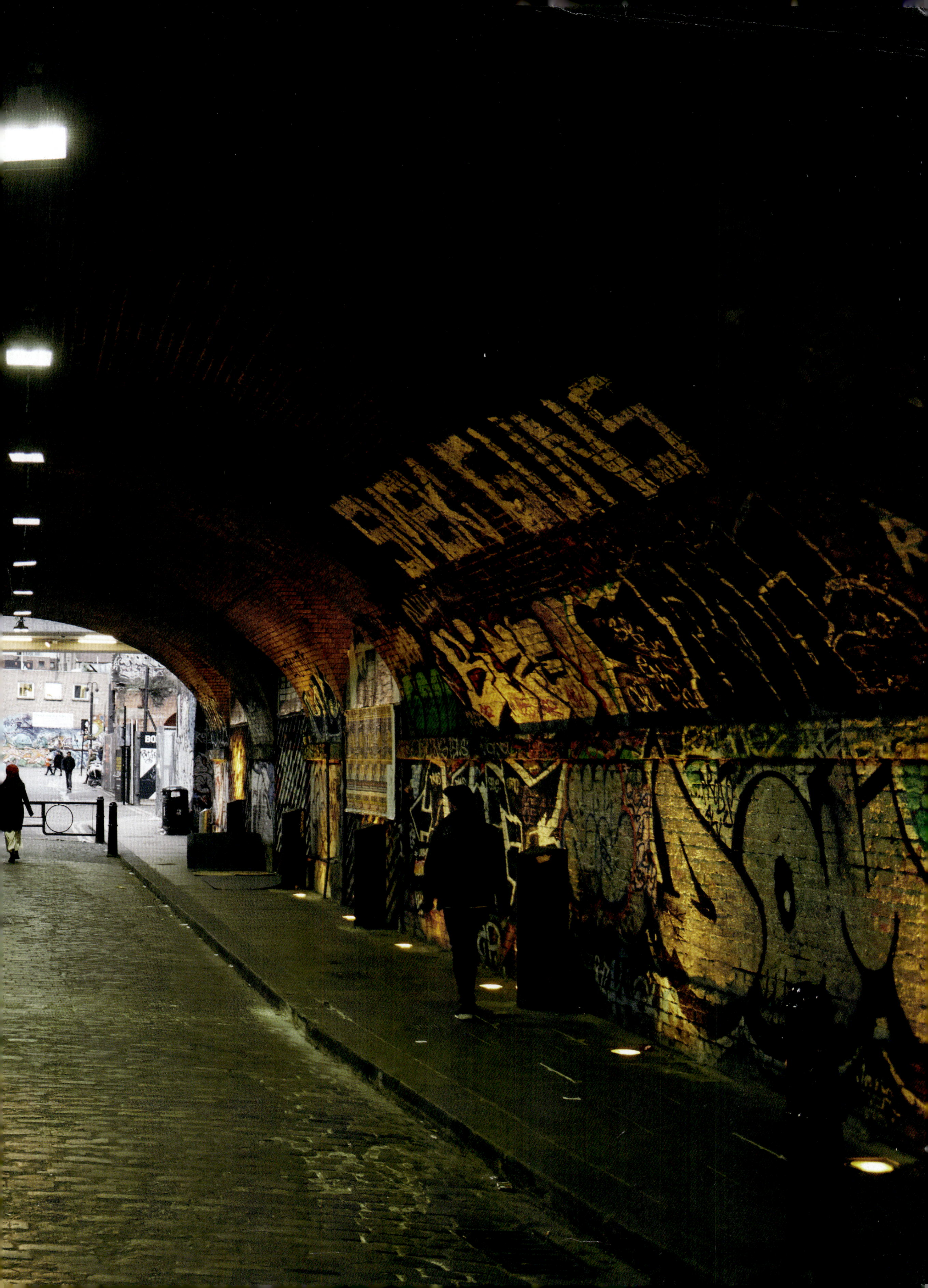